A HISTORY OF THE JEWS
IN NEW MEXICO

A HISTORY OF THE

Jews

IN NEW MEXICO

Henry J. Tobias

University of New Mexico Press : ALBUQUERQUE

Library of Congress Cataloging-in-Publication Data

Tobias, Henry Jack.
    A history of the Jews in New Mexico / Henry J. Tobias. — 1st ed.
      p.   cm.
    Includes bibliographical references and index.
    ISBN 0–8263–1390-6 Paper
    1. Jews—New Mexico—History.   2. New Mexico—Ethnic relations.
I. Title.
F805.J4T63   1990
978.9′004924—dc20   90–39798

Design by Susan Gutnik.

To Charles E. Woodhouse:
able scholar, dedicated teacher,
imaginative co-worker, and
consummate friend

Contents

Preface

To the best of my knowledge this is the first attempt to write a general history of the Jews in New Mexico. It is my belief that there can be no definitive history. The historian's efforts to depict the past will always fall short of the whole of reality. But without the attempt to describe the broad processes at work, one is left only with fragments. My purpose is to integrate facts and events to provide a broad picture. The very attempt to define and explain the historical terrain provides a social cartography by laying out the local and national conditions that have affected the Jews in New Mexico and their adaptation to these conditions from the time of settlement to the near present.

The problems encountered in writing such a general history, covering nearly a century and a half, are many. One dimension involves the documentation upon which the history rests. It is usually the case that the closer one gets to the present, the greater the quantity of materials extant. For the mid-nineteenth century each slip of paper is important because there are so many fewer of them available to reveal that era to us; in the late twentieth century we seek relief from the tidal wave of paper that engulfs us.

This condition affects both the presentation and the internal balance of the work. The relative scarcity of materials and persons, as well as the absence of formal institutions in the early period, pushes the historian toward biographical and anecdotal description from which analysis and conclusion are drawn. In more recent times, the much larger population and the existence of institutions which generate mass information allow a less anecdotal and personal approach and require a presentation based on analysis and conclusion drawn from the plenitude of data available.

Some persons may be put off by this partial shift in description. They may find biography intrinsically more interesting than the statistical accounts of mass change. Given the difference between the sizes of the population a century ago and now, one can easily see that anecdotal treatment of recent times would tell far less about the community as a whole than it would have when there were only a handful of persons. History moves beyond biography. It should tell more about a community than it does about individuals.

One of the unique values of a general history is that it links the past and present into a living process. Through description of both continuity and change and by coming as close to the present as is practical, the work should involve not only the past available through historical study, but also the connections between that past and the present. Generally, only historians talk to each other about the past resurrected by the study of documents. When the living are involved, a much broader dialogue becomes possible. People become aware of their own place in time and process and gauge themselves in the context of community, polity, and nation.

General as this history of New Mexico's Jews may be compared to the more limited descriptions attempted up to now, it is still a small part of the history of the Southwest, of the United States, or of the history of the Jews or the Jews in the United States. There is, however, an integral and reciprocal relationship between the smaller setting and the larger. The history of the Jews in New Mexico would be incomprehensible without knowledge of the broader world. Knowledge of what is uniquely local, in turn, informs and modifies the general, and the result is fuller comprehension for all. No greater justification for local history, it seems to me, is necessary.

Acknowledgments

Although the author must assume responsibility for whatever appears in a printed work, it does not necessarily follow that he did the work alone. So important are the institutions and persons who aided me in the process of creating the finished product that it would be fair to say, whatever its quality, it would have been a poorer work without that aid.

Even though I retired from the University of Oklahoma during the course of working on the book, I cannot forget either that institution or those friends and colleagues who aided me. The support of the Faculty Research Council of the university allowed me to travel and acquire materials throughout various stages of research. The staff at the Western Collection at the university went far beyond its necessary obligations to help, pointing out and purchasing materials vital to its progress.

My colleagues went out of their way to support me. The expertise of William Savage, Thomas Hagan, Norman Crockett, Richard Nostrand, and Lowell Gudmundson helped me to avoid the pitfalls of the unwary newcomer into the field of southwestern American history. David Levy provided his ample wisdom about judgments in general. Helga Madland gave me her superior knowledge of the German language where mine was in doubt. My graduate student, Rae Wineland Newstad, patiently allowed me to test ideas and conjectures on her patient good nature; I hope she has recovered and forgiven me.

New Mexicans were also generous in their support. Stanley Hordes of Santa Fe, both as an administrator of the state archives and as a friend, read portions of the manuscript in which his expertise is great and pointed out matters I had not considered. I also called on and received the advice of Professors Noel Pugach and Howard Rabinowitz of the history department of the University of New Mexico and Tomas Atencio of the Southwest Hispanic Research Institute at the University of New Mexico. Professor Jeffrey Brown of New Mexico State University gave freely of his materials.

Aside from interviewees, whose materials appear as part of the text and bibliography, persons in various communities aided me. The dedicated efforts of Fay Blake of Albuquerque to increase knowledge of crypto-Jews and her generosity in sharing that information were invaluable. Richard Kaufmann of Albuquerque, who has great knowledge about contemporary Albuquerque Jewry, did in several days what would have taken me weeks to accomplish. Elisa Simon, then director of the Jewish Community Council of Albuquerque, allowed me to forage freely in its warehouse for materials. Yale Weinstein of Albuquerque provided valuable leads as did Jan Bronitsky of Temple Albert. Seymour Beckerman of Roswell provided me with valuable information on the community to which he belongs.

I leave a special place for Charles Woodhouse for his reading and rereading of the manuscript and his patience with my false starts and qualms.

Various library and archive staffs not only fulfilled my requests for materials, but also provided advice and information I would have missed on my own. The staff at Special Collections of the Zimmerman Library of the University of New Mexico led by Rose Diaz deserves very special mention. So does the State Records Center and Archives at Santa Fe. The American Jewish Archives at Hebrew Union College in Cincinnati opened their rich resources to me with great generosity as did the Baker Library at Harvard University. And local depositories, such as the Silver City Public Library and the Chaves County Historical

Museum, were equally helpful. So too were the staffs at New Mexico State University's Rio Grande Historical Collection at Las Cruces and the DeGolyer Library at Southern Methodist University in Dallas.

And at the end of research and writing stood my contact with Mr. David Holtby of the University of New Mexico Press. His tolerance and good nature, as well as his knowledge, helped greatly to carry the process to fruition.

I thank them all.

Introduction

Travelers to New Mexico motoring from the East become aware
of an unusual dimension in their perception of the landscape.
At first the spectrum of color in the semiarid region appears
limited to an infinite blue sky, a foreground of earth-tone hues,
and masses of blue shades in distant mountains. After a time
the travelers begin to discern nuances previously undetected.
Some may find this new subtle diversity fascinating, almost
haunting. I experienced this phenomenon in my early days in
New Mexico.

I use this metaphor of color to make a statement about ethnicity in New Mexico. Social descriptions of the area are often
made along bold tripartite cultural lines: Indian, Hispano, Anglo. A closer examination, however, reveals a far more complex
composition which softens the distinctions between the dominant colors. The term *Indian* hides differences among tribes as
well as between pueblo and nomad. *Hispano* cloaks distinctions
between those who consider themselves of Spanish descent and
those of mixed Spanish and Indian background. And *Anglo* ig-
nores a range of religious, racial, and ethnic diversity all too clear
in other parts of the United States.

It is in the recognition of these nuances that one may place
the history of the Jews in New Mexico. By the dictates of the
tripartite ethnic description they are Anglos and belong to that
most recent period in the history of the area associated with its

attachment to the United States. Yet they have a hue of their own. Without recognition of that distinction their ethnic color would be lost and that more complex, variegated society of reality would not be seen. The same may be said, of course, for any other ethnic distinction that is ignored or not seen.

🐾

The history of the Jews, like that of any group, is a complex affair. Moreover, like every group, it has its own unique characteristics. Unlike communities which migrated into frontier areas as distinct, compact masses, like the Mormons, for example, the Jews came as individuals or family members. They made their way within the general population without presenting themselves primarily as Jews. Their condition upon arrival granted them neither the wealth nor the numbers to impose themselves as a moral, social, or economic force upon New Mexico, had they the intent to do so. On the contrary, in order to survive and succeed, they found it necessary to adapt themselves to the conditions laid down by the existing social and geographic environments. The skills and energies they employed to interact and adapt to their new homeland become one of the themes which this study pursues.

The Jewish immigrants came, like most Anglos, in pursuit of economic opportunity. Unlike many other western frontier pioneers, they did not come to till the soil. Between their appearance in the middle 1840s and World War II they were, using the term broadly, mainly merchants. Their specific occupations dictated where they lived and their approach to the general population. As sellers they sought to relate to as wide a population as possible. As buyers they had to deal with suppliers both in New Mexico and in the East. All of these factors lead us to other major themes of this work: how the Jews made their living, how they fared economically, how they dealt with the communities already established, and what they contributed to the building of new communities that arose from the Anglo appearance in New

Mexico. One also must consider how they fared in the face of the great technological changes that have marked the history of New Mexico.

If the activity of the Jews in New Mexico were defined only by their individual occupations, one could speak of the presence of Jews but not necessarily of a Jewish presence. Another major theme arises, therefore, out of their awareness of themselves as Jews. It was out of that consciousness that Jewish institutions developed. The Jews expressed themselves as Jews in how they married and built families, in the creation of their religious and social institutions, and in how they deported themselves to the non-Jewish world in which they were a small group. These questions are fundamental for this work, for the development of a stable, permanent Jewish community (insofar as human societies are ever permanent) is an important measure of failure or success.

While the thematic content noted above carries throughout the entire work, the chapter organization rests largely on a consecutive chronology. Its subdivision and periodization rest mainly on events basic to the history of New Mexico and to the history of the Jews. One thematic exception to this arrangement is the issue of crypto-Judaism and the Spanish colonial component of New Mexico's history. The chronology of events places the discussion of this issue first, while its nature largely removes it from the events which concern the rest of the work, at least until the very end.

Beyond this exception, the major divisions are simple. Two chapters deal with the German-Jewish immigration against the background of an American occupation and the early decades of Anglo settlement. The next two chapters revolve around the changes introduced by the railroad—a major occurrence in New Mexico history—and its effect upon the Jews. The last chapter focuses on the background of New Mexico as part of the new

West, the introduction of major national defense facilities, national social trends, and the reaction of New Mexicans to those events.

Limitations of space and availability of certain kinds of materials incur the arbitrary need to stop somewhere. The year 1980 seems to serve that purpose adequately, and I have stayed as close to that date as materials and style allow.

ᴀᴏ

Not the least of the problems confronting the historian of the Jews is how to locate and define them. The circumstances in which Jews have found themselves have not always proven conducive to openness. The whole question of crypto-Judaism in New Mexico lies shrouded in the issue of who is a Jew and who is not, a problem as difficult for Jews to solve as it is for non-Jews. Under the conditions of need for secrecy it is almost impossible to speak of numbers or anything else. Each layer of disguise adds to the difficulty of discovery and even definition.

A great gulf in the nature of conditions exists between colonial and Mexican New Mexico and American New Mexico. But the problem of identification did not end with political change. Whereas, during the Spanish era the policy of exclusion engendered the Jewish reaction of secrecy, ironically, during the American era the very openness of a society in which one did not need to identify oneself in religious terms allowed its own kind of anonymity. The census did not ask questions about religion. Social forms and pressures might arouse the curious concerned with religious identity, but evasion, if one wished to practice it, was not difficult, and records requiring statement of religious identity were nonexistent. One must also note that for a long time after the Anglos came to New Mexico there were no institutional structures around which Jews gathered and could be known.

The problem of identifying Jews involves two important questions for the researcher. The first revolves around the quantitative issue of numbers and location. Self or family identification and open association in institutions are the safest criteria.

Restriction to these standards, however, would leave out un-known numbers of persons, who, by their own wish or the ab-sence of ties, found no reason to make their presence as Jews known. The picture produced by reliance on only these safe cri-teria might well underrepresent the Jewish presence.

To overcome this problem and to achieve greater accuracy, the researcher must resort to less direct methods. Leaning on social characteristics based on historical experience, the scholar may rely on family names, birthplace, the practice of certain customs, and close business or social ties.[1] Although use of them is almost unavoidable, these criteria are far from foolproof. Judg-ment based on less than these four sorts of information becomes quite tentative. Excessive reliance on such data may exaggerate numbers beyond reality. The solution is to treat such data as fac-tors of possible rather than certain identification.

The second problem of identifying Jews revolves around a qualitative definition of Jewishness. How does one treat an iden-tified Jew who does not follow the practices of the Jewish tradition and does not associate in the institutional life of the Jewish community?

In matters concerning the building of formal Jewish institu-tions, active membership alone suffices to establish identity. The members of congregations and social organizations, the open practitioners of Judaism, recognize themselves and are recog-nized by others as Jews. But persons who do not participate in formal institutions cannot be summarily excluded from the ranks of Jews. Anyone born to Jewish parents and converts to Judaism will be considered Jewish. If identifiable, the nonparticipant Jew will be included in any qualitative measurement unless that per-son specifically refused to identify himself as a Jew for any reason.

Even with the most specific of definitions, however, there will be ambiguity. In this study, I have relied on the safest criteria noted for certainty and have included secondary criteria as pos-sible identifiers. The results may not provide the simplest and clearest exposition in the text, but I believe the method serves the best interests of accuracy and reality.

Hispanic New Mexico and Its Jewish Question

$$\boxed{1}$$

Were there any Jews in New Mexico under Spanish rule? Until a few years ago scholars leaned toward an indefinite but essentially negative answer. Rabbi Floyd S. Fierman, a dedicated investigator of Jewish history in the southwestern United States, faced the problem in 1960, at the outset of his scholarly quest. He turned for advice to France V. Scholes, a leading historian of colonial New Mexico. Fierman reported Scholes's view that "there appears, in fact, to be very little positive evidence regarding Jews in seventeenth-century New Mexico and Arizona. Those who are occasionally described in the Inquisitional documents as *judíos* were, more often than not, characterized as such by their enemies." Scholes added, "That those persons were actually Jewish, I seriously doubt." Taking his cue from this analysis, Fierman devoted himself to investigating Jews in the Southwest after 1850, that is, when New Mexico became part of the United States.[1]

In 1976, Fay F. Blake, a lay researcher in Albuquerque, investigated a different set of circumstances. Intrigued by evidence of Hispanic Jewry in New Mexico, she informed Jacob R. Marcus, dean of American-Jewish historians, that "there seems to be general agreement [among local historians] that there were Jews among the early settlers, but no one admitted it, since it was illegal [for Jews to reside in New Spain], so sorting them out from among all those 'Conversos' [Jewish converts to Christianity] could be very difficult indeed!"[2]

The problems encountered by Blake to learn about them were formidable. Beyond the obstacles posed by secrecy and the difficulty of establishing documentation, lay the issues of relevant interest and accessibility. "The materials to which I have had access," she noted, "have not usually presented a Jewish point of view and, in some cases, have tended to gloss over the very information most useful to me because the authors' interests lay in another direction."[3] Moreover, she found approaching potential informants "ticklish." Traditional Hispanic society and its problems with outsiders were (and are) sensitive matters in New Mexico. Religious and economic issues within Hispanic society at times make potential informants reluctant to reveal themselves. "Many descendants fear that their land grants would be open to question," she reported, "if it were established that the ancestors to whom the grants were made were Jews, and therefore held illegally. . . ."[4] Such barriers might give any researcher pause about the chances of success.

The conflicting views presented above raise difficult problems. But difficulty in evaluating evidence does not close an issue, it only leaves an answer in abeyance. Materials have come to light in recent years in published form, in typescript, and in the living behavior of Hispanos that make a fresh inquiry and discussion of a crypto-Jewish presence in New Mexico timely and necessary. In the interest of producing as multifaceted a picture as possible of the Jewish experience in New Mexico, it is important to describe, at least briefly, the state of the question at the time of writing.

❧

New Mexico's history did not occur, of course, in isolation. Formulating a complete picture requires that one transcend the present political boundaries and examine New Mexico within the larger context of colonial New Spain. Questions about Jews in colonial New Mexico must also refer to the broader issue of their existence in New Spain.

Geography pervades all questions about New Mexico. Herbert E. Bolton, a giant figure in the study of the Spanish borderlands, pondered the spatial relationship of New Mexico to the rest of New Spain. Writing of Oñate's expedition of conquest into New Mexico in 1598, he described the Spanish effort with an instructive analogy: "Like an athlete gathering force for a mighty spring," he mused, "the frontier of settlement leaped eight hundred miles into the wilderness, from southern Chihuahua to the upper Rio Grande." There, "colonists settled among the Pueblo Indians, Friars built missions, soldiers warded off attacks of relentless Apaches, and civilians founded a semi-pastoral society."[5] For the Spanish colonies in general, the frontiers were extended and held by "the *conquistador*, the presidial soldier, and the missionary," in short, by the agents of the state and the church.[6] The purpose of this activity was clear. Oñate's expedition was "an opportunity to spread the Faith, exploit Indian labor and protect the Empire."[7]

The geographic position of New Mexico in colonial New Spain emerges from Bolton's words. It was a remote area far from other colonial centers. Moreover, once hopes of wealth envisaged in the myth of "Seven Cities of Cíbola" dissolved, France Scholes's description of New Mexico as "an isolated, poverty-ridden frontier province" appears accurate enough.[8] The Spanish crown and its viceroy were disappointed in Oñate's results and considered abandoning the enterprise. Only the persistent appeals of the Franciscans brought continued royal subsidy for the missions and, with it, a permanent Spanish presence in New Mexico.[9] A scholar of the settlement process in the colonial north, echoing and augmenting Bolton's view, summarized the relationship this way: "Explored early, colonized early, and yet a remote, exposed, and isolated frontier late in the Spanish colonial period, it was similar to an island outpost."[10]

That condition certainly affected the character of New Mexico in important ways. Its distance from other centers of New Spain and the attendant difficulties of travel did not permit colonists ready access. Furthermore, the needs of the state and the church controlled the expeditions from the south. In time, however, the clerical-military cast of this demography softened. More settlers came in, and the soldiers themselves became settlers.

The initial period of settlement of New Mexico by a Hispanic population took place from Oñate's expedition of 1598 to 1680. One hundred twenty-nine soldiers and a possible total population of six to seven hundred arrived as the original force.[11] They suffered for a time from mutinies, battle casualties, and desertion. By 1680 there may have been as many as 2,900. It appears likely that much of this growth stemmed from natural increase rather than immigration. Only very small numbers of soldiers came between 1610 and 1680, and they, we are told, married the daughters and granddaughters of the first colonists.[12].

In 1680 the northern Indian pueblos revolted and drove the settlers southward, killing missionaries and colonists and taking women and children captive. As a result, when Don Diego de Vargas launched his campaign of reconquest in 1692, his mission became one of recolonization. The original Hispanic settlers proved too small a remnant to maintain their communities alone.[13] Between 1700 and 1800 new settlers arrived sporadically, and the heavy increase of population came from the intermingling of the settlers with newcomers as well as with Indians.[14]

If the body of existing scholarship is correct on the Spanish-led colonization of New Mexico, what does it permit us to conclude about the presence and persistence of secret or crypto-Jews? With access to New Mexico restricted to official and formal expeditions of soldiers and their families and clerics, it would not seem easy for hidden Jews to have escaped the investigations that preceded the making up of the lists of colonists. Nor could the presence and power of the priests have offered favorable conditions for surreptitious entry. Furthermore, the character of social life and the probable unavoidability of intermarriage would not appear to favor the continuous existence over generations of crypto-Jews even if some had made it through the geographic, social, and legal barriers. Such considerations alone, however, do not preclude absolutely their coming to New Mexico.

ᨀ

Before they could appear in New Mexico, Jews had to be present in New Spain since the northerly route from Mexico was how colonists arrived. That crypto-Jews lived in Mexico seems beyond dispute.[15] What is more difficult to establish, however, is their number, character, and the course of their evolution over generations. On some of these matters scholarship has differed widely. The least of the differences turns on their ultimate fate. That, a modern scholar tells us, was extinction. "The Mexican Jew of today is not the descendant of colonial times," Seymour Liebman asserts. "The descendants of the colonial Jews have assimilated and converted."[16] Martin Cohen, another modern scholar who looked at crypto-Jews through Inquisition history and trial records, concluded that "the manifestations of secret Judaism in the last century of colonial New Spain were the distorted death gasps of a movement whose fate had been sealed long before."[17]

The primary obstacle in researching and comprehending the crypto-Jews lies in the cloak of secrecy that surrounded them. The reason for maintaining secrecy lay in the ban that prohibited Jews from emigrating to New Spain. The right to go there, with few reservations, belonged only to "peninsular Catholic Spaniards."[18] It is Martin Cohen's view that "there is no evidence that any Jew, that is [any] non-New Christian, reached New Spain during the sixteenth century, and scant evidence for the balance of the colonial period."[19] The general agreement about the presence of persons practicing Judaism in New Spain refers to Spanish or Portuguese converts to Christianity who engaged in secret or, at least, discreet adherence to Jewish practices.

The condition of crypto-Jews in New Spain of necessity draws us into the issue of how and why they originated. The roots of crypto-Judaism stem directly from a series of anti-Jewish actions in Spain and Portugal over a long period of time. The central act supporting such policies, however, was the creation of the Spanish Inquisition. "The Jewish-converso issue," one scholar asserts, "was fundamental to the Inquisition's establishment." [20]

Scholars differ widely, however, on the weight and emphasis of the Inquisition. Some stress its broad purposes, which went far beyond purely religious attacks on the Jews into economic and political themes. [21] Advocates of this view point out that the actions against crypto-Jews in New Spain were sporadic and confined to the 1580s and 1590s and later, in the 1640s. Others stress the dominance of the anticonverso or heretic theme in the activity of the Inquisition.

Whichever interpretation one accepts, however, there seems to be no doubt that anti-Jewish campaigns over a long period of time profoundly affected the behavior of the Spanish and Portuguese Jews. A wave of conversions followed Jewish massacres in Spain in 1391. A Spanish edict ordering conversion or expulsion in 1492 and the forcible conversion of all Jews in Portugal in 1497 became landmarks of Jewish history.

The effects of these far-reaching events upon the Jews of Iberia were both immediate and cumulative. Without doubt there were New Christians who practiced Judaism very privately (and heretically, from the Catholic viewpoint) long before Columbus's voyages. Those Spanish Jews who converted, but continued to practice their old faith surreptitiously, gradually lost touch with normative Judaism. So far had the process gone, Martin Cohen asserts, that "it is a generally accepted fact that the Spanish New Christians had been successfully absorbed into Catholicism by 1580." He contends further that a "significant proportion" of the rabbinate elsewhere regarded these New Christians as Christians, not as Jews. [22]

If doubt exists about the "Jewishness" of New Christians in

Spain, then what can one say about their counterparts in New Spain? Cohen, who studied the life of Luis de Carvajal the Younger, the most learned of Judaizers who was martyred in New Spain in 1596, says of his subject that he knew only a few words of Hebrew, no traditional Judaism, and his views reflected a heavily Catholic background.[23] The teachers and leaders of the crypto-Jews, described as rabbis, had "amazingly scant" knowledge even of crypto-Judaism. Their claim to leadership rested on that slim knowledge "and their sacrificial devotion to their faith."[24] If Jewish practices in Iberia had suffered from a decline in traditional Jewish learning and from Catholic influence, then the impact upon a much smaller and more isolated population over a long period of time in Mexico would appear even more devastating.

Scholars do not all agree, however, on the information and conclusions offered by Cohen. Seymour Liebman places considerable weight on the devout adherence to Jewish practices, despite their forced conversion, of Portuguese Judaizers who came to New Spain in some numbers in the late sixteenth and early seventeenth centuries. His judgment rests on the forcible nature of the Portuguese Jewish conversion of 1497, which enveloped many Jews unwilling to convert. Liebman goes so far as to assert that in seventeenth-century New Spain "the word Portuguese was almost synonymous with Jew."[25]

The problem of secrecy raises the issue of numbers. Supporters of Cohen's position, relying on Inquisition data, see small numbers of Judaizers, "with nuclei exceeding a hundred only in a few exceptional instances."[26] Liebman, on the other hand, speaks of "a substantial Jewish population in the early seventeenth century" and cites sources that indicate a population of five hundred Jews in the city of Mexico alone during that time.[27]

The historians' differences diminish as they measure developments over centuries. Available evidence, Cohen claims, fails to reveal the existence of "appreciable numbers" in the eighteenth century.[28] Liebman's conclusions lead in the same direction. At the turn of the nineteenth century, he says, "there were Jews in various parts of the colony . . . but the practice of Judaism had degenerated to a few rites and superstitious beliefs." The issue of Judaism "had fallen to the state of being a minor concern of the inquisitors."[29] Replying to Liebman's description, Cohen adds that this was true because Judaism was "no longer important in New Spain."[30] Liebman's conclusion, cited earlier, that the colonial Jew was extinct completes the logic of this development. But it leaves a large question: if Jews or Judaizers could not survive in the more southerly provinces, what were their chances on the more isolated New Mexico frontier?

The use of the southern provinces of colonial Mexico as model for the history of the crypto-Jews in New Mexico has a spatial component as well as a quantitative and qualitative one. Jews or Judaizers (relapsed converts) lived in many parts of the colonial empire. One of the best known of the communities is associated with the career of Luis de Carvajal, the uncle of the ill-fated martyr of 1596. A conquistador and colonizer, Carvajal became governor of an enormous tract called Nuevo Leon centered around present-day Monterrey and stretching from Tampico to the vicinity of present-day San Antonio. Having created this subempire, Carvajal invited his extended family to join him. The terms of his contract with the crown did not require the customary proof of Old Christian lineage. When Antonio Perez, who accepted the contract as agent for Philip II, fell into political difficulty and faced high-level investigation, this lacuna came to light. Meanwhile, in New Spain, Carvajal became involved in conflict over jurisdictional matters with the central authorities in Mexico.

The result of all this political turmoil was the revelation of the governor's own Jewish ancestry and a much more intimate connection with Judaism among some of his family members. The Inquisition brought him to trial and, though absolved of practicing Judaism himself, he remained convicted of abetting and concealing Jewish apostates.[31] The information developed about his kin brought the full weight and punishment of the

Mexican Inquisition against them in the last decade of the sixteenth century and even later.[32]

The example of Nuevo Leon indicates how crypto-Jews could scatter over the empire. That dispersion did not, however, guarantee any long-term success for their survival. The Inquisition caught some of them. But in time it became less concerned and effective, particularly in areas distant from the capital. Under these circumstances, the opportunity for escape from the Inquisition's clutches would seem to have increased. When Liebman speaks of the seventeenth and eighteenth centuries, he contends that "the Jews of Nuevo Leon lived free of molestation."[33]

Nevertheless, Liebman still felt that the Judaizers tended to disappear. He concluded that the absence of religious persecution, their isolation from other Jews, and the lack of learning "made it inevitable that the minority . . . would dissolve or assimilate into the majority."[34] Writing of Carvajal's colonization, Oakah Jones noted that his arrest and condemnation seemed to destine Nuevo Leon for abandonment. His successor repopulated towns and granted encomiendas to deserving livestock raisers. Few of the original settlers remained.[35]

Whether one accepts or rejects the authenticity of the Judaizers as Jews, the erosive course of their evolution seems clear. Those who escaped the reach of the Mexican Inquisition apparently did not escape the filtration process of assimilation. They could not avoid the effects of their secret existence in isolation, the continued dilution of an already slim knowledge of their faith, and the pressures of living in an environment so culturally alien to their beliefs.

At best those historians who talk of crypto-Jewish extinction point to the remnants of customs left behind—cultural fossils which illustrate that certain Jewish beliefs and customs once existed. Liebman describes the use of *pan trenzada* (braided bread which resembles challa, the Sabbath bread of the Jews) in Merida where crypto-Jews had lived during the colonial period. Yucatecan bakers still throw a piece of dough into the fire as do Orthodox Jewish women who bake bread as a reminder of the sacrifices made in the Jerusalem temple. However, "the Yucatecan bakers do not appear to be aware," says Liebman, "of the origin of this custom."[36]

❦

The evidence in New Mexico itself for a crypto-Jewish population does not differ materially from that in Mexico. As noted earlier, the general conditions of settlement did not favor their entry. Some specific facts buttress this view. Even before Oñate's expedition, an illegal march by Castaño de Sosa lieutenant governor of Nuevo Leon in 1589, to conquer New Mexico, incurred the interdiction of crown and viceroy. A decree forbade Carvajal's lieutenant or anyone else from attempting the conquest. The king, moreover, made quite specific "that no one named Caravajal [spelling varies] should be chosen" to carry out such an action.[37] It would appear that a sharp eye controlled who entered New Mexico.

Nor do Inquisition records studied thus far alter a skeptical outlook. In the seventeenth century serious conflict existed between church and state in New Mexico. In the course of this warfare the charge of practicing Judaism was levelled formally at one governor, Bernard López de Mendizabal, in 1663. Tainted by information that an ancestor had been tried and sentenced by the Inquisition, the governor faced evidence gathered against him and his wife by associates and servants.[38]

In 1664 the Inquisition suspended the trial against Doña Teresa, the governor's wife. By then she had spent twenty months in prison. After her release she stayed among friends and relatives in Mexico City. López himself died in 1664, but in 1671 he was absolved of the charges of Jewishness by verdict of the Inquisition.

Prominent members of the López faction also felt the weight of accusation. Francisco Gómez Robledo and his family too were accused of being Jewish.[39] He was a son, Scholes noted, of Francisco Gómez, a Portuguese, who had lived in New Mexico over fifty years, and Ana Robledo, daughter of the conquistador Pedro

Robledo. His indictment summarized testimony that Gómez and his father were Jews. Witnesses claimed knowledge that Gómez was circumcised and that his brother had a "little tail" as part of his anatomy.[40] Gómez was nevertheless acquitted in 1664.

After these trials, in which the authority of the Inquisition had been invoked through the Franciscans, its relationship to ordinary ecclesiastical jurisdiction in New Mexico was redefined. Nonintervention became the policy after 1665, Scholes tells us, "to prevent loss of prestige and respect for the tribunal."[41] In the eighteenth century church power waned in New Mexico and the Inquisition could not reverse the process.[42]

Scholes was not impressed with the qualifications of the accused López and Gómez Robledo as Jews—neither was the Inquisition. Fray Angélico Chávez, in his investigation into the origins of New Mexico families, leaves open the possibility that Francisco Gómez, Francisco Gómez Robledo's father, may well have been of Jewish extraction.[43] Speaking of the subsequent fate of the Gómez Robledos, Chávez noted that seven children had been born to Francisco Gómez and Ana Robledo and concluded that "apparently, not a single male of the famous Gómez Robledo family returned to New Mexico with Vargas for the name is not met again, except in connection with the daughters of Andres [a son of the original Francisco] who made much of it."[44] Whatever the religious past of the Gómez family in Iberia, they denied any connection to Jewishness in the seventeenth century.

If Scholes's evidence for crypto-Jewish penetration into New Mexico were the strongest available, then the case for a Jewish presence there would still appear fairly weak. The Liebman-Cohen analyses for deterioration of Jewishness under conditions of ignorance, isolation, and fear carries weight if Jews did enter the northern province in the seventeenth century since those factors would indicate only minimal chances of Judaism's survival.

This conclusion, however, does not end the matter. Neither the state of documentation nor specific scholarly study on Jews attempted thus far rule out the possibility that crypto-Jews did enter the province of New Mexico. Liebman and Cohen both conceded that the ability of the crypto-Jews to hide their beliefs and customs exceeded the capacity of the Inquisition and the alien social environment to root them out.[45] Isolation and lack of learning may have produced assimilation in the provinces, but it is not clear that they erased all sense of identity.

Neither does the watchfulness of authorities to prevent crypto-Jews from entering New Mexico prove that the avenues of access were successfully closed. Just as Nuevo Leon could be used as a refuge by some crypto-Jews, New Mexico too might have been viewed as one. Crypto-Jews were quite prepared to feign Catholicism and to serve as soldiers if their survival was at stake; what better means of displaying one's loyalty to the crown or easier way to go where one wished?[46]

The late 1590s were a time of great activity by the Mexican Inquisition against crypto-Jews as well as the Spanish march into New Mexico. The muster rolls of the Oñate expedition included family names similar to those of conversos and even names of persons cited as fugitives by the Inquisition.[47] After the Vargas conquest, the Gómez Robledo daughters returned to New Mexico, and the family tree, we are told, "fans out across the genealogical landscape" with possible traces of Jewish ancestry.[48] At this point, one may at least suspect that the border could be breached.

Such evidence alone cannot erase the heavily skeptical outlook of traditional historiography toward a Hispanic-Jewish presence in New Mexico. However, as suggested at the outset, a growing body of evidence which has been accumulating during the last fifteen years or so points to the existence of Hispanos holding to traditional Jewish or hybrid Judeo-Catholic customs, familial consciousness of a Jewish past as well as a continuing existence, and a growing willingness and awareness on the part of some to bring these matters into the open. Why such evidence should emerge at this time is best left to later discussion.[49]

The newly emerging evidence varies widely as to type. Some of it rests in legal documents. One Hispanic genealogical researcher of her own family, who considers herself Jewish and belongs to an Albuquerque congregation, has traced her lineage back to survivors of the 1680 Pueblo Revolt through civil documentation—muster rolls, deed transfers, and the like.[50] The courts have awarded land grant title of converso heritage back to 1692.[51]

Another type of evidence is speculative—circumstances which seek explanation. An early Protestant missionary in the late 1880s, in speaking to Hispano youngsters over a number of years, realized that the only Bible stories he ever heard from them were from the Old Testament. He reported this curious state of affairs to his daughter.[52] In 1979 an Albuquerque physician, seeing a Star of David around the neck of one of his Hispanic employees, inquired why she wore it. She replied that her mother, on her deathbed, had bidden her "to return to the old religion."[53]

Other data point to a crypto-Jewish presence but do not necessarily claim linkage with the seventeenth century. One family, with a clear memory of its Jewish traditions and which still lit candles to Moses as a saint, migrated to New Mexico from old Mexico in the late 1890s.[54] The theme of extinction in both places becomes less certain.

Even practicing Hispanic Catholics show awareness of a Jewish past. One speaks of a toy he played with in his childhood known in Yiddish as a *dreidel*, a spinner, which is used during the Jewish celebration of Hanukah.[55] In all likelihood, far more persons of such background exist than those who claim to be Jews.

Paul J. Citrin, rabbi of Temple Albert in Albuquerque, adds evidence of recent vintage. He speaks of discussions with persons "who trace their lineage to Marranos, who are not practicing Catholics, and who clearly are members of the Hispanic culture of this area."[56] A Hispanic member of his congregation who "rejoined the Jewish faith," estimates that some fifteen "Marranos" belong to Temple Albert.[57] Systematic analyses of their backgrounds, apparently, do not exist.

Similar kinds of anecdotal evidence have appeared also along the Rio Grande in Texas. Researchers have discussed the links between Nuevo Leon and Texas and speak of crypto-Judaism in terms of "hushed family tradition hardly ever openly discussed." They eat "pan de semita" during Lent, which approximates Passover in time, "made of flour, water, butter, and mineral or vegetable oil (pork lard is never used) . . . a kosher product." Richard G. Santos, who describes himself as a descendant of Sephardic Jews notes, "There are a great number of us who still hold to oral and cultural traditions which are unmistakenly of Sephardic Jewish origin."[58] Although not directly connected with the discussion of crypto-Judaism in northern New Mexico, the existence of similar phenomena not too far distant adds weight to the possibility of a continuing presence.

Some Hispanos who are no longer Jews by religious definition still find their lives deeply affected by their heritage. The Reverend Symeon Carmona, a Russian Orthodox priest, who belonged to a Jewish congregation for a time, has described his own family's secret adherence to Jewish traditions, the use of Ladino in prayers by female members, as well as his mother's food preparations on Friday and her lighting of candles on that day. When he learned of his heritage at the age of twelve (fear of disclosure made it dangerous to tell younger children of their Jewishness), it produced a difficult identity problem for him. At the time of writing, Reverend Carmona has a Star of David on his glass door and estimates that there are as many as 1,500 families in New Mexico who keep secret their Jewish origins.[59]

Scholars have now begun to examine broadly the heritage and history of New Mexico Hispanos to sort out the roots of Jewish and Spanish culture as manifested in language, folklore, song, literature, and culinary practices.[60] They seek to examine a living cultural tradition or one of which there is still a living memory. The evidence points logically to cause—the existence of a Jewish legacy.

The presence of crypto-Jews was not completely unknown even among Anglos. Mary Austin, a writer who lived in New Mexico and who did some social research in the late teens of the twentieth century, noted in a description of Taos County that "there does not seem to be any of the Spanish Jew among these old settlers, such as may be traced further south in New Mexico."[61]

But what was only dimly known among Anglos, it would seem, was well known among the Hispanos themselves. A recent informant told an interviewer, "When I was growing up . . . I was constantly being beaten up. We were made fun of, because we were called *Judíos*, or *Matadores de Cristo*, Killers of Christ. They would gather, you know, that we were different."[62] And on another plane, there are the words of the Catholic scholar Fray Angélico Chávez, linking himself directly to "the famed Jewish family Carvajal" as "my direct ancestors."[63]

However tenuous the evidence reaching the eyes and ears of scholars to date, the future seems to promise more—not less. That, of course, is an expectation and not a conclusion. How much material of a persuasive scholarly nature can be gleaned from records, what may be drawn from existing customs to link the past with the present, remains an open question. Nevertheless, whereas in 1960 the search seemed to lead to a dead end, in the late 1980s a new awareness of both past and present makes scholarly pursuit a worthwhile challenge and a necessary task.

Migration and Settlement: The German-Jews, 1846–1860

Who the first Anglo-Jew in New Mexico was, is uncertain. There is some evidence that one Paul Levi, presumably of French background, lived in Spanish colonial Santa Fe as early as 1773. John Rowzee Peyton, an American colonial who wrote of his captivity in the Spanish province, told of Levi's presence, described him as a Jew and related an account of Levi's role in his escape.[1] Fray Angélico Chávez, in his researches into family names in Mexican New Mexico, records the presence of Simon Levi, married to Candelaria Chávez, who bore a son, Jose Manuel, on December 31, 1835 at Taos.[2] Simon Levi's Jewishness is conjectural, resting only on name recognition. Whether the two Levis were related is unknown.

Chávez also records the name of Jose Francisco Rubin, "25 years old and a native of Nueva Ullorca (New York)." He was the son of "Santiago Rubin and Maria Tomasa Bruce, and was baptised at Taos, April 5, 1828. He married *Maria de Jesus Gallegos*, August 30, 1828.[3] Both name recognition and adult baptism allow the possibility that Rubin was at least originally a Jew.

Avid investigators might turn up other candidates. But the earliest of the Santa Fe traders who can reasonably be considered a Jew was Albert Speyers. We know him through the eyes of others as a figure of considerable and varied talents. Speyers's obituary in the *New York Times* of December 24, 1880 speaks of his role as agent for Jay Gould and James Fisk in the gold speculations that resulted in the stock market's Black Friday of 1869 and his trading activities around 1840, when he carried goods from California to Vera Cruz and made a small fortune.[4]

The depiction of Speyers's career as a trader to Santa Fe comes to us from other sources. His contemporaries placed him on the Santa Fe Trail as early as 1843 and described him in 1846 as "a man of great energy of character—nothing daunts his courageous spirit."[5] Dr. A. Wislizenus, a German immigrant engaged in travels of scientific inquiry who attached himself to Speyers's caravan in 1846, described him as one "very well known in the Santa Fe trade for his energy, perseverance, and fearlessness."[6] Speyers was a tough and seasoned veteran who knew his way about the dangerous countryside as well as in high political circles in New Mexico.

A direct reference to Speyers's religious background comes from James Webb, himself a well-known trader on the trail who settled in Santa Fe for many years. Travelling with Speyers's train, Webb related a tale of how Speyers purchased a painting which, the latter was convinced, was an old master brought from Spain by the seller's ancestors. Webb, unconvinced, commented, "So much for being a Jew and a judge of property and knowing a good thing whenever they see it."[7] Dr. Wislizenus merely described Speyers as "my enterprising countryman."[8]

But Speyers's Jewishness carries some doubt. His obituary offered other options. "The funeral services," the item noted, "will be held in St. Mark's Church."[9] It is possible that Speyers, who left a wife and four children, converted at some point, but it is also at least possible that he was not a Jew at all.[10]

There is even more doubt about the Jewishness of another important early figure in the Santa Fe trade who has been identified as a Jew. William J. Parish, author of the most scholarly of works about German-Jewish–owned businesses in New Mexico, described Eugene Leitensdorfer, a well-known Santa Fe merchant, as a German Jew.[11] Parish's own sources throw no light on the subject. Webb's editor described Leitensdorfer as a native of

Carondelet, now a part of St. Louis, who began his career as a Santa Fe trader in 1830.[12] Leitensdorfer's father, who wrote of his own colorful religious past, made no mention of Jewishness, although he discussed his family's Catholic expectations, and it is highly doubtful that his son was a Jew.[13]

By contrast, the earliest person to be involved on the Santa Fe Trail who was unquestionably Jewish and who settled in Santa Fe was Solomon Jacob Spiegelberg. A younger brother, Lehman, dated Solomon Jacob's arrival in New Mexico as 1844.[14] Although some dispute surrounds that date it seems clear enough that the presence of the first Spiegelberg in New Mexico predated its taking by the Americans.[15]

〜

What brought Solomon Jacob Spiegelberg to New Mexico? The question of motive is often raised in reference to the coming of Jews to the West. Although one does not find them among the earliest trail blazers, they are often not far behind as traders on routes such as the Santa Fe Trail, as peddlers behind settling farmers, and as adventurers in the California Gold Rush or other mining bonanzas.[16]

The question may reveal more about the hidden assumptions of the questioner than the motives of Jewish westerners. Twentieth century Americans, Jews and Gentiles, are accustomed to images of the Jew as an easterner and large city dweller. There is, of course, considerable evidence to support that perception, but it is not wholly correct in historical perspective. It suffices for our present purposes to note that a census of American Jews published in 1880 located them in every state and territory except Oklahoma.[17] In 1877 more Jews lived in California than in any state except New York.[18] Despite popular notions, some considerable Jewish dispersion existed across the length and breadth of the American continent.

The movement of Jews across the continent can be readily linked to the general migration in which the whole American nation participated. America itself was a frontier to Jews and other immigrants of the nineteenth century and, commentators tell us, "attracted the maverick, the bold in spirit, the adventurous in life and thought as well as those who left home for wise and prudent reasons." Those who went west "were the restless spirits unbounded by conventions and undisciplined by traditions."[19] They often went as individuals—young unmarried males—or single families.[20] Indeed, these characteristics contributed to the historian's difficulty in finding them, for, as individuals many quickly lost their identity and disappeared into the surrounding population.

The coming of Solomon Jacob Spiegelberg to the United States, however, reflected factors not necessarily shared by the entire American or immigrant population at large. Although German Jews were known in eighteenth-century America, their disposition to emigrate increased sharply after the end of the revolutionary and Napoleonic era in Europe.[21] From the 1830s to the 1880s the wave of immigration from the German states defined the ethnic background of American Jewry.

The reaction against cosmopolitan humanism and Napoleonic innovation undertaken by the restored regimes after 1815 fueled this exodus. It was under a dominant mood of "nationalistic and pietistic-mystical beliefs," wrote Selma Stern-Taeubler, that "the concept of the 'Christian-Germanic' or 'German-Christian' state arose." Insofar as these goals affected Jews, she concluded that "if one conceived of the state as a community of those who lived, had lived, and were still to live, with every hope for moral and religious development related to Christianity, there could be no place for Jews in this community."[22] The German states sought to apply pressure upon their Jewish population through social and economic regulation, which often restricted civil rights granted earlier, or to force them into patterns of life alien to them. They sought to deflect young Jews from commerce and channel them into agriculture and handicrafts.[23]

However "healthy" some may have regarded that process, it could not be accomplished without trauma. In Bavaria, a source

of large numbers of emigrants, limitations on the right of residence and on marriage, whether one had a trade or not, made
migration for many young Jewish men almost a necessity if they
expected to lead normal lives.[24] Added to this were a variety of
taxes which only Jews paid and the occurrence of intermittent
outbreaks of open anti-Semitism. The issue of military service
also spurred the young to leave. Indeed, the latter reason is often
the only motive suggested for the departure of Jews. It should be
noted, though, that even if it caused some Jews to depart, non-
Jewish Germans also emigrated to evade military service.

Conditions in the Germanies were generally conducive to
emigration. This is borne out by the fact that between 1820 and
1880 alone nearly three million Germans left their homeland,
and Germany gradually assumed first place among the sources of
immigration to America.[25] The Jews, then, were not alone in
responding to unfavorable conditions in their country of birth by
leaving. Some of the reasons, economic, political, and even religious, were common to all who departed; others were responses
by Jews alone to their own condition.

Exactly how many Jews left is difficult to measure. American
census materials do not separate Jews from Germans. A survey
by the Union of American Hebrew Congregations in 1877 estimated the total number of Jews in the United States at 190,000
and assumed that the great majority of them came from Germany.[26] As with the general migration from the German states,
Jewish numbers appear to have increased greatly after the revolutionary disturbances of 1848. One estimate places 15,000 Jews
in America in 1840 and 250,000 at the end of the seventies.[27]

Many new Jewish immigrants set their sights westward, moving out of the coastal Northeast soon after they arrived. Although
by 1850 New York counted fourteen Jewish congregations, Cincinnati had four, St. Louis two, and San Francisco two. The
South also witnessed a considerable influx of Jews in the 1830s
and 1840s. Congregations existed in Georgia, Louisiana, Ala-
bama, Mississippi, and Kentucky.[28] With this continuous out-

ward flow it was inevitable that when the Southwest opened as an area of settlement, Jews would also appear there.

Historians of the American Jews have suggested that German Jews, as one of the paths of their dispersion, followed or accompanied the movement of German immigrants. "In general," Eric Hirshler noted, "the German Jew joined and was part of the great stream of German immigration. . . . Often he found in familiar customs and in the German language a certain help in making a start, often also security in sounds of his fatherland." [29]

Germans settled in Missouri, and particularly in St. Louis in large numbers. Gottfried Duden, who in the late 1820s published a famous account of the American West with emphasis on Missouri (subsequent editions appeared in the 1830s), may have been responsible for the surge of immigration there. [30] By the 1840s, letters from newcomers to the homeland spoke of Germans owning one-third of St. Louis and of Missouri as becoming Germany for America. [31]

The relationship of Missouri to the Santa Fe Trail provided its own context for movement to New Mexico. St. Louis was the early financial anchor of the trail in the East. From there to its starting point at Independence, Missouri, the trip was relatively easy. Through Kansas and farther west, however, it involved considerable hardship. Nevertheless, many German immigrants took the risks of engaging in trade on the trail and the German-born population of the New Mexico Territory was already high in the census of 1850 as compared with other European immigrants. If one excludes those two-thirds of New Mexico's foreign born who defined themselves as Mexican (a definition made necessary by the changed political boundaries after 1848), then one immigrant of each 3.4 in the territory was German-born as compared with one in four for the whole United States. [32] Of 786 non-Mexican foreign-born whites in New Mexico in 1850, 229 were from the Germanies. Only Ireland, with 292, provided a higher number of newcomers. [33] In 1860 the number of Germans in New Mexico reached 569.

As far as is known, German-Jewish immigrants made up the entire Jewish population of New Mexico in 1850. The exclusiveness of that pattern appears to be a product of the relationship of the Missouri Germans to the trail, the relationship of the German Jews to other German immigrants, and of the familial and old friendship ties of the German Jews to each other. And behind those factors lies the limiting environment of the trail itself.

In the absence of direct evidence it is impossible to pinpoint the reasons for Solomon Jacob Spiegelberg's appearance in New Mexico. It is clear, though, that after he arrived there he found employment in the establishment of Eugene Leitensdorfer, the Tyrolean immigrant's son from the St. Louis area.[34] Whether the trail of Germans in Missouri or the Santa Fe Trail itself beckoned to him is unknown. It is not even clear that "the land of enchantment" was Spiegelberg's intended final destination. He may simply have responded to the call westward and the opportunity provided by the Santa Fe Trail.

❧

For many of those who followed the first modern Jewish settlers into New Mexico the question of why they came may be answered specifically. A relative in America and an assured opportunity to work provided a place to go and a clear motive for going. Solomon Jacob Spiegelberg's brother Levi arrived in 1848, and Elias, another brother, came in 1850. Brothers, indeed, formed an important segment of the first generation of Jewish newcomers to New Mexico. By 1860 one could count among them the Beuthner brothers of Taos, the Zeckendorfs of Albuquerque, and the Seligmans and Staabs of Santa Fe. Two more Spiegelbergs joined their brothers in Santa Fe in the fifties. In Mora one could find the Biernbaum brothers. Perhaps a third of the total Jewish population of New Mexico can be accounted for in this manner by 1860.

Other family ties increase the share of Jews in New Mexico related to each other. The Ambergs and Elsbergs of Santa Fe were cousins. So were the Zeckendorfs and Spiegelbergs. The Spiegelbergs and Staabs, too, were kinfolk.[35] Taken together, the number of related Jews passed half the total of the small Jewish population. The picture presented by this considerable stratum of joint family ties distinguishes those early Jews who settled in New Mexico from other western images of the Jew as a lone peddler or shopkeeper.

The insularity of New Mexico, the difficulties of traversing the Santa Fe Trail, and the relative lack of New Mexico's economic importance as compared to other locations clearly accounts for the kind of society New Mexico's Jews presented in the early decades of their residence. In large degree they came because brother, cousin, or acquaintance called for them or made an initial place for them when they arrived.

Beyond the process of going to New Mexico and arriving because it was at the other end of the Santa Fe Trail or because one's relatives were already there lies the question of purpose: What were they going to do? Although written a few years later, a letter from the young Phoebus Freudenthal from Las Cruces to his brother in Germany expressed with boyish certainty why he thought all came to New Mexico. "Of course," he noted, "New Mexico is good only to earn money. It is a place, as everyone says, that God made last of all."[36] Whatever intent the immigrants had when they left their homeland, there is little doubt that when they arrived in New Mexico they engaged in business ventures. In 1850 all Jewish males in the territory (there were no females) described their occupation in the census as merchant or clerk.

On the basis of expectation and opportunity it appears almost axiomatic that these early German-Jewish immigrants would seek to engage in business. "Practically all German Jews began with peddling," Rudolf Glanz asserts.[37] Solomon Jacob Spiegelberg may have done so. We are indebted to Rabbi Isaac Mayer Wise, a leader of the Jewish Reform movement who came to America in 1846, for a classic description of the hierarchy and development of Jewish peddlers:

(1) The basket peddler—he is as yet altogether dumb and home-
less; (2) the trunk-carrier, who stammers some little English,
and hopes for better times; (3) the pack carrier, who carries
from one hundred to one hundred and fifty pounds upon his
back, and indulges the thought he will become a business man
some day. In addition to these, there is the aristocracy, which
may be divided into three classes: (1) the wagon-baron, who
peddles through the country with a one or two horse team;
(2) the jewelry-count, who carries a stock of watches and jewelry
in a small trunk, and is considered a rich man even now;
(3) the store-prince, who has a shop and sells goods in it. At
first one is the slave of the basket or the pack; then the lackey of
the horse, in order to become finally the servant of the shop. [38]

Here was the Jew of many parts of the frontier and the rural
West.

America, however, was not all of a single piece. The peddler
could not function in the Plains as he had in the East and Northeast. Peddling was feasible where a settled but not a dense population existed. When population became concentrated enough
to warrant the establishment of permanent stores, the peddler's
activities became restricted, although they did not necessarily
disappear. [39]

On the other hand, the peddler could not operate where
population was too sparse, the obstacles of climate too great, and
the danger to life and limb omnipresent and overwhelming.
These conditions, which applied to portions of the Great Plains,
forced entrepreneurs to look beyond them, farther west, where
they could operate. To pass through these dangerous plains required, at the very least, a peddler who was a "wagon baron" in
Wise's terminology, with the means to find sufficient credit, the
capacity to collect and transport goods in adequate quantity, and
a method of cooperative defense which could overcome the natural and human obstacles so that goods could reach the desired
market. This is what the trade and organization of the Santa Fe
Trail permitted and accomplished. Had Wise classified them, he
might have called the Santa Fe traders "super peddlers."

Beyond this broad picture of America lay the conditions specifically imposed by the environment of New Mexico. Before American authority supplanted Mexican, the economy of the province was, as Parish put it, "essentially feudalistic." Up to 1821, under Spanish rule, barter was the chief form of trade within its boundaries.[40] Such trade as existed beyond those limits moved via caravans to and from the south, a pattern as old in some ways as the Spanish occupation itself. This activity lay under the control of merchants in Chihuahua who held the New Mexican traders under their financial sway. Goods, particularly ironware, fabrics, and delicacies, were taken north, and sheep, wool, hides, nuts, and salt, south. The Chihuahuans gained considerable advantage from currency exchange since the peso was not standardized, and they provided credit sources—all to their benefit.[41]

With the Louisiana Purchase and Mexican independence from Spain established, American traders looked westward. Zebulon Pike, in his famous trek through the area in 1806–7, had noted the cheapness of New Mexican produce and the high cost of imports brought in from the south.

Contemplation of the prices brought by finished goods whetted the appetite of the Americans.[42] Soon after they first rolled their wagons across the Santa Fe Trail in the 1820s, however, they found a restricted capacity among the New Mexicans to absorb their wares.[43] At the same time, the Americans discovered the "royal road" to the south and in time their trade based no small part of its economic rationale on the transshipment of goods from Santa Fe into the interior of Mexico. In his work on the Mexican-New Mexican route, Max L. Moorhead summed up the advance of the new American branch of that trade in this way:

> In 1822 seventy men . . . with three wagons had carried $15,000 worth of goods, mainly of American manufacture, to Santa Fe, and had taken about $9,000 of it on to Chihuahua. In 1846 caravans engaging 750 men and 363 wagons had

*taken approximately $1,000,000 worth of goods, a large part of
it foreign, to Santa Fe, and had sold all but a very small
amount of it in Chihuahua and other interior cities.* [44]

The effects of this new trade made a strong impact on all the
parties involved—Mexicans, New Mexicans, and Americans.
The difference in price between goods brought in via the Santa
Fe Trail and those freighted in from the south was one crucial
factor in the change. As a result, the Chihuahuans found their
monopoly over the New Mexican trade broken. The governor at
Chihuahua explained to his superiors that the success of the
Americans resulted from the long Spanish neglect of New Mexico, internal duties, and the problems of geographic distance
from the south. New Mexicans, in turn, found they could sell
their surplus of goods imported from the United States in Chihuahua for hard cash, bringing the provincial treasury increases
which pleased the local authorities. [45]

For the Americans and New Mexicans, the Santa Fe trade
produced a reorientation of perspective. An east-west axis of interest cut into the traditional north-south axis. New Mexico
slowly became linked to American goods. Textiles, iron tools,
and drugs became more readily available. Moreover, Americans
and Mexicans started to become accustomed to each other. This
new cultural relationship did not always run smoothly, but a
number of Americans became residents, married New Mexican
women, learned Spanish, and maintained good relations with
the local population.

The American victory in the war of 1846–48 with Mexico
produced major political and economic changes. The position of
Chihuahua changed from that of an interior to a border province. What had been the leg of a prosperous commerce was broken and took years to mend. [46] What the war shattered in one
place, however, it replaced elsewhere. Wartime conditions and
postwar uncertainties assured the presence of a considerable military force in New Mexico for an unforeseeable length of time.
The revolt at Taos in 1847 and the widespread danger from the

nomadic Indians led to the creation of a number of forts. The presence of troops and forts, in turn, produced a need for a continuing stream of supplies. This new market gave merchants opportunities to trade in ways and on a scale heretofore unknown, affecting the structure of business, finances, and the kinds and quantities of goods needed.[47]

It is within the framework of these changing conditions that one must consider the fortunes of the early German-Jewish immigrants to New Mexico. They clearly affected the course of action adopted by Solomon Jacob Spiegelberg. Having worked as a clerk for Eugene Leitensdorfer, Solomon Jacob apparently signed on with Colonel Sterling Price for the Chihuahua campaign. There are indications but no direct evidence that he served as a sutler, provisioner for the troops.[48] Other evidence implies that he went south as a merchant. He may have done both. In 1846, on his return, Solomon Jacob founded the house of Spiegelberg. At that point he received an appointment as sutler to the newly established Fort Marcy at Santa Fe.[49] Rather than viewing the war as an obstacle to trade, Spiegelberg saw in the new conditions an opportunity to advance his business fortunes.

Others, too, were drawn into the framework of army needs. The military expenditures for grain and forage surpassed all other outlays combined.[50] By 1852 Joseph Hersch, who had been operating as a merchant, had acquired a gristmill in Santa Fe and a contract to deliver 50,000 pounds of flour to the army in Santa Fe.[51] Hersch held grain and corn contracts with the army throughout the 1850s. Up to 1859 he had received orders totalling 711,500 pounds of flour.[52]

Such experiences typified the changes that occurred in New Mexico after the American takeover. The merchant middleman became a key person in supplying troops with both local and eastern produce as well as being a supplier to the local population. In the process, the "itinerant peddler" of the Santa Fe Trail became a sedentary merchant or shopkeeper.

The changes, however, could not have occurred overnight.

Dealing with a later period, William Parish, the leading scholar of business history in New Mexico, attributed "a spectacular change in the conduct of frontier business" to the appearance of the German-Jewish merchant in New Mexico. But when he referred to the late Mexican and early territorial years, he pointed out that "when the German-Jewish merchant came to New Mexico at the close of the 1840s, his bed had already been made for him by an enterprising freelance American trader. . . ." [53] Parish similarly warns us against exaggerating the character of this early trade, which, he held, was not "much above the level attained by the beginning petty capitalist who deals in the products of the local countryside, supplemented on an unplanned basis by the imports of the traveling merchant." [54]

The evidence supports a picture of spirited growth. But the forts and armed points in New Mexico were not all established simultaneously. Fort Marcy was created in 1846; Fort Union, near Mora, in 1851. The number of troops present was not large. The total military establishment in New Mexico in the period 1851–61 averaged 1,700 men for the entire territory. Fort Marcy had only 67 soldiers in 1858. [55] Such indications permit the assumption that numbers did not demand mercantile heroics in terms of supply or the unearthing of extraordinary credit sources.

It must also be taken into account that the lower stages of peddling as understood elsewhere in the country were more unusual in New Mexico. Merchants involved with quantities of goods that exceeded those handled by the foot peddler existed from the very beginning and commerce in New Mexico cannot be said to have passed through that stage in a significant way. This development did not prevent peddling completely. American rule changed legal trading conditions in New Mexico, opening new opportunities for internal civilian commerce. Although illegal, a measure of retail trade had been practiced by Americans under Mexican rule as far south as Chihuahua. [56] Now, many of these restrictions ceased. General Kearny's code of government allowed merchants and peddlers to operate under license. Peddlers were defined as persons dealing "in the selling of goods . . . other than the growth, produce, or manufacture of this Territory, by going from place to place to sell the same." [57] This exclusion might have been made to provide some protection to customary local internal trade and economic patterns.

An early and seemingly rare example of a Jew who engaged in peddling briefly was Nathan Appel, who arrived in Santa Fe in 1847. He "explored the surrounding countryside on a number of trading adventures, selling merchandise, 'at a very high price' in the villages north of Santa Fe." [58] Appel's ventures must have turned out well. By 1852 he had married, moved to Socorro, and set up a store. [59]

                                                                ᐱ

How did the early Jewish New Mexicans fare? A difficult problem of many frontier studies intervenes here—the matter of stability. The history of any people in a fixed location leans heavily on those who stayed. Transients leave fewer traces and associations than permanent residents, however important they may be.

It is an open question whether the early arrivals from the United States to New Mexico intended to stay. Economic opportunity and welfare were the touchstones in such decisions. New Mexico was no farming frontier for the early Anglo immigrants. Wherever trade and mining bonanza were the initial attraction in the West, problems of transience arose. Outside of the few Anglos who married and settled in Mexican New Mexico there were many who merely did business there or passed through. In the early territorial period many who came could only make their decision about long-term residence with the passage of time, among them appointed officials, soldiers, and prospectors, as well as traders.

A comparison of Jewish names in the 1850 and 1860 censuses shows considerable impermanence. In 1850 there were possibly sixteen Jews in the population schedules based on name, occupation, and birthplace data. Of those sixteen, only six remained in the census of 1860. While there is evidence of why one person, Solomon Jacob Spiegelberg, left, and an account of the death of Elias Spiegelberg (a roof fell upon him while he slept), there is nothing known of why the other eight (half of the total) departed. Writing in 1850, James S. Calhoun, the Indian agent, ventured the opinion that as a result of Indian unrest, "at least half of American immigrants had left the Territory." [60] The numbers are too small to judge whether Jews were more or less inclined to leave than non-Jews, but the scanty data suggest, at least, that the rate of departure was roughly the same.

Some evidence dealing with those who left may be suggestive of their condition as compared with those who stayed. All who had left by 1860 were still under thirty years of age in 1850 and all were single in that year and without other family. Although caution as to any conclusion is in order, one may ponder the presence of family as a factor of stability. If economic difficulty or brighter prospects elsewhere were among the reasons for leaving, then their youth and relative mobility certainly made it easy for them to go.

Evidence of their economic well-being may also help distinguish between those who stayed and those who left. Those who stayed did well. Levi Spiegelberg was nearly thirty in 1860, had recently married, and advanced his fortunes from a declaration of no real estate in 1850 to $15,000 worth in 1860—no small sum in those days. In addition, he revealed his personal estate to be $50,000 in 1860. [61] No personal estate figures were available for 1850. Joseph Hersch had $300 in real estate in 1850 and claimed $40,000 in 1860 and another $20,000 in his personal estate. [62] Simon Rosenstein, in Albuquerque, listed $600 of real estate in 1850 and $500 in 1860. His personal estate, however, amounted to $22,000 in 1860. [63] There can be little doubt that New Mexico's economic climate agreed with them.

Those who stayed had usually attained estates of five figures by 1860. In the one case where this was not so, that of Nathan

Appel, he had moved several times during the decade and was, by 1860, already in Arizona (then still a part of New Mexico). One wonders whether his declared worth, some $6,300 in 1860, and the five-figure estates of those who stayed, represents a kind of break point between those who found it economically worthwhile to remain and those who did not.[64]

ᴄ᪥

The issue of stability apart, these early success stories should not be taken as evidence that the road was an easy one. Territorial New Mexico was a dangerous place, where lawlessness and violence were daily fare. In 1849, R. H. Weightman, a well-known attorney and political figure in New Mexico, represented Simon Rosenstein, who had been arrested by soldiers of the garrison at Albuquerque, confined to the guardhouse, and while blindfolded, "*stripped*, and *bound* and *scourged*." This, Weightman related, occurred while Rosenstein was "peacefully engaged in the prosecution of his lawful business as a trader, or merchant." Attacking the arbitrary behavior of the government itself, Weightman described these events in Congress where he was serving as the territorial representative.[65] Again in 1855 the unfortunate Rosenstein suffered an assault upon his person.[66] Danger went hand in hand with success in these turbulent years.

Like many others, the Jews suffered losses at the hands of the Indian raiders. In 1851 Joseph Hersch lost animals in a raid near Santa Fe.[67] There was even loss of life. A Mr. Goldstein was the victim of an encounter with Indians, along with others near Wagon Mound around 1850 based on private papers found near the putrified bodies, which were buried in a common grave.[68]

The rough side of frontier society also had its impact on some of the Jews. The gambling, often described by contemporaries as a great evil, tempted some. Speaking of a Jewish trader to whom James Webb, the Santa Fe merchant, was a creditor, John Kingsbury, Webb's agent, recorded that [Selig] Weinheim "was doing a good and profitable business, had good credit, but suffered himself to play off all his profits and much more, deceived his best friends and countrymen."[69] Kingsbury commented to Webb that even "such men as Sampson Beuthner," another well-known Jewish merchant, played "as heavy as anyone."[70] Whether loneliness or character contributed to this condition, the participation of a number of Jews in such activities is unquestionable.

Drink, too, had its Jewish adherents. Simon Rosenstein, who allowed card playing in his store, was apparently too drunk on one occasion to intervene in an alleged cheating incident involving Judge Kirby Benedict, which could have ended in tragedy.[71] Rosenstein's drinking became a factor in his divorce from his Hispanic wife in 1866, possibly the first involving a Jew in the territory.[72] Without generalizing, it is easy to imagine that Jews on the frontier engaged in the customs and activities of the rougher elements of Anglo society. Some, like Rosenstein and Weinheim, overdid it. Perhaps, too, the avoidance of all such amusement would have isolated them to a degree intolerable for themselves and for their relationship with others.

🎵

How the Jewish newcomers progressed through the first generation of existence in New Mexico involves their social as well as their economic well-being. As suggested by the census data, they were young when they came. Solomon Jacob Spiegelberg was eighteen or nineteen when he left home. His brother Levi was eighteen when he arrived in 1848 and brother Elias the same age when he left Germany.[73] Joseph Hersch was the oldster in 1850 at the age of thirty.[74] They were not unusual. Out of eighteen merchants and clerks born in Germany and living in Santa Fe County in 1850 (including the above-named persons) only four were thirty or older.[75] No doubt, their immigration (Jewish and non-Jewish) reflected conditions imposed in the old country. By comparison, of thirty-seven Anglo newcomers, merchants and clerks, thirteen were over thirty.[76]

The marital condition of the young immigrants indicated both their youth and their newness in the country. Only one Jew, Simon Rosenstein (Rosenstan in the 1850 census), was married.

He was thirty years old. Of the eighteen merchants and clerks from Germany in Santa Fe County, only one, at the venerable age of forty-five, had a family. The Anglo arrivals, too, built families only slowly. Of thirty-seven merchants and clerks, only three had families. By contrast, the Hispanic-surnamed persons in commercial pursuits reflected a higher degree of family building. Of nineteen, nine had families.

At best, up to 1860, the number of Jews living in New Mexico was small and can only be fixed approximately. A perusal of the population schedules of 1850 permits a possible total of sixteen. The census, however, was probably not complete. Nathan Appel, for instance, who claimed residence after 1847, is not enumerated. William Parish noted nine merchants in his totals for the years 1845–49, but his list includes names not noted in the census.

By 1860, the Jewish population had at least doubled to thirty-two, with a possible maximum of forty-three. The rate of increase exceeded the general population growth of New Mexico and stayed roughly even with the rate of German immigration into the territory if one uses the maximum figure of forty-three.[77]

The passage of a decade showed its effects on their social condition. In 1850, only one Jew had been married. In 1860 there were at least six families with Jewish male heads. Some of them were newcomers who arrived during the fifties, while others were among those already listed in the 1850 census. The first American but non-New Mexican-born Jewish children appeared in the 1860 census rolls. Nevertheless, the young and single still dominated the list, indicating continuity in the pattern of immigration. All of the Jewish adult males were still German-born.

If nuclear family building came slowly to the young immigrants, they were not, as noted earlier, devoid of family ties. The readiness with which young male relatives followed their predecessors suggests that family additions served both their economic and social needs in this country as well as solving their problems in the old homeland. The brothers and cousins surely provided a strong sense of trust which, in turn, allowed a certain flexibility in business arrangements and an edge against loneliness not as readily available to an individual. Although one cannot argue for it conclusively out of these family relationships, it nevertheless seems likely that the most impressive successes among the Jews in business by 1860 were those involving family firms, particularly those among brothers. The fraternal tie may well have provided the most stabilizing economic and social condition for the first generation of immigrant Jews in New Mexico.

How Solomon Jacob Spiegelberg occupied himself in the mid-forties had not changed much by 1860 in terms of economic activity. In the 1850 census all the Jews were merchants or store clerks, and the heavy majority of them still were in 1860. At most only a minor broadening of activities occurred. There were several soldiers who possibly were Jews, a clerk of the Ninth Territorial Legislative Assembly, and, possibly, a confectioner.

Together with most Anglos, the Jews tended to stay around Santa Fe. In his study of German-Jewish merchants, William Parish found eight out of nine there in 1850 and nearly two-thirds (sixteen out of twenty-five) in 1860.[78] The larger figures derived from census data, however, add places of residence. To Parish's listing of Santa Fe and Taos in 1850, those data add Albuquerque. In 1860 Parish found merchants in Santa Fe, Albuquerque, Las Vegas, and Taos and in rural areas.[79] The census allows us to add Los Lunas, Mora, Arizona County, and several forts. Although Santa Fe clearly remained the major center of attraction, Anglo residence had spread to other communities, and the Jewish settlers were part of that expansion. In addition to their residences by 1860, Jews had licenses to trade at one time or another in every county which existed: Bernalillo, Doña Ana, San Miguel, Rio Arriba, Taos, and Valencia.[80]

🐾

How did the first generation of Jews in New Mexico fare as Jews? Information on their spiritual condition is scarce. Young single males, few in number and occupied with their economic affairs, probably did not provide the best example for demonstrating the open practice of Judaism. Nevertheless, there are signs that they did not forget that they were Jews. As early as 1848 a reference to their presence in Santa Fe appeared in *The Occident*, a periodical published in Philadelphia devoted to Jewish affairs. In 1856 the same publication noted that there were at least four subscribers in New Mexico.[81]

Our first clear indication that they had not abandoned their customs came in 1860. An item carried in *The American Israelite* in 1881 recalled the "first Yom Kippur held at Santa Fe" at the home of Levi Spiegelberg. The whole Spiegelberg clan, the Solomon Spiegelbergs (no relation apparently to the family of Solomon Jacob), two Staab brothers, two Dittenhoffers, Louis Gold and son, Joseph Hersch, Louis Felsenthal, Aaron Zeckendorf, Herman Elsberg, Herman Ilfeld, and Philip Schwartzkopf attended.[82] The assemblage probably included the whole Jewish population of the town at the time.

Why did 1860 become the date for the "first" commemoration of its kind? There can be no certainty, but some thoughts may be offered. Levi Spiegelberg had married within the year and brought his bride, Betty (age seventeen), to Santa Fe from Germany. Possibly the new arrival evoked memories and provided an opportunity heretofore absent for a proper observance of the solemn Day of Atonement. The newcomer and Mrs. Solomon Spiegelberg were the only two "Hebrew ladies" in town. Mrs. Solomon Spiegelberg had been present, but there is some speculation that the two Spiegelberg families did not get on too well.[83] The new arrival may have provided the reason for a social rapprochement and the holy day a religious occasion on which differences were supposed to be forgiven.

The event impressed the anonymous correspondent deeply. The company remained together all through the day fasting and praying, and, the writer recalled, the thrill of the old days "rushed through our souls." He reminisced, "It was a strange crowd in that Catholic country, where Indian fights, murders, broils, and fandangos were every-day occurrences. . . ."[84]

The observance of that Day of Atonement, however, may reveal its exceptional character. Prior to 1860 there is no sign of public religious expression, no sign that Jews joined together as Jews to pray or sought to form a congregation of any kind, or whether they observed dietary laws, although conditions in New Mexico would have made that difficult at best. It may be that those who felt the need prayed privately and quietly all through the years.

Whether they allowed themselves to express their religious feelings openly also appears moot. We do not hear of Sabbath closings. In New Mexico, as in many other places, the pressure of business conditions may not have permitted them to place themselves at such a competitive disadvantage. They may simply have had to forego their traditional ways. Of course, there is also the possibility that those who had decided to move to remote areas where they would encounter problems in fulfilling the requirements of religious observance had already discounted their religious needs in advance.[85]

All the same, it is equally clear that the German-Jewish New Mexicans in general did not hide their Jewishness or seek to forget it. The first generation of non-Hispanic Jews must have had greater problems in perpetuating themselves as Jews than did those who came later. The census data of the early territorial period indicate that insofar as Jews married, they did so mostly with Hispanic women. Four of the six married Jewish males did so. Three of those four lived in relative isolation as Jews. Only Levi Spiegelberg, who had done very well economically, returned to Germany and married a German-born Jewish girl, while Solomon Spiegelberg, who was thirty-five in 1860, arrived in New Mexico already married to his German-born Jewish wife with four children born in New York.

A sense of their intentions can be seen in the letter of the young Emanuel Rosenwald, who later became an important figure in Las Vegas. Still in Baltimore in 1860, he wrote to a friend in the West, "I must not forget to tell you, that if you would come here, I would introduce you to some very beautiful Hebrew ladies."[86] The few marriages that took place and the choices made suggest tentatively that economic factors as well as isolated conditions contributed to the exercise of marriage options. Those who had the resources could extend the range of their search to the East Coast and even the old country.

❧

How the German-Jewish immigrants fared as Jews is only half answered by a description of their internal religious and social life. The other half of the answer rests on how they got along with the non-Jewish population among whom they lived. The Jews were an infinitesimal fraction of one percent of the total population and even of the Anglo population of the territory. Clearly, it was they who had to adapt to existing conditions. There is no sign that they came in with great resources with which to influence any of the constituencies with whom they had to deal to do things as they might have wished. They had to accept the reality of a settled Hispanic population and its traditions, the givens of American practices and laws, and the circumstances of the moment. Hispanos and non-Jewish "Anglos," the common designation for non-Hispanics, would be their customers and suppliers, as well as their neighbors. More than other newcomers, the Jews had to learn to get along in New Mexico.

It seems safe to say that the Jews were regarded and regarded themselves as part of the Anglo newcomers who came to New Mexico from the 1840s on. The cultural separation of Anglos from native New Mexicans dictated that. Moreover, the contingent of Anglo merchants and traders, a small community of common activity and interest even while they were competitors, ensured a considerable degree of interaction, cooperation, and trust. Personal trust meant much, and differences based on religion or ethnic background, whatever they meant in the East or the old country, had to give way to the need of the newcomers to rely on one another.

That did not mean, however, that hostile attitudes toward Jews endemic in Christian culture did not reach New Mexico or that Jews or others in New Mexico were oblivious to differences. As noted earlier, Webb had expressed his stereotypical views of Speyers. Informing Webb of Weinheim's gambling misfortunes, John Kingsbury described them in his initial impression as "a Jewish swindle," although he softened his judgment later.[87]

Kingsbury's comments reveal, in addition, elements of collective concern among Jews for the wrongdoing of one of their own. "We have had considerable excitement the past weeks in our little Jerusalem of Santa Fe," he remarked, when he introduced the subject of Weinheim to Webb. "The whole Jew outfit are more or less interested in this nest." He added with amused disdain, "the excitement is really laughable."[88] The Jews were apparently disturbed by the notion that the disgrace of one of their fellows might reflect on all, and Kingsbury, in his stereotypical way, was willing, at least initially, to attribute Weinheim's behavior to an assumed collective characteristic.

Materials indicate both competition and cooperation within the commercial community. Webb's letters and papers (which date to 1861) include correspondence from the Beuthners in Taos, Simon Rosenstein in Albuquerque, and Moses Sachs in Los Lunas. Invoices for purchases include the firms of Spiegelberg and Connelly and Amberg of Santa Fe.[89] Webb discussed business affairs with the Spiegelbergs in Boston, watched their activities and those of the Beuthners, and rented a store to "the Jew Abrahams" in 1853.[90] Henry Connelly, later governor of the territory, wrote Webb in 1854 to get Mexican blankets from Joe Hersh [Hersch]. "If he has the articles," Connelly wrote, "I would take it as a favor if you would get them of him, as he is owing me, but at the price that you would give them. . . ."[91]

Partnerships, a major form of business organization in the

territory, were organized not only between relatives but also between unrelated Jews as well as between Jewish and Gentile Anglos.[92] For a time Henry Connelly and Jacob Amberg joined forces in the fifties. So too did Charles P. Clever, a German immigrant and later an important political figure in territorial politics, and Sigmund Seligman.[93] In both cases family members later joined the original arrangement. When the partnerships dissolved, they did not necessarily end friendships. Such results allow for the interpretation that open attitudes, mutual trust, and respect characterized many of these arrangements.

The ease of the commercial interrelationship of Jews and Christians proved important to the well-being of the former. Pointing up the importance of the new businessman, Howard R. Lamar asserts that "the American merchant-trader and the military were to dominate New Mexico from 1846 to 1870."[94] The need to protect the Santa Fe trade and the property of the American traders was a crucial factor in the coming of the war with Mexico. The leading figures of early civil government, Charles Bent, General Kearny's choice as governor, Supreme Court justices Joab Houghton, Carlos Beaubien, and Antonio Jose Otero, were traders. So too were Eugene Leitensdorfer, who became auditor, and William S. Messervy, the first territorial delegate to Congress, who was Webb's partner.

The business connections of some of the Jewish merchants with these first political leaders were strong. Henry Connelly, who had married into an influential Mexican family and became governor in 1861, was, as mentioned earlier, a partner of Jacob Amberg. Joab Houghton had been a member of Eugene Leitensdorfer's mercantile house and knew the Spiegelbergs well enough to write about Solomon Jacob's early days and a "farewell tribute" to Emanuel Spiegelberg in 1868.[95] Charles Clever, who had also worked for Eugene Leitensdorfer and had become a partner of Sigmund Seligman, developed his own political career in the fifties. He became adjutant to Governor Connelly in 1861.[96] Such ties were strong enough so that in 1852 Solomon Jacob Spiegelberg advanced the territorial legislature four thousand dollars to pay its members' salaries. The sum was repaid in 1853.[97]

Clearly, German-Jewish merchants were well known and accepted among the Anglo leaders who acquired political influence. One secondary source even characterized the Jewish merchants as a faction or party in their own right.[98] Outside of their family-oriented businesses, hiring, and aiding the creation of new businesses by relatives, there is no sign that they collaborated; rather they competed with each other, as did all others. If they found some comfort in each other's company as co-religionists, then that appears to be the limit of their association. Indeed, their connections with the top elite of New Mexico might indicate that they attributed as much economic and political value to those ties as to any "intra-Jewish" connections which might have isolated them beyond any value their small numbers could provide.

Their business connections, however, do not appear to have carried the German-Jewish merchants over into political activity. It may be that the old Anglo settlers who had intermarried with Hispanic families formed a fairly exclusive political and social elite of their own in early territorial days.[99] The Jewish immigrants did not join them in marriage and in the early days did not serve in any political capacity.

The Jews may well have shunned the public limelight in these early years. Solomon Jacob Spiegelberg turned down an appointment as an election judge for militia officials in 1851 on grounds of inexperience and for business reasons.[100] Only Louis Felsenthal, who served as an assistant marshal for the 1860 census in Socorro and as clerk in the House for the Ninth Territorial Legislative Assembly, could in any sense be considered a political appointee.[101] Some of the non-Jewish German immigrants, by contrast, did become involved in political appointments early, among them Charles P. Clever, John H. Mink, and second-generation Eugene Leitensdorfer. There is insufficient evidence, however, to account for these behavioral distinctions in any conclusive fashion.

The Jews also involved themselves heavily in the new institutions which were formed. The Masonic order and the Odd Fellows were the earliest organizations created.[102] The Masons' Montezuma Lodge was chartered on May 8, 1851.[103] Its early membership included the most illustrious Anglo New Mexicans: Ceran St. Vrain, Kit Carson, and Charles Bent among them. The lodge brought together men of similar sentiments and provided a dimension of social life and forms of mutual benefit heretofore nonexistent for Anglos. Soon after its formation, the lodge, together with the Odd Fellows, established a cemetery. On travel through Santa Fe in the mid-sixties, James F. Meline reported that the Hispanic population referred to the lodge as "the American church."[104] In a society without Protestant churches or Jewish congregations, such organizations fulfilled functions difficult to organize otherwise.

Jewish membership in the Masonic order came early. Flora Spiegelberg, the wife of Willi, believed that all five brothers joined and that Solomon Jacob was among the first members in the early fifties.[105] Levi Spiegelberg's name was among the incorporators in 1854.[106] Some other early Jewish members included Albert Elsberg, Jacob Amberg, and Joseph and Solomon Beuthner.[107]

Another dimension of social purpose and cultural responsibility toward their surroundings can be seen in the creation of the Historical Society of New Mexico in 1859. Some of the same persons who created the Masonic presence involved themselves in this enterprise to collect and preserve historical records and artifacts related to the natural history of New Mexico.[108] Although the membership of the society and the Masonic Lodge overlapped heavily, the nature of the society, with its cultural, rather than its ethical base, included a broad ethnic and religious spectrum of Santa Fe society.[109] Lansing Bloom, who edited the minutes of the society for publication, pointed out the organization's cosmopolitan character by noting that "representatives of the Jewish race" were among its members.[110]

Indeed, Jewish members were present from the beginning. Although they were not charter members, Louis Felsenthal, Zadok Staab, and Albert Elsberg joined immediately after the society's founding. Bernard Seligman joined soon after. And Jewish and non-Jewish members alike were early contributors of items to the collections set up by the new organization.

Although the Masons and the Historical Society served different purposes and attracted, to some extent, different constituencies, they both reflected a new sense of belonging and social tone in Santa Fe. If, on one hand, they drew like-minded persons together, on the other, they were somewhat exclusive organizations. Masonry had its own set of rules for admission, as did the historical society. Entrance into the latter came through recommendation and a vote of three-fourths of the membership.[111] Jews were clearly accepted into the emerging social and cultural network that was growing up among the more educated or wealthier segments of local society.

🙾

How these first German Jews got on with Hispanos as compared with Anglos is difficult to judge in the absence of a body of documentation. It is possible that the Jews found Hispanic culture less forbidding than did native-born Anglo newcomers. American-born non-Jewish Anglos often appeared surprised that people in the Southwest were "different," and they sometimes judged the native New Mexican population to be inferior to themselves for cultural, racial, or religious reasons.[112] To European immigrants, coping with another new language may have been less strange and arduous than for native-born Americans. To Jews the differences between Catholic and Protestant may have been quite unimportant. Parish pointed up "a minimum of cultural inhibitions" and "the penchant for seeking business wherever it could be found" as factors in the success of the Jews.[113] Perhaps the simple consideration that they had a greater sensitivity towards prejudice than their fellows may have come into play. But it is difficult to weigh such matters as if they were fact, and in the absence of data from these early years such judgments remain unproven, even if plausible.

🙞

No earth-shaking event marked the year 1860 in New Mexico. Their commemoration of the Day of Atonement together symbolized a generation of immigration, settlement, survival, and success, and the Jews of Santa Fe celebrated it in full measure in accord with their customs and beliefs. That in itself was a landmark in their eyes.

The Golden Age of the German-Jewish Merchants, 1860–80

The years 1860–80 marked the golden age of the German-Jewish merchant settlers in New Mexico. Some of those who had come in the forties and fifties achieved success in their business and a high degree of acceptance in their social affairs. They were joined by a new generation of pioneers who added to their numbers. Changes occurred, too, that reflected the passage of time. The pioneers of the first generation became established residents, and long-term settlement allowed a social evolution to take place within the Jewish community. The end of the period came with the noteworthy changes wrought by the arrival of the railroad in 1880.

The early sixties, above all else, found America involved in a vast civil war. Although the major events of the conflict were relatively remote from New Mexico and the scale of combat there did not match what took place in the East, the territory neverthe-less suffered invasion and was the scene of troop movements and pitched battles. As a result, the civilian population and the economy suffered some disruption and destruction.

New Mexico's involvement came about largely as the result of plans forged by General Henry H. Sibley, an officer with

Southern sympathies who had been stationed in the territory. He sought to conquer New Mexico for the Confederacy. Sibley may even have envisioned the capture of the entire Southwest from as far north as Colorado and Utah to the Pacific as well as some of the northern provinces of Mexico.[1] He believed that with a force raised in Texas he could combine the support of Confederate sympathizers in southern New Mexico, anti-Unionist Mormons, and pro-Southern elements in California.[2]

One key to Sibley's campaign plans lay in solving the problem of logistics. He conceived the operation as a self-sustaining one initially with the troops carrying only enough supplies to maintain themselves enroute to the battle theater. Once there, he counted on the capture of forts and garrisons in New Mexico proper and the accumulation of local produce to take care of his troops' needs.[3]

Sibley's vision brought him into a line of direct conflict with that small group of merchants which made up New Mexico's Jewish population in the early sixties. Having long been engaged in acquiring supplies for the army, the outbreak of the war led them into taking on increased responsibilities of this sort. Henry Lesinsky, who had only recently become a merchant after his arrival from California where he had been a prospector, was living in Sabinal in 1861. The war brought business to a standstill, but Lesinsky worked to supply grain for the Union forces of General Edward R. S. Canby. When Sibley's forces took control of the area, Lesinsky's house was plundered. Aware of the function that he was serving for the Union army, Sibley, Lesinsky believed, sent scouts out to arrest him. Lesinsky, at that point, joined General Canby's troops.[4]

In its early phases Sibley's campaign made good advances. In March 1862 his army occupied Albuquerque and then Santa Fe itself. Those victories, as well as several smaller operations, appeared to accomplish some of what Sibley had sought to do. Confiscations by his Texans of Union supplies and the stores of the local merchants brought a sense of well-being.[5] Despite their successes, however, the Confederates did not gain sufficient materiel to sustain them for long. That, in part, was the result of efforts by Union troops east of Santa Fe to deprive them of supplies and the behavior of the Texans themselves, who vandalized the town to some extent and dissipated their new-found wealth.[6]

Like Lesinsky farther south, Jewish merchants in Santa Fe felt the effects of Sibley's presence. The Spiegelbergs became sutlers to the New Mexico Volunteers, holding that appointment from July 1861 to July 1864.[7] Their store was among those that suffered confiscation. Flora Spiegelberg, the wife of Willi, who was himself in Santa Fe during the occupation, reported that fifty thousand dollars worth of merchandise passed into the Texans' hands.[8]

The behavior of the occupying troops in Santa Fe produced some danger for the inhabitants. Aware of the problems that accompanied armies of occupation, Sibley warned the women of the capital not to appear in public. Despite this cautionary step, with few diversions available, one day Levi Spiegelberg took his young wife on a buggy ride to nearby Indian pueblos to view the dances and crafts. The next morning an old pioneer visited Spiegelberg and warned him not to venture forth again with his wife out of fear she would be kidnapped. The brothers henceforth kept an armed vigil over her at home. Drunken soldiers, too, endangered life and limb when they entered the Spiegelberg store and demanded goods without payment. On one occasion a soldier's demand for a box of cigars without payment nearly led to Levi Spiegelberg's death.[9]

Other Jewish merchants also felt the Confederate presence. Letters seeking compensation for losses came to the secretary of the treasury from Louis Gold, who lost $2,300 dollars of clothing and staples, Albert Elsberg, over $4,300, and Joseph Hersch, over $3,100 of similar goods.[10] Part of the Amberg-Elsberg losses may have come from the Confederates' use of three teams of horses for transporting stores in April 1862, the bill for which was signed by General Sibley in the sum of $330.[11] The losses were, no doubt, hard to absorb but not crippling. The Spiegelbergs, apparently, never received any compensation for their losses. Flora Spiegelberg referred to the existence of warrants, which the family held as souvenirs.[12]

In all, the Confederates remained in Santa Fe only a few weeks. A costly battle at Glorieta, a few miles to the east, and the threat of a northward move by General Canby toward Albuquerque sent them into a retreat from which they never recovered. After mid-April, the territorial government, which had evacuated to Las Vegas, returned to Santa Fe. In terms of military engagements, the war in northern New Mexico was over.

Like other New Mexicans, Jews also served in the armed forces of the Union. A fair number acquired commissions. Solomon Spiegelberg—not of the brothers—was a captain by appointment of General Canby. Louis Felsenthal recruited a company of volunteers and became a captain in the summer of 1861.[13] Bernard Seligman reached the rank of captain and the position of quartermaster, while William Zeckendorf and Marcus Brunswick, too, became officers. There is no sign that any New Mexican Jews joined with the Confederate troops in New Mexico.

ᔐ

Whatever the short-term effects of the Civil War upon the Jewish population, they did not alter any long-term patterns of immigration. As noted earlier, at least thirty-two Jews were present in 1860, and perhaps there were a dozen more on the basis of name recognition. In 1870 there were about sixty minimum and perhaps as many as eighty-five. At the end of the period in 1880, there were about 180 clearly identified Jews with about 220 as a maximum.[14] The national survey of Jewish population compiled in 1877 by Jewish agencies cited 108 in residence in New Mexico, a reasonable estimate without the more comprehensive census data.[15]

The enumerations of the census allow only decennial attempts at precision. In a mobile society there were those who came and went rapidly in the years between census taking. And if some were persuaded to move by better prospects, it cannot be assumed that they were all badly off. Otto Mears, who worked for both Elsberg and Amberg and then the Staabs in the mid-sixties, moved on to Colorado to become wealthy and politically influential by dint of his talents.[16]

Clearly, Jews did not come to New Mexico in large numbers either before or after the Civil War. Neither did other Anglos. In 1877 the territory ranked forty-fourth of forty-nine states and territories in its Jewish population.[17] In total population it ranked forty-first in 1880. Despite its growth, New Mexico still ranked near the bottom nationally in its place as a residence of Jews. Rounding off the figures within the territory, Jews accounted for five-hundreths of one percent in 1860, one-tenth of one percent in 1870, and two-tenths of one percent in 1880. All in all, that amounted to a quadrupling of their percentage of the total population in twenty years and a considerably higher rate of growth than the population of the territory in general.

Despite the infinitesimal size of the group, to some they appeared more numerous than they were in actuality. As a population engaged in commerce, they settled with few exceptions in the larger towns, presenting an image of density which seemed to magnify their numbers. The highest concentration lived in Santa Fe County where seventy-odd Jews represented about seven-tenths of one percent of the total population in 1880. In San Miguel County, with Las Vegas as its urban center, about the same number of Jews lived in a county with twice the population of Santa Fe County, that is, about thirty-five hundredths of one percent.

Within the towns Jews could appear even more heavily settled by virtue of their concentration. The censuses showed that family members and clerks lived either close to or with each other. Moreover, their places of business or employment were situated on or near the plazas typical of the central districts of the towns. And not least of all, the Jews formed a considerably larger portion of the merchant than of the general population, the signs of their stores standing out plainly for all to see. In 1850 they represented over 7 percent of all merchants in an agrarian society and in 1860, 16 percent. Those figures fell to 9 percent in 1870 and rose again to 12 percent in 1880. Their presence in the most conspicuous parts of the towns could easily give the impression of far greater numbers than actually existed.

Travelers to New Mexico who strolled the plazas and wrote of their experiences noticed them. Some made stereotypical comments about their presence. Writing of his visit to Santa Fe in 1866, James Meline noted changes that had taken place there over a decade. The influx of American goods had led the black shawl to replace the reboso. These items, he related, "appear to find ready sale at the mercantile emporiums of Isaac, Jacob and Abraham."[18] In 1870, William A. Bell, an Englishman engaged in surveying possible rail routes through New Mexico, remarked of Santa Fe, "A large proportion of the traders are of German-Jewish extraction, and, taking them all in all, they are by no means a bad set of fellows, and well suited to the position they occupy. . . ."[19] In 1881, John G. Bourke wrote impressionistically of Santa Fe and the changes that had taken place in a decade, noting, "the narrow streets, still lit at night with camphine torches or filled by day with a motley crew of hook-nosed Jews, blue-coated soldiers, senoritas wrapped to the eyes in rebosos. . . ."[20] The visitors appeared fascinated by the exotic picture of Jews in the Southwest.

The factors attracting Jewish immigration to New Mexico did not change after 1860. The frequent use of family and friends by newcomers as leverage for employment remained. Brothers continued to arrive as a sizable proportion of the immigration. A number of those who came between 1860 and 1880 would be counted among the most successful and best known of the German-Jewish contingent, among them the Bibo clan, the Eldodts, and at the economic apex, the Ilfelds and Rosenwalds. Other combinations—cousins, nephews—related to the above families or to each other, included the Freudenthals and Lesinskys in southern New Mexico and the Gusdorfs in Taos, who were related to the Staabs. Their individual attributes did not change. They still came mainly as young, single men.

In 1870 all of the adult males living in New Mexico still originated from the German immigration. Only in the census of 1880 do unquestionably Jewish American-born adult males appear. Even then they were too few to alter the essentially Germanic ethnic flavor of New Mexican Jewry. Perhaps the best known of these American Jewish families were the Pragers, who came from Pennsylvania and would make their mark after 1880 both in Roswell and in Albuquerque.

The passage of time inevitably affected the social character of the population. The stabilization of their circumstances and their maturity allowed the men to marry. Overwhelmingly unmarried in 1860, and despite the continuing influx of young, unmarried males, New Mexican Jewry slowly began to present a picture of nuclear family life. By 1870 nearly one-third of the males had married and a decade later, nearly half were married.

The pattern of marriages also took on a new character. On the basis of only one example between 1846 and 1860, it was suggested that only successful persons could afford to follow their ethnoreligious urges and marry German-Jewish wives. The increasing number of successes in business in the sixties seems to bear this out. Whereas up to 1860 marriages with local Hispanic women had exceeded all others (of the few who did marry), by 1870 marriages with German-Jewish wives surpassed all others (seven out of eleven wives to Jewish males were of this background). Moreover, those who married German-Jewish women were persons who had achieved some degree of financial success. Among them were Henry Lesinsky, Louis Sulzbacher, Joseph Hersch, Abraham Staab, Aaron Zeckendorf, and Simon Lowenstein.

In the seventies, the pattern of wives' birthplaces shifted to some extent. Marriages to women from the states nearly equalled those with German-born women. By that time, perhaps, the pool of eligible women stemming from the German-Jewish immigration but born in the United States had become sufficiently large to make the trip to Germany less necessary than before. Whether German or native born, the women were overwhelmingly Jewish. One must conclude that religious affiliation remained an important condition for the New Mexican Jewish men in their selection of mates and that they sought to maintain their identity even as their direct ties with Germany slowly began to decline.

The appearance of children followed the increase of marriages. Only four Jewish families had offspring in 1860. By 1870, eight families had them, and in 1880, twenty-four Jewish families had no fewer than seventy-two children sixteen years of age or younger.[21] Between 1870 and 1880 in particular the nuclear family began to take its place as a social characteristic of the Jewish population, producing a more complex community than had existed earlier.

The issue of raising children as Jews now became a consideration. Among observant Jews the practice of circumcision of male children is important. In 1872 an item in *The Israelite* related that the Reverend M. A. H. Fleischer of Denver, at the solicitation of the Jewish citizens of New Mexico, had visited the territory in June "and circumcised a large number of children at an advanced age." Happily, the correspondent announced, the hosts were pleased with the results and "at the scientific manner in which the operation was performed."[22] An unsigned circumcision record, that of Dr. John Elsner, carried entries of operations performed on one Louis Amberg in 1867 at the age of twenty-seven in Black Hawk Territory in Colorado and a visit to Santa Fe in 1875 to accommodate Edward Samuel ben Abraham, son of Abraham Staab on December 7 at the age of four weeks and Eleazor ben Hirsch, son of Herman Ilfeld at the age of eight days on December 8.[23] The Jews were forced to reach out beyond their isolated geographic area if they expected their needs as Jews to be fulfilled.

In 1876, the first bar mitzvah ceremony in New Mexico took place in Santa Fe. The young boy inducted into manhood was Alfred Grunsfeld, a nephew of the Spiegelbergs and son of Albert

Grunsfeld, after whom Congregation Albert in Albuquerque was named a generation later. [24] Here were further signs that the needs of the young as Jews were stretching the community into performance of services which the old joint male families did not need.

Such matters came under discussion in the seventies. The state of religious education disturbed some. Among the complaints voiced by one Jedidjiah of Santa Fe in 1877 in *Die Deborah*, a German language Jewish weekly emanating from Cincinnati, was his concern for the lack of schooling and instruction for the young. "Everything is lacking here," he wrote, "the congregation, associations, synagogue, clergy, teacher, school and every kind of instruction." [25] There can be little doubt that the growth of the nuclear family contributed strongly to his misgivings.

Beyond the specific needs of the young, signs of a general desire for a more organized religious life emerged in the seventies. As is known, Jews had long been celebrating their major holidays in New Mexico, but now people began to seek regularity in their religious practices. In 1874, a letter to *The American Israelite* described a holiday observance in Mora. There persons had congregated from as far away as fifty miles to participate. "Service," we are told, "was held in the orthodox 'minhag' (custom), a young lawyer of intelligence and high standing at the New Mexico bar (possibly Louis Sulzbacher) performing the duties of chasan (cantor)." [26] Those present resolved to establish a congregation. The driving force behind this effort in a community of scant population was Benjamin Loewenstein. [27] Although nothing came of this resolve, clearly a need was being felt and discussed.

A more contentious expression of this feeling appeared in *Die Deborah* in 1877. Jedidjiah's letter from Santa Fe noted above strongly protested the state of religious affairs among the Jews in the city. Admitting the difficulty of circumstances in "this wilderness here in the Rocky Mountains," he nevertheless countered that Las Vegas, Santa Fe and other towns contained "Jehudim" (perhaps a sarcastic use of the term *Jews*, implying big shots) enough whose financial condition would not be strained by doing something for their ancestral Judaism. But, as he saw it, even the holiest day, Yom Kippur, was thought of as a "mezumen (money) making" rather than a "minyan (religious association) making" time.[28]

Jedidjiah's criticism received fortification and substantiation from one G. several months later. He described a meeting of Jews in Santa Fe several weeks prior to the High Holidays at which it was agreed to hold services in the Germania Hall. When only eight Jews showed up on the first day of Rosh Hashanah, however, "the pioneers of Judaism in the Far West," he noted sarcastically, "who, by the way, had their stores open," refused to release several Jewish clerks from work for a few hours to join the services to meet the required number of ten for a minyan. G.'s point, like Jedidjiah's, was that "the Almighty Dollar is closer to the Jews of Santa Fe than our holy religion."[29]

One might note here that public religious observance was not totally lacking. In 1872 the Santa Fe *Weekly New Mexican* reported that "the plaza presented a grim appearance on Saturday—most of the stores were closed in consequence of the Jewish holiday."[30]

Nevertheless, the point of the criticism was clear. The resources for community building were present. There were enough persons to participate even if they were not plentiful, and there were finances enough. Only the proper attitude was lacking and that, apparently, among the expected leaders.

Jedidjiah's letter drew its response in defense of the Santa Fe "Jehudim." A respondent, who signed himself as Trebla, praised both Spiegelberg families, Solomon's and Willi's, for their efforts in setting up the Germania Hall for Yom Kippur services and for their participation in the events.[31] The writer also alluded to the fact that two years earlier, at the time of the first bar mitzvah celebration in New Mexico, money had actually been donated for the building of a temple in Santa Fe.[32] Again, nothing had come of that gesture.

Even in this response, however, the thrust of the facts

pointed up the changes that were taking place. Private methods of expressing religious feelings and identity were falling short of what some Jews on the scene wanted. Their increasing numbers and the intensity of their feelings, as well as the needs of their families, demanded a more public and formal organization. That recognition would only come to fruition in the eighties.

The increasing numbers of Jewish women in the sixties and seventies affected the cast of the Jewish community. The sparse data of the 1860 manuscript census indicates that the women did not engage in the family's business affairs but generally took care of home and children. Those who were well off, such as Levi Spiegelberg, could have servants; those less well off, might not.

The home in this period often involved more than the simple nuclear family. Frequently other family members joined to form a relatively sizable group in the household. Servants also lived in. Thus the care and work involved took considerable time and energy.

The manuscript census of 1870 underscored the emerging pattern of the sixties. Jewish women are virtually all described in their occupation as "keeping house." Matilda Lesinsky in Las Cruces, Rebecca Loewenstein and Paulina Sulzbacher in Mora County, and Mathilda Zeckendorf in Albuquerque are all listed in this fashion. Only in the household of Samuel Kohn in Las Vegas, a dealer in wool and pelts, do we find Yetta Kohn described as a seamstress.

With few exceptions, the pattern had not changed by 1880. Wherever listings occur in the census, the wife or other adult female family members are described as housekeepers. Life's fortunes, however, brought some changes. Yetta Kohn, now widowed, became a dealer in wool and hides, possibly finding it necessary to take over her husband's mode of livelihood. For several of the Bibos, women other than wives fulfilled the role of housekeeper. Nathan Bibo's sister, Lina, a widow, kept house for him in Bernalillo and even took charge of the store when business elsewhere took him away.[33] Hispanic wives of Jewish men also listed themselves as housewives.

Their function in the households of New Mexican Jewry presented one side of the role which women played in New Mexico. Quite another dimension appeared in the seventies with Flora Langermann Spiegelberg, the wife of Willi Spiegelberg, who arrived in Santa Fe in 1875. Born in New York and educated in Germany, she made the family home a social center for her husband's widespread economic and political contacts, which included upper-class Hispanos, leading political figures, high-ranking army officers, and visiting dignitaries.

Flora Spiegelberg's biographers depict her as a middle-or upper-middle class exponent of European culture.[34] Her cultural and material standards, which the family was fully capable of supporting, clearly impressed Santa Feans and endeared her to such persons as Bishop Lamy, so far removed from his own European homeland, and Governor Lew Wallace. The wines, European cuisine, her collection of paintings, as well as her piano renditions of Chopin and Mendelssohn, reflected some of what upper-class Santa Fe had left behind in the East or what others knew dimly. In this sense she represented a phenomenon of no mean cultural dimension by the standards she presented.

ᔣᔅ

As at the beginning of the German-Jewish period of immigration in the mid-forties, economic good fortune served as the decisive theme in attracting newcomers. In the small amount of published literature on those Jewish immigrants, it has been axiomatic to point out their success. From many indications that general assessment is correct and the outlines of it had already been laid out by 1860. A few comparisons based on census materials illustrate that judgment. In 1860, about 43 percent of the Anglos and 89 percent of the Hispanos in Santa Fe declared neither real nor personal property.[35] Almost half of the Anglos reported no personal assets and two-thirds no real property.[36] By contrast, 84 percent of Jews reported personal wealth and two-thirds no real property.[37] Clearly, some meaᵴure of wealth among Santa Fe's Jews, who composed the bulk of the total Jewish population of New Mexico in 1860, appeared far more common than in the rest of the Anglo population. This was especially true of personal wealth. In terms of real property, the Jews were at the same level as the rest of the Anglo population.

The level of wealth also reflects the relative well-being of the Jewish population. In 1860, 11.6 percent of Santa Fe's Anglos reported holdings of ten thousand dollars or more.[38] Among the Jews, 33 percent reported wealth at that level. The combined reported wealth (real and personal) of the Anglos was $1,474,864 in 1860 and that of Hispanics, $548,050.[39] The combined wealth of the Jewish population was $220,000. This meant that the share held by Jews was 14 percent of Anglo wealth and about 10.5 percent of the total wealth of the town. When one takes into account that the size of the Jewish community was about one-half of one percent of the population, then the share held by Jews appears quite large.

A decade later, in 1870, the picture had not changed markedly. The total wealth of the Anglos rose a bit—to $1,642,100, of the Hispanos, $628,450.[40] For the Jews, their total wealth had reached $230,000—14 percent of the Anglo wealth and slightly over 10 percent of the Santa Fe total. The percentage of Anglos with over ten thousand dollars decreased slightly from 11.6 to 10.3 percent; the percentage of Jews in this category also dropped from 33 to 31 percent.[41]

Nevertheless, neither in 1860 or 1870 were individual Jews the wealthiest persons in the territory. No Jew approached the wealth of Ceran St. Vrain or the Dold brothers of Las Vegas in 1860. Levi Spiegelberg reported the highest amount among Jews in that year—$65,000. St. Vrain, by comparison, reported over $200,000 and the Dolds $76,500 each. In 1870, Lehman Spiegelberg reported $77,000. Lucien B. Maxwell, in Colfax County, indicated $170,000, largely in real estate holdings.

A different, although incomplete, picture of the relative financial standing of the Jewish merchant community emerges from commercial rating services which had begun to penetrate the territory after the Civil War. Bradstreet's *Commercial Report* for 1872 evaluated 194 businesses, twenty-one of which belonged to Jews. Over 14 percent (seven of forty-nine) of the firms rated A or higher had Jewish proprietors.[42] That represented one-third of all Jewish firms rated and under one-fourth of non-Jewish–owned firms. The data support a picture of well-being.

The census of 1880 did not carry data on wealth. The record of comparative economic performance becomes much more difficult to trace and is often fragmentary and anecdotal. However, there is more than sufficient illustration to demonstrate that some Jews were doing very well. The top merchant families in particular prospered in the seventies. Researchers single out some of the firms for special comment. "Four large commercial firms," asserts Terry Lehmann, "were the basis of Santa Fe's commercial prominence, Spiegelberg Bros., Johnson and Koch, S. Seligman and Bro., and Z. Staab and Co."[43] Three of the four belonged to Jewish families. In 1872 the Spiegelbergs transacted a volume of business estimated at between $500,000 and $700,000. In a letter to the Comptroller of the Currency supporting the formation of the Second National Bank by the Spiegelbergs in 1872, Jose M. Gallegos, New Mexico's delegate to the Congress, estimated their capital at two million dollars.[44] The Staabs, in 1874–75, transacted sales of $600,000 in the wholesale trade alone.[45]

Other sources indicate the scope of the operations of the largest Jewish firms. The Spiegelbergs displayed their confidence in 1874, proposing to the superintendent of Indian affairs of New Mexico, Colonel L. Edwin Dudley, "to supply all rations needed for the Indians of New Mexico. . . ."[46] In his well-known history of New Mexico, Ralph E. Twitchell described the scale of the New Mexico trade by using the Seligman firm as an example. Depicting it as "one of the big concerns engaged in the 'Santa Fe trade,'" he cited the loading of 83 wagons carrying about three tons each at Kansas City for them. The transportation charges on one caravan came to $30,000, the value of the goods to $125,000, and the profit to $51,000.[47] Given the size of the economy of New Mexico, such figures are impressive.

One cannot judge the entire community by the economic

condition of its most successful members, but generally merchants did well. Jews represented an important segment of the total merchant community, and a very large proportion of the Jewish working population were part of it. In 1860, of twenty-five adult males, seventeen were merchants and seven were clerks. In 1870, of thirty-six adult males, twenty-four were merchants and ten were clerks. In 1880, of seventy-one adult males, fifty were merchants and fifteen were clerks. Their concentration in mercantile pursuits was so heavy, they have almost the appearance of a caste. The Jewish population as a whole was well positioned to prosper.

Between 1860 and 1880 the merchants of New Mexico appeared as a full-fledged type. They are best described by William Parish in his studies of German-Jewish merchants. These sedentary merchants were, he noted, "not content merely to sell but desirous to enlist and control the petty capitalist farmer and his supply of produce for eastern shipment."[48] Their success rested on their ability to acquire scarce monetary exchange where no efficient system of indirect lending existed and where purchases had to be hauled long distances.[49] The most successful of the German-Jewish merchants, as well as non-Jewish merchants who engaged in similar types of business, fit into these conditions which were typical of entrepreneurs operating in regions not well developed in capitalist enterprise.

The context became complex. They needed capital to buy goods in the East and sell in the West. They needed to advance capital in the West to buy and sell both in the East and West. No narrow retail operation could satisfy the demands of these arrangements. They bought from New Mexican farmers for the army and for the Indians; they also bought in the East for all their customers. They sold commodities purchased in the East to the local population and had to supply credit for their local producers to produce and buy. In seeking to extend the range of their operations, they set up relatives and friends to open and acquire

markets wherever they could be supported. They became who-
lesalers as well as retailers, and the spread of their operations
carried them far beyond the limits of Santa Fe into a large area
of the entire territory and, for some, beyond.

Although their primary economic activity remained, for
most of them, their stores, the nature of their operations as well
as opportunity, led them into a diverse economic life. Most notable was the move into banking. Until 1870 no banks existed in
New Mexico. The large merchants played the role informally.
The safes of such persons as Abraham Staab became the "de-
pository of large sums of money belonging to the native representatives throughout New Mexico, in the handling of which Abraham Staab served as advisor and trustee." [50] Large purchases from
Staab involved the use of property as security, a function of mortgage banking. [51] Staab, it would appear, followed the pattern of
commercial and mortgage banking used by Spiegelberg. [52] The
Spiegelbergs even issued their own scrip as early as 1863, and,
outside of the use of gold and silver, their paper was probably
more highly regarded than bank notes. [53]

Even after banks appeared, however, mercantile houses long
remained de facto bankers for many of their customers. [54] A Hispanic storekeeper near Taos described to a traveling salesman
from whom he would not buy how he feared theft and did not
trust banks. Charles Ilfeld held his cash for him for "maybe ten
years." [55]

The first attempt to create a bank occurred in 1863. The
legislative assembly had granted a provisional charter in that year
to create a Bank of New Mexico, but congressional approval,
which was necessary to sanction the bill, was never obtained. [56]
Among the ten prominent New Mexicans who sought that charter were Jewish merchants Levi Spiegelberg, Sigmund Seligman,
and Gustave Elsberg. [57]

In 1870, Lucien B. Maxwell, having sold his Beaubien and
Miranda land grant, applied for and received a bank charter in
Santa Fe. His bank, the First National Bank of New Mexico,
became the first in the territory. A few months later, in 1871,

Stephen B. Elkins and Thomas B. Catron in association with others, took over Maxwell's bank.[58] The Spiegelbergs, who were not included in the new directorship, moved quickly to charter a bank of their own. Formed in 1872 as the Second National Bank of New Mexico, four of the brothers: Solomon and Levi of New York, and Lehman and Willi of Santa Fe, became principal stockholders.[59]

The purpose for the creation of the Second National Bank raises some questions. The Spiegelbergs might have feared the loss of opportunity to negotiate their own monetary exchange and to protect their own credit operations.[60] Elkins, seeking to prevent the creation of another bank, attributed their motivation to "the fact that in our organization we did not have any of the jews to take stock."[61] The original shareholders of the Second National included only one possible Jew, Adolph Guttmann, besides the Spiegelberg brothers themselves, who held a majority interest.[62] Whether the Spiegelbergs felt stung by what they interpreted as an anti-Jewish snub is moot, but they did not or could not enlist heavy Jewish support, suggesting theirs was a family rather than a Jewish communal response.

The Spiegelberg bank was the most ambitious venture in banking involving Jews, but not the only one. Toward the end of the seventies, Joseph Rosenwald in Las Vegas became one of the organizers and directors of the San Miguel National Bank.[63] In the eighties and nineties, the coming of the railroad and the growth of new towns would spark a much more rapid expansion in banking facilities.

Since land served at times as security in the credit relationship between the merchant and farmer or herdsman, it too became a factor in the economic activity of the Jewish merchant. The issue of land in New Mexico had some special dimensions which distinguished it from such matters elsewhere in the United States. Title to all property in New Mexico was a difficult problem throughout the territorial period because of the complexity of the land grant issue. The basis of the problem lay in the provisions of the Treaty of Guadalupe Hidalgo under which the

United States agreed to respect property rights held under Spanish and Mexican grant.[64] Differences in legal traditions and use, involving, among other issues, communal rights and boundaries, led to lengthy negotiation and litigation. Claimants, of necessity, turned to attorneys to settle their disputes. The attorneys often received their fees in land, and some acquired large amounts of it by this process.

The holding of real estate among Jewish merchants may well require special studies before definitive statements can be made about it. Insofar as the census materials reveal anything, they tend to show that the acquisition of land before 1880 was distinctly secondary for them. Their personal wealth far exceeded their real wealth and the latter form was not out of line with percentages cited for other Anglos.[65] One does not find ready evidence of the urge to accumulate latifundia characteristic of Thomas B. Catron, whose holdings of two million acres made him one of the largest individual landholders of American history.[66]

Yet, there is evidence of landholding. Most of it appears to be in and around the urban areas where the merchants lived. The Spiegelbergs had a long history of such acquisition before 1880, particularly in Santa Fe itself.[67] It was not unknown, too, for Jewish entrepreneurs to become involved in sheep-raising ventures. Henry Lesinsky became a partner of Benjamin E. Davis on his San Augustin Ranch on the east side of the Organ Mountains, where some 7,500 head grazed in the mid-seventies.[68] On the other hand, although the big Santa Fe and Las Vegas merchants had frequent contacts with Catron, he does not seem to have involved them in his land accumulation ventures.

William Parish has advanced the theory that land accumulation might have proven ill advised for the merchants. The control which the merchant qua banker could exercise on the supplier of agricultural products could easily become oppressive. The relationship with such suppliers was often kept comfortable by the merchant's ability to aid his debtors to solve financial dilemmas rather than pressing his advantage as creditor. The merchant may well have done so out of the necessity to guarantee his sources of supply and to protect his monetary exchange. The merchant did not want his supplier to lose either face or property.[69]

Perhaps the most telling argument against heavy land acquisition by the merchants lay in the character of use of capital. The key to it would have been its liquidity. Heavy land purchase would have hampered that. Moreover, until the middle of the seventies, the value of land was low. Summarizing his subject's career, Catron's biographer noted that "he sought land, and few if any persons . . . acquired more. . . . As his empire grew, disposal of property in exchange for cash created tremendous problems which led to the ultimate loss of most of the property he owned."[70] It would not have made good sense for the merchants, who in any case do not appear to have had Catron's love of acreage, to choose that path of investment or to burden themselves with land at the expense of endangering their sources of supply and customers.

Beyond merchanting and its extension in banking and land holding, many of the German-Jewish merchants also engaged in ventures typical of the developing economy of New Mexico. The lure of mineral wealth had long attracted prospector and investor. The Spiegelbergs had a history of interest in mining which dated at least to the sixties. Lehman Spiegelberg served on the board of directors of the Willison Silver Mining Co. in 1872. Henry Lesinsky, who had spent years as a prospector in Australia and California and came to New Mexico in 1859 to join his uncle Julius Freudenthal in business, found his knowledge of mining and related activities in high demand in the southern parts of the territory and Arizona. He was a partner of Bennett Brothers Co. in its Cibola Reduction Works at Silver City and moved heavily into copper mining in Clifton, Arizona.[71] In time, it became his major interest.

Investment formed only part of the picture of the merchants' activities. They also became involved in service functions. With Bennett, Henry Lesinsky subcontracted to run the Southern US

Mail and Express Route in 1868, providing weekly service between Albuquerque and Mesilla. In 1870 Barlow, Sanderson and Co. sublet to Bennett and Lesinsky their contract to deliver mail between Mesilla and Tucson.[72] They also began to act as agents for national firms. An advertisement in the *Daily New Mexican*, March 22, 1872, announced the availability of Sigmund Seligman's services on behalf of the Merchants' Life Insurance Co. of New York.[73] In like manner, Lehman Spiegelberg received appointment as general agent of the New York Insurance Co. for New Mexico in 1873.[74] Their business places also served in many instances as post offices. The list is legion: Julius Freudenthal was postmaster at Belen from 1865 to 1868, Morris Bloomfield at Elizabethtown in 1868, Alex Gusdorf in Taos in 1875, Nathan Eldodt at San Juan in 1870, and Charles Ilfeld at Tiptonville after 1876.[75]

One branch of business took on a special and new significance after the Civil War—the Indian trade. A treaty with the Navajo returned to them a portion of their traditional homelands in northwestern New Mexico and Arizona after they had languished for several years at Bosque Redondo. Apache reservations were also created, although in a more scattered fashion, while their conflict with the whites continued to plague the territory. As a consequence of existing fears and actual hostilities, the size of the military grew after the Civil War. A student of the army calls the period between 1868 and 1880 the one of greatest expansion of military posts. Many of these posts adjoined or were close to the newly established reservations.[76]

Both tribes received certain forms of support from the federal government in return for their acceptance of the new conditions. The Apaches "settled down," as one author put it, "to a life of rations," while agents sought to encourage farming among them.[77] The Navajo received seed and agricultural implements for specified periods of time and certain articles of apparel and blankets or the raw materials to make them.[78] The new arrangements opened expanded markets for trade.

After the Navajo moved back to their old lands, Indian agents appointed licensed traders to deal with them. It was the trader's task to obtain the supplies required by the tribes.[79] In 1871 the commissioner of Indian affairs disallowed the purchase of large quantities of supplies from the traders themselves—they were to act only as buyers—since such purchases were seen as disadvantageous to the government and offered a classic conflict of interest when buyer and supplier were one and the same.[80]

The Spiegelbergs were among the first to move into the re-established Indian trade. When the Navajos moved to their reservation in August 1868, the first trading license issued at Fort Defiance went to Lehman Spiegelberg. He named his brother Willi and one Henry O'Neill as his clerks, and they had the right, not later granted to others, to trade at the agency or anywhere on the reservation.[81] Willi Spiegelberg, in turn, was the first trader at Fort Wingate in July 1868.[82] Lehman did not remain long on the reservation but took an active role on behalf of Spiegelberg Brothers as wholesale merchants in the trade.

Jewish merchants generally took a prominent role in the business of supplying the Indians in the seventies. Well set up to bid on the government's needs through their eastern and local contacts, the names of Spiegelberg, Rosenbaum, Zeckendorf, Schuster, and Rosenthal appear repeatedly in the reports of awards made. In the seventies, the Spiegelbergs were probably the dominant firm, with the Staabs second.[83] Most often they bid on and received contracts for the Southern and Mescalero Apache agencies, as well as the Abiquiu, Navajo, and Cimarron agencies and the San Carlos agency in Arizona.[84] The commodities provided included coffee, sugar, beef cattle, flour, medical supplies, hardware, tobacco, matches, and services such as transportation.

One can only indicate by example the quantities of goods sold in the Indian trade. The report of the Board of Indian Commissioners to the secretary of the interior for 1873 showed that Z. Staab and Co. received contracts for coffee and sugar for $4,772.40, 90,000 lbs. of flour for $5,287.50, and another contract for coffee and sugar for $6,752.10—a total of $16,812.[85] In

1876 the Spiegelbergs' contracts included orders for 3.5 million lbs. of beef cattle at $5.14 per hundred pounds and 250,000 lbs. of flour for the Mescalero Apaches at $4.45 per hundred.[86] The volume of business and the profits netted must have been high.

Between 1860 and 1880 New Mexico's traditional appearance began to change. Santa Fe remained the largest town and the center of commerce. Slowly, however, new focal points of population and trade grew and new areas opened to settlement.

Las Vegas, on the eastern side of the mountains and at the edge of the plains, assumed second place as a population center. Not that it was a new area of residence. The vicinity of the future town had accumulated some two thousand inhabitants in the 1830s with the issuing of land grants by the Mexican government.[87] Its location made it a natural port of entry into New Mexico for the Santa Fe Trail, and the Mexican population found trade and catering to the traffic of the trail conducive to economic growth. The establishment of Fort Union in 1851 to the north further enhanced the position of the town as a supply center and improved the cash condition of the community. But the numbers housed at the fort did not remain constant. In 1854, for example, there were 142 men at the post, and that remained typical of the fifties.[88] In 1865, however, there were 807.[89] Even with such numerical fluctuation that increase was marked.

The expanded opportunities offered by Indian and army needs demanded a search for supplies locally as well as purchases in the East. That meant opening up new stores and depots in strategically located areas. In turn, the number of locations in which such enterprises could be found run by Jewish merchants increased. In 1860 Jews lived in only half a dozen places in New Mexico. In 1870 they were present in at least eleven locations and in 1880, in no less than sixteen. In 1860 Albuquerque, Taos, Mora, and Los Lunas had Jewish residents, as well as Santa Fe. In 1870, Las Vegas, Las Cruces, Ocate, and Laguna had been added. R. H. McKay, an army medical officer reporting for duty in southern New Mexico about the turn of the decade, noted that "the commercial interests [of the area] were conducted by so-called foreigners: Americans, Germans and Jews, the latter predominating."[90] By 1880 La Mesilla, Silver City, Georgetown, Tecolote, and Bernalillo, among others, were included in the dispersion.

The issuance of commercial licenses reflected the spreading operations of the individual merchants. Already in the fifties, Joseph Hersch, deeply involved in supplying the army with milled grain, had reached into Taos and San Miguel counties from his Santa Fe base. He was the only merchant with licenses in three counties during the decade. The Taos-Santa Fe axis also involved the Elsbergs and Ambergs and Louis Gold. Besides Hersch, the Taos–San Miguel county connection included Henry Biernbaum, while Simon Rosenstein operated in Bernalillo and Valencia counties. The Zeckendorfs engaged in business in Santa Fe and Bernalillo counties during the decade.

Judging by the paucity of licenses in the early sixties, one must assume the Civil War played havoc with normal business. Starting in 1866, however, the number of Jewish firms involved in multilocation businesses and the number of locations for individual firms greatly increased. The most far ranging were the Spiegelbergs, who in the sixties and seventies operated in San Miguel, Bernalillo, Grant, and Santa Ana counties, as well as in their primary base, Santa Fe. The Zeckendorfs, already located in Santa Fe and Albuquerque, made the latter their base, and moved into Grant and Mora counties. In the seventies Maurice Trauer did business in Colfax, Grant, Mora, and Santa Fe counties. These entrepreneurs appear to have had the largest number of operations. However, it was quite common for Jewish businessmen, and others, to operate in at least two places. The Staabs, for instance, had a long record of licenses in Taos in the seventies, the Rosenwalds in Mora as well as San Miguel, the Lesinskys in Grant, as well as Doña Ana.[91]

In addition to the expanding number of outlets which appeared as branches of already established firms, the sixties and seventies also witnessed the creation of new ones. It became common for the relatives of the Spiegelbergs, the Staabs, and others to start businesses of their own, and not in Santa Fe. The older families may well have encouraged migration to other parts of the territory as response to stimuli offered by the economy, either to avoid excessive competition or crowding in Santa Fe itself, which grew less rapidly than some of the newer areas, or simply to take advantage of the rising opportunities presented elsewhere.

In this manner, the Zeckendorfs moved into Albuquerque in the fifties for the Spiegelbergs and then with their aid became an independent entity in the sixties. Difficult times after the Civil War led them to move farther out into Tucson, where they engaged in supplying forts and in varied enterprises reminiscent of the experiences of earlier Jewish merchants. In time, Tucson became their primary location.[92] Similarly, the Amberg and Elsberg cousins took Herman Ilfeld into their firm. They aided Adolph Letcher to open a store in Taos and to act as their agent to purchase grain for the forts in the later sixties. Herman's brother, Charles, joined Letcher in Taos, and, when they determined that the economic situation there had deteriorated, Letcher moved to Las Vegas with the support of Amberg and Elsberg. In time Charles Ilfeld began to build a sizable empire of his own. In the seventies the Staabs used relatives Alexander and Gerson Gusdorf in like manner in Taos.[93]

Despite the ties of kinship and financial support among many of the firms, they remained essentially competing entities. This can be seen readily in the bidding for the Indian trade. Zeckendorfs and Spiegelbergs frequently bid on the same contracts, and the Staabs and Spiegelbergs did so constantly. An outsider, Frank Warner Angel, who came to New Mexico in 1878 as a special investigator for the Departments of Justice and Interior to look into the violence in Lincoln County, commented in his notes on the Spiegelbergs and Staabs that they should be used against each other.[94] It is also noteworthy that when the Spiegelbergs created their Second National Bank in 1872, neither the Staabs nor any other known Jewish merchant joined them.[95]

Another dimension of their relations appears through evidence of less-than-perfect behavior toward each other. Lawsuits occurred among them. In 1869 Gustave Elsberg filed suit against Jacob Amberg and Herman Ilfeld as the firm approached bankruptcy, also implicating A. Letcher and Charles Ilfeld. Amberg absconded, apparently to old Mexico.[96] In 1872 several suits were brought against Moses A. Gold by Z. Staab and Benjamin Schuster for fraud and, again, by Abraham Staab on the same grounds.[97]

The Spiegelbergs, about to turn a list of debtors over to a collection agent in 1881, rated them in terms of their credit reliability. They found co-religionists Dittenhoffer, Bibo, and William Rosenthal's debts no good and those of Joseph Hersch and Nathan Barth, the latter in Arizona, good, in a ranking which ran: good, fair, no good, and quien sabe.[98] Individual traits, not universal trust nor good faith in co-religionists guided their judgment.

Nor were the relatives always kind and considerate of each other. A nephew of the Zeckendorfs who came to clerk for them in Tucson in 1871, returned to New York after three months. He revealed to persons in the territory "that his uncles were not able to pay their debts" and gave that as his reason for departing. The nephew told all this in strict confidence, but the information reached the sharp ears of R. G. Dun's investigators.[99]

The new locales, particularly Las Vegas and Las Cruces, became centers in their own right and not mere tendrils of Santa Fe. While Jewish merchants, as noted above, had already begun to do business in San Miguel County in the early fifties, and had an established presence in Mora, their numbers grew and took on a permanent appearance in Las Vegas after the Civil War. The names of Marcus Brunswick, the Rosenwald brothers, Joseph and Emanuel, and Adolph Dittenhoffer appear as license holders. In 1867 they are augmented by Isidor Stern, Adolph Letcher, and Simon Rosenstein.[100]

By 1870 there were at least half a dozen Jews in Las Vegas. In 1880 there were forty-eight as a conservative minimum and perhaps as many as seventy. Given the small numbers of Jews in the entire territory, such an increase over a decade represented a major addition in terms of how those persons could view themselves as a community. By 1880, Las Vegas roughly equalled Santa Fe in the number of its Jewish residents.

Some of the new settlers did not duplicate the experience of the youthful immigrants of the forties and fifties. As a second, and later, commercial center, Las Vegas drew merchants from other areas of New Mexico and elsewhere. That has already been shown by the license-holding patterns described and the actual lock and stock moves of such firms as Adolph Letcher's. His move, with his future young partner, Charles Ilfeld, involving a hundred mules to cross the mountains, was no small feat in 1867.[101]

Other settlers were new but had considerable experience elsewhere. The Rosenwald brothers, for example, had migrated to the United States in the early fifties. A series of business ventures led them from early family connections in Staunton, Virginia, and Baltimore westward to Iowa and then to Wyandotte and Lawrence, Kansas, and on to Denver and Leadville, Colorado (then called California Gulch). For a time during the Civil War, Joseph Rosenwald held a sutlership for a Kansas regiment at Fort Smith, Arkansas.[102]

The lively state of the economy and the skills and capital of such men as Ilfeld and the Rosenwalds allowed their fortunes to advance rapidly. Three years after their settlement in Las Vegas became permanent, the Rosenwalds were deeply engaged in supplying corn (300,000 lbs. in an 1869 contract) and beans to Fort Bascom.[103] The Letcher-Ilfeld firm, soon after their arrival, also supplied hay and grain for army forts. Previous experience and their economic condition, as well as rapid expansion, may well have contributed to their sense that Las Vegas had an identity of its own and had to do things its own way. In terms of Jewish community building, this would become quite evident in the early eighties.

No other town approached Santa Fe or Las Vegas before 1880

in the size of their Jewish populations. A number of towns, however, had several Jewish families, often related, working together. Las Cruces, with its Lesinsky-Freudenthal clan, to which the Solomon family may be added, was one such place. Their numbers were too few to allow more than the appearance of an extended family. The distance of Las Cruces from northern New Mexico was great enough to produce a different axis of economic attachment than one sees in the relationship between Santa Fe and Las Vegas and other northern communities such as Mora or Taos. These southern families spread their interests gradually throughout the southwestern part of the territory, partially on the basis of the discovery and exploitation of copper. They established bases in Silver City and eventually Arizona. Like their coreligionists in the north, the southern families would become involved in a variety of enterprises, generally prosper, and duplicate the northern experience.[104]

A different sort of experience emerges, however, from the activities of Jews in more isolated areas, often so difficult to learn about. Sometimes such persons operated as filaments stretching from Santa Fe or Las Vegas. They lived alone as Jews and did not attain the level of wealth acquired by their centrally located employers or principals. Yet their lives were as real and meaningful for the history of the territory and its Jews as that of their coreligionists in the main cities.

The Bibo family represents a saga of this type. A veritable clan, seven of the children eventually came to New Mexico, all inspired by the tales of their grandfather, who had spent eight years in America between 1812 and 1820.[105] Nathan Bibo arrived in Santa Fe in 1867, where his brother Simon had preceded him. Friends of the Spiegelbergs from Germany, they were at first employed by that family and continued to have business dealings with them and the Staabs throughout the years.

In 1868, Willi Spiegelberg asked Nathan Bibo to manage his business with the Navajos at Fort Wingate. So began a long-term association with west-central New Mexico and the Indians. In time, Nathan joined his brother Simon, who located himself at

Cebolleta. The brothers collected corn from the local Indian farmers off the reservation, who gradually increased their acreage as demand rose from Fort Wingate and other military posts. In the early seventies, the Bibos, along with Solomon Barth "occupied every ox team available" to deliver corn to Forts Defiance and Wingate.[106]

While at Cebolleta, Simon and Sam Bibo opened, with enormous difficulty, a road to supply troops in the White Mountain area of Arizona, "calling for the first time to attention . . . that New Mexico and not California should be called upon as a matter of advantage and economy to the government, to furnish this new post," Camp Apache.[107] The hardship and labor, as well as the dangers, of buying corn, loading it, and getting it to the troops, as described by Nathan Bibo, depict a harsh mode of existence quite different from the scenes of Spiegelberg domesticity or Staab's Saturday night poker sessions.

In 1872 Nathan Bibo established a store of his own in Bernalillo.[108] Francisco Perea, the fabled leading citizen of the town, prevailed upon him to build the store and allowed him to buy "120 yards of land at a very reasonable price" as an inducement.[109] In addition to his regular trading activities Bibo planted orchards and grapevines and enjoyed visits by occasional dignitaries such as General W. T. Sherman and Lew Wallace. He built the government station and had stable room for the mail contractor and stage line.

Nathan Bibo's relationship with the Indians and his closeness to the common farmer revealed something of a social conscience in him. From his account, they trusted and admired him, and he served at times as a go-between for them with the army. He, in turn, never forgot their help. In later years he became an advocate for them against deprivation and neglect.[110] He sympathized keenly with the lack of opportunity for education suffered by the younger Hispanic population. "It seemed to me," he noted, "all the richer classes wanted was to keep the poor poorer, dependent upon their magnanimity, and have them at their beck and call; to keep them working for $8 to $10 per month, as they had been from times immemorial." For his part, he did his best to teach and advise them in any way he could.[111]

♋

The success of the New Mexican Jewish families could occur only within the framework of a generally harmonious atmosphere between Jew and Gentile. The relative openness of western society remained characteristic of business and social relations of the two elements of New Mexican society. This was especially evident in the predominantly masculine business world, but also visible elsewhere.

Nowhere is the private and public nexus of goodwill more apparent than in the tie between Archbishop John B. Lamy and the Spiegelberg and Staab families. The personal attachment of Lamy and the Spiegelbergs went back to 1852 when the bishop, en route to New Mexico, tended to the dysentery-stricken Levi Spiegelberg on the Santa Fe Trail.[112] The friendship they established lasted throughout the years.

After Willi Spiegelberg married Flora Langermann, the points of contact grew even closer. The well-educated young woman and the prelate conversed in French, discussed the fruits of their gardening, and exchanged gifts.[113] The prelate regularly sent fruit, wine, and flowers to the Spiegelbergs on important Jewish holidays.[114] The Old World tie, no doubt, played a role in creating a mutual sympathy.

The friendship also received public expression. In 1869 Lamy laid the foundation of the St. Francis cathedral, which is still a landmark in Santa Fe. The Spiegelbergs were among the larger contributors, donating five hundred dollars to the building fund for the contemplated structure.[115] Civility and humaneness between Jew and Catholic had clearly superseded parochialism.

The Lamy-Staab relationship was also close. Out of their acquaintance arises the intriguing story of Abraham Staab and Lamy's cathedral. Staab apparently provided Lamy with large sums for the construction of the building.[116] When the cathedral was completed, above the main entrance a triangle was inscribed with the Hebrew letters for Yahweh, called the Tetragrammaton, within it. The bishop, Flora Spiegelberg reported, pointed it out to her on a tour of the site while it was still under construction. She interpreted its presence as a sign of his universality and tolerance. [117]

In his biography of Lamy, Paul Horgan explains the presence of the inscribed stone simply: "Some said this was done by Lamy out of gratitude for Jewish support—though theologians pointed out that the triangle and the Hebraic letters symbolized the Holy Trinity enclosing the Godhead, a device long known in traditional use by the Church." [118] A letter addressed to this author suggests a more direct relationship between Staab, Lamy, and the inscription. The account runs as follows:

My grandmother's second husband, a Mr. Berlette, was the tinsmith who did the gutters, et. al. on the cathedral. From them we learned this account of the very large donation which the merchant made. Lamy virtually haunted the premises while the cathedral was being built and knew and chatted with all his workers quite freely. He told my grandfather directly, and in turn, Berlette told my parents, and father told me in turn, and I had my grandmother confirm the story. . . .

There was a group of Santa Fe business men who played poker almost without fail, on Saturday nights. Lamy often went to talk to them, not joining their game, merely visiting. Grandmother asserted that he was a fascinating raconteur . . . so he was always a welcome visitor. One evening, it was noticed that he seemed preoccupied and not his usual, vivacious, vocal self. Someone asked, "What's the trouble, Bishop? You're not yourself tonight?" To that he responded that he doubted he would live to see the cathedral finished. When pressed for his reason for the doubt, he admitted he had again run out of funds and would not even be able to roof the structure. The Jewish merchant asked how much he thought would be needed to complete the structure. Lamy estimated somewhere between ten and fifteen thousand dollars.

"If you'll promise to do something I'll ask of you, I'll give you the money you need."

"I'll have to know what you want me to promise before I can commit myself," the Archbishop replied.

"I want you to engrave, in the keystone of the arch of the main entrance the Hebrew for Yahweh."

The Bishop replied that no one could object to doing that, and he would do it.

The merchant wrote out a check for the required amount, and handed it to the Bishop, and work continued. . . . [119]

New Mexican author William Keleher offered a version of events which coincides with the essence of the story cited in the letter, but changes the setting. His source was Louis Ilfeld, Staab's son-in-law, who related that he heard Staab himself tell the story many times. [120]

Denials of the negotiation came from Rabbi Floyd Fierman and others. Fierman argued against it on the basis of Staab's character, that he would not place anyone, much less the Archbishop, at a disadvantage. Fray Angélico Chávez guessed that it was done out of cordial relations with the Jewish pioneers. [121] Neither argument proves or disproves a request by Staab. Whether a grateful archbishop would use it as a gesture of friendship with or without a request remains moot. On the basis of evaluation of evidence, however, Keleher's source appears the strongest to this author, but its authority is less than definitive.

But that Staab might have had a good bit more than a casual acquaintance with Lamy has its own circumstantial basis. The well-known Sister Blandina Segale noted in her journal for 1878 that she had been assigned the duty of entertaining Mrs. Staab and her children. Mrs. Staab was depressed and needed attention, although the sister complained that she had "no attraction for entertaining wealthy ladies." A few weeks later she noted that Staab had asked her to accompany his wife and children to Europe. Unsympathetic, she commented, "I believe he thinks money can do anything. . . ." [122] Somewhat later she was informed that Archbishop Lamy wanted her to accompany the Staab family to the rail terminus near Trinidad, Colorado and she complied with his request. [123] The solicitousness of the archbishop toward the Staabs appears to have exceeded that required of a minor friendship.

The growth and dispersion of the Anglo population produced a continuation of what had begun to happen in Santa Fe earlier with respect to the creation of an institutional network to link males seeking social intercourse that expressed common interests and needs. Probably no organization fulfilled that function more than Freemasonry. At the lodges, Jew and non-Jew met in common ceremony in one of the few formal structures where intermingling between persons of differing faiths could occur. Besides Freemasonry, the gaming table and the bar remained, but they were insufficient for many. Protestant as well as Jew needed a more civil social environment. Freemasonry even provided for burial ground at a time when religious organization was scarce or totally absent.

As new lodges opened, Jews joined and frequently took prominent roles in their activities. Las Vegas became the second site in New Mexico for a lodge. Formed at Fort Union in 1862 within the military, the source for a number of lodges, the Chapman Lodge became permanent in 1866 and moved to Las Vegas in 1867.[124] Among its masters were Louis Sulzbacher, Emanuel Rosenwald, and Charles Ilfeld.[125] When death came, many were buried in the Masonic cemetery, as were members of their families of later generations.[126]

Other lodges chartered in the sixties and seventies included the Aztec Lodge at Las Cruces, formed in 1867. Charles and Henry Lesinsky, who owned the building in which the lodge met, and Aaron Schultz were members, and Henry Lesinsky held many important posts in it.[127] The Silver City lodge, chartered in 1873, included Hyman Abraham and Aaron Schultz after he moved from Las Cruces, and the Union Lodge at Watrous, where Simon Vorenberg served as master, was chartered in 1874.[128] The Abraham clan of Silver City, too, lie generation upon generation in the Masonic cemetery.[129]

The German Jew in New Mexico also retained an ethnic dimension of German culture which produced its own points of contact with non-Jewish German immigrants. Many never lost their love for their native tongue, and since they existed in sufficient numbers to nurture their interest, they organized cultural and social activities to express them. In Santa Fe they formed a singing club, of which Bernard Seligman became president, a German Aid society, of which Lehman Spiegelberg was treasurer, and a Germania Club in 1875, headed by Solomon Spiegelberg.[130] It was at the hall of the club that Jewish holidays were commemorated in the late seventies. When the Franco-Prussian War broke out in 1870, the German immigrants demonstrated in favor of the homeland and even evoked the public sympathy of Governor Pile.

Participation in public events, too, offered an important sign of identification with the larger community. The celebration of the Centennial at Santa Fe on July 4, 1876, allowed expression of that unity and also demonstrated the high status of some Jewish citizens. Of the thirty-eight persons selected as the General Committee of Arrangements, five were Jews: Willi Spiegelberg, Sigmund Seligman, Z. Staab, Noa Ilfeld, and Solomon Spiegelberg. The procession which marked the festivities included a float with thirty-nine young ladies, each representing a state or territory of the Union and included Sallie and Helen Grunsfeld.[131] A year later, upon the death of ex-governor Donaciano Vigil, a meeting of citizens selected Lehman Spiegelberg and Solomon Spiegelberg to make the arrangements for his memorial.[132]

The Jewish citizens could be the source of public occasion themselves. When Lehman Spiegelberg returned from a trip to Germany in 1872, a military band greeted his return.[133] The death of Sigmund Seligman in 1876 likewise drew considerable attention in the press, and his pallbearers included William Ritch, the territorial secretary, and Anastacio Sandoval, a Hispano merchant, as well as Seligman's co-religionist peers.[134]

The growth of social institutions, however, did not spell the end of less genteel forms of recreation, particularly gambling. The Saturday night poker sessions, which included Abraham

Staab, were well known. Some went beyond private parties. Marcus Brunswick in Las Vegas even had brushes with the law over it. He was cited in San Miguel County on March 20, 1867, by Attorney General Clever as one who "did unlawfully keep a gaming table called Monte andando" among other games.[135] He was again cited in 1870 for playing poker at the house of Charles W. Kitchen.[136] Apparently incorrigible, he was cited a third time in 1873 and pled guilty to criminal charges of keeping a gaming table called Faro.[137]

Business and politics emerged in the post–Civil War era in a new form. The beginnings of political parties and, perhaps, the start of the land grant problem, may well define the underlying conditions of the new combination. The most dramatic single expression of the new politics rested in a shadowy formation which became known as the Santa Fe Ring. Indeed, so informal was it that it is difficult to date its creation and even prove its existence.[138] Howard Lamar defined the ring as "essentially a set of lawyers, politicians, and businessmen who wanted to run the Territory and to make money."[139] The rise of a Republican party organization and the activities of Thomas B. Catron appear linked at the heart of the matter.

Given the power attributed to the Santa Fe Ring and the wealth of the most successful Jewish merchants, the question of their relationship to it arises. Only one name appears to have warranted a close enough tie to be included in its membership, that of Abraham Staab.[140] The evidence, however, is slim. One writer suggests that Staab invested in military warrants on Catron's advice.[141] In 1877 we learn that Colonel Nathan A. M. Dudley, the commander at Fort Stanton, suffered a court martial and was relieved of his command. Dudley blamed his problems on contractors who had, he believed, provided inferior corn to the post which he had rejected. These contractors, he insisted, were connected with the ring. The specific contractor named was

Staab.[142] Staab certainly did business with Catron. In general, however, Staab does not appear in any way close to the land-oriented activities of the ring or its leader's political activities.[143]

If Staab had a possible connection with the ring, the other leading Santa Fe Jewish merchants had far less. Abraham's brother, Zadok, was a Democrat who attended his party's territorial convention in 1870.[144] But then, some scholars who defined the ring did not consider it a group sharply defined by party lines. The Spiegelbergs seem to have had no connection with the ring, although they too had their business connections with Catron. Lehman Spiegelberg and Catron were associated in the incorporation of the Willison Silver Mining Co.[145] Nevertheless, this Spiegelberg and other persons protested Catron's appointment as United States attorney in 1870 on grounds that he had Southern sympathies.[146] In 1872 the Seligman, Spiegelberg, Staab (Z. Staab & Bro.), and Guttmann, Friedman & Co. firms, as well as C. P. Clever and Mayer Kayser, signed a statement attesting to the good character of August Kirchner, a Santa Fe butcher. This statement was attached to an affidavit in which Kirchner described an attempt by Catron to use him to bribe members of the Legislature.[147] Such actions, at the very least, cannot be construed as friendly. It was in this period, too, that Catron's First National Bank was formed, which did not include the Spiegelbergs.

Given the economic prominence of the German-Jewish merchants in the post–Civil War period, their personal political ambitions appear rather limited. The reason may lie in their overriding concern with their businesses and the demands these made upon their time and energies. Another reason may lie in the character of New Mexican politics. The latter has been described as "based more on family alliance, cultural ties, anti-Americanism, church faction and crass economic interest than on any party principles."[148] Bitter factionalism made politics a morass and might have also given caution to the German-Jewish immigrants against seeking too public a role in which they might become readily identifiable as targets. Yet, some involvement for persons of prominence was probably unavoidable, and economic interest may well have demanded it.

The career of Charles P. Clever, a German immigrant who came to New Mexico in the mid-forties, indicates some of the pitfalls into which involvement in politics could lead. As noted previously, Clever was, between 1854 and 1861, a business partner of Sigmund Seligman but in time moved into the study of law and a political career. Admitted to the bar in 1861, he was appointed United States marshal and then adjutant to Governor Henry Connelly. He also became attorney general, in which capacity he served from 1862 to 1867.[149]

In his capacity as attorney general, Clever backed Governor Robert B. Mitchell in his conflict with Secretary of the Territory W. F. M. Arny over the latter's actions and appointments as acting governor when Mitchell was in Washington.[150] Clever thus found himself embroiled in one of the bitterest disputes of early territorial New Mexico's political history. In this atmosphere, in 1867, Clever ran for the position of territorial delegate to Congress as the Democratic candidate. He appeared to win the election and took his seat in Washington only to find the results contested by J. Francisco Chaves, the Republican candidate, who eventually prevailed.

That such problems arose in the factionalized politics of the territory was not unusual. Before the affair ended, however, Clever found himself attacked in the *Daily New Mexican* and described as an "Apostate Jew and now a Catholic," who, "when he came to New Mexico fifteen years ago . . . was a German of the Hebrew persuasion. . . ."[151] Clever's Jewishness is less than established and the newspaper did not take him to task for his alleged faith but for the implied opportunism of his conversion. However, the fact of religious adherence was raised.

By itself the article might be regarded as a trivial curiosity. During this trying conflict, however, the adherents of Governor Mitchell, who attacked the territorial legislature which opposed him, were, in turn, attacked by his opponents. One of them, Manuel Romero of Sapello, addressed a letter to Aniceto Salazar, which was published on December 24, 1867. In it, he declared:

> *Now what I recommend to you is to pitch into this nest of Jews, and don't let go of them and to this end it seems good to me that you send to Congress resolutions against a party of men which is causing the inhabitants of this unfortunate Territory great injuries to free ourselves from which it is necessary to cut them up root and branch; so don't be dismayed, give them blazes until the devil gets them. War!! War with them!!!* [152]

The attack on the "Jews" collectively, some of whom supported Mitchell and, therefore, Clever, demonstrated that not all New Mexicans regarded their presence kindly. Although the attack in print was an isolated instance, it nevertheless indicated that involvement in the passionate personal politics of New Mexico could draw forth latent anti-Semitic feelings among persons who viewed Jews as predatory outsiders.

Even if they limited their desire for public office, the linkage of business and politics at times benefitted the Jewish merchants. A letter from William Breedon, attorney general of the territory and chairman of the Republican Central Executive Committee on behalf of the Spiegelbergs, backed their offer to supply Indian rations. "I am convinced," the author noted, "that the interests of the Government and also of the Indians would be advanced by the acceptance of the proposition." [153] The letter appeared on the stationery of the Republican party's Central Executive Committee.

But the influence of the large merchants also produced its opponents. William Clinton, a major in the superintendent of Indian affairs office in Santa Fe, complained to the commissioner of Indian affairs about the local purchasing practices: "There are but four prominent merchants in this place, Mssrs Spiegelberg Bros, Staab and Bro., Seligman and Bro., and Johnson and Koch . . . . they each and all think that they are entitled to a share of all monies spent by the Government, whether for Indians or any other purpose."[154] To the major, the merchants appeared arrogant.

ᴂ

Up to 1880 it seems reasonable to describe the German Jews of New Mexico as part of the Anglo population. Yet, they were distinct as a subgroup, however much they participated as individuals in the business and public life of the territory. Cultural and religious background served as the factors which kept them (or by which they kept themselves) distinct. Traditions and marriage patterns are the primary indicators for this development.

By the nature of how they made their livelihood, the Jews interacted heavily with non-Jewish Anglos. They participated actively in the creation of social institutions among the Anglos and in public affairs to a more limited extent. Acceptance in Anglo society, at least at the class and social levels at which they engaged in it, heavily outweighed any slight they might have felt as the result of the occasional outbursts against them. Louis Ilfeld is reported to have commented, "I guess if Charles Ilfeld stayed in New York and worked there some may have referred to him as a 'Kike,' but he came to New Mexico and is known as Mr. Ilfeld."[155] Respect may be the key to how the Jewish community as a whole was regarded by their Anglo brethren.

It is more difficult to judge the early relationship between the Anglo Jews and the Hispanic population in the absence of a printed literature. It is clear, however, that marriages of Jewish men and Hispanic women occurred, that Hispanics worked with and for them and were, in general, their suppliers as well as their customers. Hispanos were included on the Second National Bank's board of directors.[156] Personal friendships existed. Charles Ilfeld related how an old Spanish don allowed him to borrow as much as he needed (five thousand dollars) at a difficult financial moment in the early seventies without a note.[157] Nathan Bibo's sympathies toward the plight of Hispano youth have been noted.[158] On an individual basis, it would appear, a broad range of contact existed between Anglo Jew and Hispano, and much of it was no less than civil and, at times, was more than that.

There is a body of literature which attempts to deal with the larger questions of Anglo-Hispanic relationships in New Mexico and the Southwest. Some of it challenges the concept of a peaceful, passive Hispano after the Mexican-American War. In reaction to the Anglo intrusion, Robert Rosenbaum asserts, "Mexican Americans did resist, did try to protect themselves against the realities of United States rules, and they are still resisting."[159] Bound by family and region, and buttressed by pressures of race, religion, language, and custom, they sought to retain their way of life. Physical separation often permitted many, not the elite or upwardly mobile, to ignore the Anglo in the nineteenth century. Nevertheless, friction occurred out of misunderstanding, mutual ignorance, and, at times, the fact that Anglo and Hispano society did not necessarily want the same things.[160]

How much the Hispano distinguished the Anglo Jew from the general Anglo population is difficult to know without special study of the Hispano population. How the theme of crypto-Judaism may have influenced Hispanos for or against them is equally difficult to determine at this point. The above cited instance of a published attack on Jews seems a rarity. Possibly, Jewish Anglos were regarded far more as Anglos than as Jews, and any Hispano anti-Semitism does not appear to be a matter of significance.

ᕗ

Whether or not two generations of German-Jewish merchants carried out a "commercial revolution," as William Parish contended, their importance as part of a new and changing economic order in New Mexico up to 1880 is undeniable. They were at the center of the nexus that tied local pastoral and agricultural producers to export trade and to the federal government's policies of dealing with the Indians. In this sense, for better or worse, they helped draw New Mexico into the economic mainstream of American life and out of the relative isolation in which it had existed before.

In the success they achieved, they displayed considerable energy and perspicacity. They pitched in, moving into the most remote as well as the most populous areas, using every opportunity to establish their position as traders. Their economic activity, from the first, was strongly linked to their social order. The stream of relatives and family acquaintances that followed the first settlers allowed them to expand and solidify their businesses in an atmosphere of trust. Along with that trust, their education, talent, and prudent use of resources were the foundation on which their success was built.

Nevertheless, they still regarded the economic environment through the eyes of individual entrepreneurs. They never lived in isolation from the society in which they found themselves. They were too few in number, too dependent upon a benign and open atmosphere to be able to survive alone. The freedoms of America, the openness of the West, their acceptance of their neighbors and the reciprocal acceptance by those neighbors of them led them to participate in such measure as they were able in the economic and social life and spirit of the environment in which they lived. Just as they were sensitive to the economic opportunity which drew and kept them in the West and sustained them, they had to show sensitivity to others. Given the social character of the existing society, and their own attitudes, they did not assert themselves to create religious institutions which would separate them from the larger society, although they were beginning to feel the pressure of their restraint as their own community began to mature. Business and family were the cornerstone of their existence, not the synagogue or the ethnic community.

The plaza in Santa Fe, c. mid-1850s. The sign of the Seligman-Clever firm is visible on the right, and the Exchange Hotel is at the left. Courtesy Museum of New Mexico. Neg. No. 10685.

Bernard Seligman, Zadoc Staab, and Lehman Spiegelberg of the nineteenth century German-Jewish merchant families of Sante Fe and Kiowa Indians. Courtesy Museum of New Mexico. Neg. No. 7890.

The Spiegelberg Block on East San Francisco Street, Santa Fe, c. 1885. Courtesy Museum of New Mexico. Neg. No. 10777.

Abraham Staab residence, Palace Avenue, Sante Fe, c. 1885. Today a part of La Posada hotel complex. Courtesy Museum of New Mexico. Neg. No. 10464.

Plaza in Santa Fe with Seligman Bros. and S. Spitz store signs visible on the right, c. 1900. Historic Santa Fe Foundation, Box 98-13, No. 25265. State Records Center and Archives, Santa Fe.

The White House, in the Catron Building, in 1916, represented a new generation of Jewish merchants in Santa Fe. Cooke Collection, Box 43, No. 33708. State Records Center and Archives, Santa Fe.

Abraham Staab, brother of Zadoc Staab, leading Santa Fe merchant. Courtesy Museum of New Mexico. Neg. No. 11040.

The Spiegelberg brothers, c. 1865–70, leading merchant family of nineteenth-century Santa Fe. Photo by Sarong. Courtesy Museum of New Mexico. Neg. No. 11025.

The Ilfeld family, merchants of Santa Fe, Las Vegas, and Albuquerque. Standing left to right: Herman, Johanna, and Louis Ilfeld; seated, left to right: Charles, Wilhelm, and Noah Ilfeld. University of New Mexico General Library, Special Collections. Neg. No. 000-119-0001.

Albuquerque Jewish merchants, c. 1883. From left to right: David Weinman, Mike Mandell, Louis Kornberg, Dr. Z. B. Sawyer, and Louis Neustadt. University of New Mexico General Library, Special Collections. Neg. No. 000-119-0384.

Plaza in Las Vegas, showing Charles Ilfeld Co. building, c. 1885. Courtesy Museum of New Mexico. Neg. No. 14719.

Henry Jaffa, first mayor of Albuquerque, merchant, and first president of Temple Albert. University of New Mexico General Library, Special Collections. Neg. No. 000-119-0249.

Mike Mandell, early mayor of Albuquerque and merchant. University of New Mexico General Library, Special Collections. Neg. No. 000-119-0209.

Albert Grunsfeld, pioneer merchant of Albuquerque. Congregation Albert was named in his honor. University of New Mexico General Library, Special Collections. Neg. No. 000-119-0253.1.

Emanuel Rosenwald, important nineteenth-century Las Vegas merchant. Photo O. S. Dowe. Courtesy Museum of New Mexico. Neg. No. 103189.

Lewinson-Weinman wedding, Albuquerque, c. 1895. Such events expressed the continuity and stability of a growing Jewish community. University of New Mexico General Library, Special Collections. Neg. No. 000-119-0409.

Rosenwald Bros., c. 1915 in Albuquerque. Photo William R. Walton. Courtesy Museum of New Mexico. Neg. No. 8646.

Nathan Jaffa, merchant and banker of Roswell, last secretary of the territory, c. 1903. Courtesy Museum of New Mexico. Neg. No. 7591.

The Freudenthal family of Las Cruces, one of the oldest Jewish families in New Mexico. Phoebus Freudenthal is at the upper right, and the young Louis E. Freudenthal is seated at the lower right, c. 1905. Rio Grande Historical Collections, New Mexico State University Library.

Temple Montefiore, Las Vegas, the first synagogue in New Mexico (1886). Courtesy Museum of New Mexico. Neg. No. 132705.

The first Temple Albert, Albuquerque, c. 1905. Courtesy Museum of New Mexico. Neg. No. 8588.

A Generation of
Transition,
1880–1900

$$\boxed{4}$$

As well as any date might, the year 1880 marked the beginning of a new order in New Mexico. The most telling factor of change was the arrival of the railroad. The last vestiges of the Santa Fe Trail, which had for so long filtered access to the Southwest even as it served as its major avenue of approach, eroded before the steel rails. New Mexico had to redefine its relationship to the outside world and much more rapidly than ever since the arrival of the Anglo.

The eighties and nineties, too, served notice to the old established German-Jewish families that times were changing. The pioneers of the fifties and sixties were aging, and a new generation began to have its impact upon the social and economic order. Not that the change was cataclysmic. Good times shone on the old pioneers like the sun of an Indian summer as if to reward them for the decades of their labors. They were, however, the prologue to the rise of a new season.

❧

A single event which vividly depicts the well-being of the Santa Fe German Jews was the visit of President Rutherford B. Hayes in the fall of 1880. His appearance, the first by a president at Santa Fe, heralded, as the *Santa Fe Weekly Democrat* put it, "a new era of a business and social relation between the Territory

and the rest of the world."[1] The Jews of long standing in Santa
Fe played a major role in this festive and momentous occasion.

The Hayes party was received at the train by a special committee which included Zadok Staab. As the caravan rolled into
town the residences of the Staabs and Spiegelbergs, among others, were singled out for special attention, as were the businesses
of the above families and the Ilfeld business. In the procession of
vehicles, President Hayes's carriage included the president, the
Honorable H. M. Atkinson, the surveyor-general, and Zadok
Staab. The second carriage included Mrs. Hayes and Mr. and
Mrs. Lehman Spiegelberg. Willi Spiegelberg and the Solomon
Spiegelberg family rode in other carriages. At the point of debar-
kation, Bernard Seligman was among those introduced to the
presidential party.[2]

Nor were these families absent in accommodating and entertaining the distinguished visitors. The President and Mrs. Hayes
were guests of the Lehman Spiegelbergs and dined and slept at
their home. An evening reception held at the Old Adobe Palace
again saw the Spiegelbergs and Seligmans playing important roles
as leaders in the proceedings.[3] While the emphasis placed on the
part played by these families may appear exaggerated by the high-
lighting, the prominence of their participation in the visit is undeniable and represented a kind of landmark of recognition of the
status they had attained in the highest circles of Santa Fe society.

⤳

The impact of the railroad, while not immediately overpow-
ering, was nevertheless at once noticeable in urban New Mexico.
Most affected at first were the towns whose links with the outside
world changed as a result of their improved ability to serve as
supply and service centers and to move the products of the hinterland out. New communities emerged along the tracks, some,
like New Albuquerque and East Las Vegas, only a short distance
from their older parts. Others, like Deming and Clayton, were
totally new. Still others, like Santa Fe, which was initially by-

passed, suffered as a result of their altered and diminished positions as commercial centers.

One of the telling effects that emerged in the generation that followed the appearance of the railroad was the shift in population. Overall growth between 1880 and 1900 did not change dramatically. New Mexico's population expanded from 119,565 to 195,310—an increase of about 63 percent.[4] That rate of growth did not even improve New Mexico's ranking among the states and territories, which was forty-first in 1880 and forty-fourth in 1900.[5] The Jewish population, however, grew a good bit faster, rising from a conservative figure of 180 in 1880 to a conservative 403 in 1900—an increase of over 100 percent.[6] Taken in terms of the whole population of the territory, however, the Jews still made up a tiny fraction of the whole, about two-tenths of one percent.

More impressive than the general population figures was the impact on the towns along the railroad tracks. Albuquerque, with a population of 2,315 in 1880, had grown to 6,238 in 1900, surpassing Santa Fe. East Las Vegas, with 2,385 in 1890, numbered 3,552 in 1900 without including the older town.[7] R. G. Dun's *Mercantile Agency Reference Book of Principal Cities* for 1879 did not have any towns in the territory listed. The volume for 1885, however, included Las Vegas. It gave the population of the town as 6,500, a considerably higher figure than offered by the census of 1890.[8] Las Vegas may have been the largest town in the territory in 1900. Santa Fe, by comparison, with 6,635 in 1880 and 5,603 in 1900, showed the effects of displacement by its two chief commercial rivals.[9]

The Jewish population, heavily concentrated in Santa Fe and Las Vegas in 1880, was powerfully affected by the changes. Albuquerque had only about eighteen Jews at that time, but Santa Fe and Las Vegas had about seventy each. By 1900, Santa Fe's Jews numbered about forty while Las Vegas and Albuquerque had each passed the hundred mark by some margin. Thus the sharpest growth in Jewish population occurred where the greatest urban expansion had taken place—in Albuquerque and Las Vegas. Santa Fe, by contrast, with its decline in size and economic prominence, underwent an even sharper reduction in the number of its Jewish residents than in its general population.

⮜ৡ

In the short term, wherever the railroad produced new towns, it created the opportunity for rapid social change. The absence of institutions, the appearance of a new population, and even the resettlement of an older population, all formed the basis for the development of a new society. New Mexico's Jews, residing predominantly in towns, felt the impact of this new environment strongly, and the new conditions played no small role in the creation of a new kind of Jewish community.

The social vacuum of New Albuquerque offered an almost unlimited opportunity for organizations of all kinds to grow. Unlike the old town, there was no overwhelming Catholic or Hispanic presence. In rapid order two Masonic lodges and an International Order of Odd Fellows lodge were formed by 1883. A Germania society to promote sociability among German speakers, a YMCA, a branch of the Ancient Order of United Workmen—an insurance fraternity, and two Knights of Pythias lodges emerged, all drawing the unaffiliated population of the new town into their ranks and out of their isolation. Churches mushroomed with the Congregationalists organizing first and the Methodists and Catholics not far behind. [10]

It was in this atmosphere of rapid social combination that the first public Jewish organization in New Mexico came to life in 1883—Lodge No. 336 of the Independent Order of B'nai B'rith (Sons of the Covenant). Formed in 1843, B'nai B'rith, by the late seventies, had become a movement that could embrace all American Jewish males as an associational community by synthesizing the ideas of fraternity, mutual aid, and acculturation. [11] It served the American Jewish community, as Deborah Dash Moore put it, as "a secular synagogue" and "a model of pluralist integration." [12]

It is noteworthy that Albuquerque's Jews addressed their public identity first with an organization of a secular, rather than a religious, character. Although there are no documents to account for this choice, the character of the original membership offers some suggestive clues. The twenty-five members who signed the registration book on January 14, 1883, recapitulated, in some ways, the characteristics of the early Jewish immigrants into New Mexico. They were young—fifteen were in their twenties, eight in their thirties, and only one each in their forties or fifties. Nineteen were single and six married. All were merchants or clerks.[13] Most of them had come to Albuquerque after 1880, some from other towns in New Mexico, others from outside the territory.

In the bustling, rapidly expanding city of Albuquerque, a population of this sort might have sought points of mutual contact as Jews for their social enjoyment and a presence which gave them a public identity. They did not need Sabbath schools as their first order of business. Nor did their needs, it would appear, require a formal religious structure. If they did, the B'nai B'rith members could have readily created a congregation—even without the expense of a resident rabbi or the erection of a synagogue. The opportunities available to the residents of the new town to organize were considerably greater than for those who had come in earlier generations. The growth of B'nai B'rith itself allowed them to adopt an existing organization—a course of action scarcely possible for their predecessors.

The lodge did fairly well in its growth and development. Between the first registration of 1883 and the end of 1896, the last year before the founding of a congregation, forty-seven additional persons joined. The newer members still manifested a youthful character (twenty-five of them were in their twenties), but not as strongly as at first. Sixteen were in their thirties and six in their forties. Similarly, whereas among the original members barely one-fourth were married, twenty of forty-seven of those who joined in the following thirteen years were married—over 42 percent.[14] Although still a young man's organization, B'nai B'rith's membership displayed the effects of continuing growth and long-term existence, the maturing of its population and the increased importance of the nuclear family unit.

During the eighties, the new organization, as part of its mission, created a substructure of committees to fulfill its obligations. One of the earliest actions it undertook, in January 1883, was to look into the purchase of suitable ground for a cemetery.[15] Despite the serious nature of such a step, it was perhaps a sign of the relative youth of the membership that a number of years passed before the action was completed. Five years later, in 1888, a new committee was appointed for the same purpose.[16] The minutes of the lodge meetings refer to the formation of a cemetery association only in 1889, but the formal constitution came in 1892.[17] Urgency does not appear to have motivated them.

Like its counterparts everywhere, the lodge also concerned itself with the issue of aid for its members and charitable functions. A committee for the sick looked into specific requests for relief both in Albuquerque and for members elsewhere.[18] Special charities designated by B'nai B'rith as its own, such as an orphan asylum in Cleveland, Ohio, received regular contributions.[19] Nonmembers also received charitable attention. It was perhaps an indication of the changing social character of Jewish immigration when the lodge created a charity committee in 1891 "to alleviate and investigate wants of destitute Israelites coming to Albuquerque."[20] The lodge also drew its members into the international arena of Jewish problems. In 1897 requests for aid to schools in Rumania received consideration.[21] The presence of B'nai B'rith created a focal point for united action, a marked departure from earlier Jewish behavior, although individual Jews may have expressed their humanitarian urges all along. New Mexican Jews could now face such issues as a public presence.

In fulfilment of its description as "a secular synagogue," B'nai B'rith did provide the basis for some religious activity. By its rules it avoided the touchy issue of varied religious practices. The minute book carried a printed warning from the president of the order to the district grand lodges to "*refuse their sanction to all laws and regulations leading towards the introduction of the dogmatically religious elements into our Order."* [22] In 1884 the lodge sought to have a "young minister from Cincinnati," the seminarial home of Reform Judaism, come out for the holy days and allotted $200 for services and expenses for a rabbi that year. [23] And in 1885 the lodge appointed a committee "to notify all members . . . and other Israelites, that services be held at this Hall on Rosh ha shana and Yom Kippur." [24] National Jewish organizations sought to use the lodge to expand religious services. The Union of American Hebrew Congregations applied to it in the interest of providing religious instruction for communities without such facilities. [25]

Nor did the lodge limit itself to labors on behalf of its membership. When it scheduled religious services under its auspices, nonmembers were invited and asked to help defray expenses. Touring lecturers on Jewish subjects were arranged for and tickets sold through the lodge. In 1895, when Dr. Krauskopf of Philadelphia came to speak in Albuquerque, the lodge reported that 120 tickets had been sold. [26] The lodge's hall also served a number of uses beyond the members' direct needs. In 1895 the Ladies Hebrew Benevolent Society started a Sunday school, and the lodge granted them permission to use the facilities for instructional purposes. [27]

The existence of B'nai B'rith in Albuquerque also allowed interested persons outside the city to draw closer to the new center of activity. The original membership included Solomon Barth, who listed his residence as St. John's, Arizona. Shortly after the lodge's formation Max and Meno Oppenheim of Los Lunas joined. In the eighties and nineties, others, from Alameda, Sabinal, Bernalillo, Peña Blanca, and even as far away as Socorro and Grants sought and received membership.

Once created, B'nai B'rith served as a resource to aid other organizations. Exactly when the Ladies Hebrew Benevolent Society was formed is not certain, but that organization, as noted, used the lodge's facilities and joined with it in common committees in the mid-nineties. The strongest point of contact centered around the perceived need to provide religious instruction for the young. When the Jews of Las Vegas began to consider forming a lodge of their own in 1896, they turned to Albuquerque for advice and information.[28] In time, the cemetery created by B'nai B'rith was acquired by Congregation Albert.[29]

B'nai B'rith alone, however, could not long satisfy the needs of the growing and maturing Jewish community of Albuquerque. The appearance of the Ladies Hebrew Benevolent Society pointed up the limited nature of the men's organization. The women of the community sought an outlet of Jewish expression for themselves, and, as concerned parents, they moved to provide religious education for the next generation. Such actions point up both the youthful and male social character of B'nai B'rith.

Once the needs of the young began to receive an organized response, the creation of a congregation could not remain far behind. On September 26, 1897, a number of Jewish residents met to discuss the creation of such an organization. Many of the same persons active in B'nai B'rith took leading roles in this new stage of development. The Ilfelds, Grunsfelds, and Neustadts were as much in evidence here as at B'nai B'rith. Clearly, they did not view the lodge as sufficient to address the needs of a Jewish community. Once begun, the business of forming the new congregation moved quickly. At the September 26 meeting, officers were elected, namely, Henry N. Jaffa as president, Noa Ilfeld as vice-president, Alfred Grunsfeld as treasurer, and Samuel Neustadt as secretary.

The congregation adopted its name by auction. The Grunsfeld family received the privilege of providing the title by its bid of $250.[30] Several months later, in January 1898, a meeting of the trustees accepted the proposed name "Albert Congregation" in honor of Albert Grunsfeld, Alfred's father, who had passed away in 1893.[31]

During that September meeting in 1897 in which the congregation was founded, the group also decided to advertise for a rabbi in *The American Israelite*. The process took some time, but in December, the trustees began negotiations with Dr. William H. Greenburg of London on an offer of a two-year term at $125 per month.[32] In January 1898 Dr. Greenburg wired his acceptance, and in March he arrived and was greeted with considerable fanfare. He conducted his first service on March 18, 1898. With that act Albuquerque Jewry came of age as a Jewish religious community. Fifty members and seatholders were in the new congregation.[33]

While Albuquerque could rightfully claim the first Jewish secular organization in New Mexico, the first religious organization belonged to Las Vegas. Why did the two largest centers of Jewry in the territory create their institutions in reverse order? Las Vegas had a much larger and better established Jewish population than Albuquerque in 1880. The larger number of families and children, as well as greater material means, probably dictated the decision to seek a religious foundation first.

The Jews of Las Vegas moved to form their congregation in 1884. On October 6 of that year the *Daily Optic* made note of a lecture delivered by Reverend Dr. Joseph Glueck to a large number of Jews and Gentiles "equally." Afterwards "the Israelites" formed a permanent congregation with about one hundred members. "The Israelites," the item noted, "have cause to be proud of yesterday's work. It is not often that so small a community exerts itself for the promotion of Judaism to such an extent."[34] Dr. Glueck himself became the rabbi of the new congregation, which some time later adopted the name of Montefiore, after the noted Jewish philanthropist, Sir Moses Montefiore.

In 1886 the congregation took steps to build a house of worship. A subscription list to raise funds circulated in January of that year drew support from outside as well as from within the Jewish community. Half of those who gave were not members. Such well-known persons as M. A. Otero, J. Raynolds (who made a large contribution of $100), and A. W. Manzanares subscribed.[35] Willi Spiegelberg of Santa Fe also contributed to the fund. By mid-year a contract had been signed with architects to erect the new structure.

At about the same time a printed constitution and by-laws

appeared. It carried the names of forty-two members (heads of households), and in the preface, John H. Teitelbaum, the secretary, noted the imminent dedication of a temple and proclaimed,

> *we never will allow ourselves to be numbered with the skeptical. . . . We have been taught to remember our Creator in our youth. The recollections of our teachings are still fresh. The heroic deeds of our ancestors will never be blotted from the memory of Israel, who will forever perpetuate the teachings and practices of Faith, Hope, and Charity.* [36]

On September 26, 1886, dedication services were held with music provided by the Presbyterian choir. [37]

As with the Albuquerque community, once the Jews of Las Vegas had created one institution, others followed in fairly short order. In 1888 the congregation purchased from the Odd Fellows a portion of its burying ground as cemetery. [38] The women of the community may have organized a Hebrew Ladies Benevolent Society as early as 1887, although its by-laws appear as a written document on October 2, 1895. [39] Perhaps because of a rabbi's presence the women may have felt less pressure to take the lead in the religious education of the young. The by-laws of 1895 included a caveat that "Money in Treasury shall only be used for Charitable Benefits." [40] In 1902 the Jewish males of Las Vegas actually formed the second B'nai B'rith chapter in New Mexico, Lodge No. 545 in the name of J. E. Rosenwald. [41] With that act the two cities acquired a rough parity in their institutional development, although the Las Vegas organized community was still the larger of the two.

The Jews of Las Vegas and Albuquerque created their first public institutional networks in the first generation after the railroad appeared. Increased numbers and a new environment, the result of the railroad's entry, provided the milieu and incentive for such action. Santa Fe, however, did not undergo a similar evolution.

From the viewpoints of town and commercial development, the coming of the railroad did not mean for Santa Fe what it did for Albuquerque and Las Vegas. The fact that Santa Fe had not acquired a place on the main line was only one part of the problem for the town. Once the vaunted terminus of the Santa Fe Trail, it now became an ill-located rail stop on a branch line. It failed to generate such new energy as the rail lines had sparked elsewhere by the creation of new towns, and things remained largely what they had been before 1880. The entrenched character of the communal leadership and their established methods of doing business led them to respond only slowly to change.[42]

If the Jews of Santa Fe had not exerted themselves overly much to create public Jewish institutions during their heyday before 1880, they were hardly likely to do so when that day began to pass. Lehman Spiegelberg signaled his attitude toward the existing state of affairs in 1884. In a brief historical survey of New Mexico, he wrote, "Although times are not as good as before the railroad, the railroad is a great advantage, and begins a new development the benefits of which will be felt years hence from now."[43] Less than a decade later, in 1893, the departure of the last member of the Spiegelberg family from Santa Fe and the liquidation of the family business interests ended nearly a half century of the family's presence there.[44]

Other old line German-Jewish families, such as the Staabs and Seligmans, also did not alter their behavior toward the creation of Jewish institutions. Abraham Staab was never deeply religious, although he sought to keep his children within the fold of his heritage.[45] His children turned to other occupations and he began to suffer ill health. He had virtually retired from business early in the twentieth century and passed away in 1913.[46]

The Seligmans did not leave Santa Fe or suffer the effects of altered generational goals, remaining active both in the political and economic life of the territory and the town. Bernard's sons, James and Arthur, both educated at Swarthmore, joined the family business in the late eighties and early nineties. However, both married outside of the faith of their parents. Such actions could scarcely indicate any strong desire to forward the religious concerns of the Jews of Santa Fe.

The departure from Santa Fe of some Jews adds to the discouraging picture of institution building. In 1878 the Spiegelbergs opened a branch store in Albuquerque. They placed their relatives, the Grunsfelds, who had been working for them in Santa Fe since 1873, in charge of the new operation. Similarly, Noa Ilfeld, a brother of Charles and Herman, moved to Albuquerque in the early eighties to assume an active life in commerce and community affairs. Both the Grunsfelds, as noted above, and the Ilfeld families were important activists in the growing Jewish institutional life of Albuquerque. Such events reflect the rise of a new era elsewhere in the territory for New Mexico's Jews.

▪

Even as the Jewish population attained a new stage of institutional growth, problems of stability and continuity remained. Indeed, after institutional roots had been planted, some problems, such as the survival of the community, received public articulation for the first time. Marriage, as the key to future generations, received its share of attention. Before 1880 it seemed reasonable to assume that few, if any, Jewish males would find Jewish spouses on the local scene. The women simply were not there. The growth of the nuclear family and the maturation of children to marriageable age appeared to increase awareness of the imbalance between males and females and the consequent difficulty of marrying within the faith. Whatever balance there may have been between the gender of children born in New Mexico was offset by the immigration pattern in which males predominated heavily. The new institutional spokesmen sought to foster intrafaith marriages, but their task was not an easy one. An item in *The American Israelite* in 1885, referring to Las Vegas, lamented that "there are 25 marriageable young men and only one young lady here, hence our young men are doomed to remain bachelors, unless kind Providence intervenes for them and induces young ladies from elsewhere to come here."[47] There were, of course, other possible solutions to the problems of the young men—some married outside their tradition.

Looking at New Mexico more broadly, the author saw the same troubling situation everywhere. Although he pointed out that Dr. Glueck had performed four marriages in three months, he continued his pitch to attract Jewish females from elsewhere. He appealed for "a few young ladies from the States and Territories to ornament our society." They "would be a blessing, as it would cheer the hearts of our young men, and would have a tendency to improve society in general." In concluding his plea, the author commended New Mexico to readers, assuring them that "we have every convenience life affords in the cities of the East."[48]

All, however, was not glum. The occasional wedding of the children of New Mexican Jewish families took on the air of a triumph. The Albert Eisemann–Sallie Grunsfeld nuptials in 1884 received newspaper coverage under the subheading, "The Most Brilliant Affair New Mexico Ever Saw," in Albuquerque's *Morning Journal*. The story noted that the groom was "one of the leading wool merchants of New Mexico," while the bride was the eldest daughter of a member of the house of Spiegelberg.[49] Taken historically, the event indicated a certain coming of age in generational terms and a hope for the future, however fragile.

The ethnic character of the Jewish community, so overwhelmingly composed since its beginnings of immigrants from Germany, slowly began to exhibit signs of change. In 1880 over two-thirds of the entire adult Jewish population had been born abroad. By 1900 that portion had slipped below 60 percent. That shift might be considered modest and still speaks for the continuity of ethnic background. In the relatively stable atmosphere of the Las Vegas community, the by-laws of Congregation Montefiore of 1886 still noted that the children of members were entitled to receive "religious and German instruction" as part of their training.[50] A sprinkling of Russian and Polish-born Jews appears in the 1900 census, but they scarcely affected the Germanic component of foreign ethnicity among New Mexico's Jews. New Mexican Jewry did not reflect the vast changes that were taking place in the character of Jewish immigration to the United States in which Eastern European Jews were supplanting the older Germanic strain.

A greater change occurred through the Americanization of the community. In 1880 three-fourths of the adult Jewish males were foreign born, but in 1900 that share had fallen to two-thirds. The data on women show a similar shift. In 1880 two-thirds of the women were foreign born, but in 1900 just under half were. The pattern that was beginning to emerge in the seventies had strengthened—immigrant Jewish men who came to New Mexico were marrying more American-born Jewish women, to the point where the native-born ladies formed a majority.

Childbirth pushed the Americanization of the New Mexico community much further and faster. The vast majority of the rapidly increasing numbers of Jewish children living in New Mexico were born in the United States, and the heavy majority of those were born in New Mexico. That seems to confirm that New Mexico was still a young man's frontier and that most married after they arrived in the territory. Ties with Germany receded for the Jewish community as Americanization proceeded, although they did not disappear.

Generational differences in education and career lines slowly began to occur as the offspring of the pioneers reached maturity. The pioneer immigrants, as a rule, could not consider career changes. Work pressures and family obligations, absence of local educational facilities, and simple lack of expectation and opportunity may account for that. Louis Sulzbacher was a notable exception. He came to Mora and went to Las Vegas as a merchant, read law, and was admitted to the bar in 1870. In time he achieved some fame as an attorney. However, he left New Mexico in 1890.[51]

The children of the pioneers present a more varied picture.

Two sons of Abraham Staab entered the professions, one as an attorney and another as a doctor, leaving no able direct male successor to inherit the business. Others, seeking higher education for their children, nevertheless incorporated them into the business—Louis Ilfeld in Las Vegas and James Seligman in Santa Fe offer examples of this progression. Still others did not take this path. The sons of Emanuel Rosenwald did assume their father's business in Las Vegas, but without the level of professional education followed by the Seligmans. The picture was one in which the automatic following of sons in father's footsteps was mixed, reflecting new opportunities, individual tastes, and differing assessments of the future.[52]

ᴄᴇ

In the eighties and nineties New Mexico awakened to a new sense of connection with the rest of the country. It adjusted and expanded its administrative and economic structures to reflect the new needs and desires. The leading Jewish families of Santa Fe played an important part in these developments. To a greater extent than before, they became public and even political figures. Solomon Spiegelberg, already appointed to the Santa Fe County Commission in the seventies, ran for and was elected to the County Board in 1880 and became its president.[53] In 1882 Adolph Scligman received an appointment to the commission.[54] And at the end of the eighties, Abraham Staab served on it.[55]

Probably the most political of all the Santa Fe Jews was Bernard Seligman. He became a member of the territorial house from Santa Fe County in 1880. Subsequently, he served in both houses of the legislature, as chairman of the Board of County Commissioners, and as territorial treasurer.[56]

And when others sought office, they looked to Jewish citizens for support. In the early 1890s, Thomas B. Catron, then considering a run for the office of territorial delegate to Congress, wrote to Louis Sulzbacher, who was no longer in New Mexico, and asked him to return to aid him in his campaign.[57] Once in the race, he wrote to Ilfeld Bros. in Albuquerque, "Please do the best you can throughout the county to aid me, with every one you may be able to influence."[58]

Their appointments to a growing number of institutions created to deal with changing local political structures and to draw New Mexico closer to the rest of the nation reflected a recognition of their skills and the high regard in which they were held. In 1880 the legislature created a Bureau of Immigration to attract newcomers to the territory. Prominent citizens of each county served as its commissioners and prepared reports on local conditions.[59] Lehman Spiegelberg and Adolph Seligman joined its membership in 1880, and Willi Spiegelberg was a member in 1886.[60]

It also became customary for New Mexico to represent itself at a wide variety of economic meetings to gain favorable recognition of its existence.[61] Lehman Spiegelberg attended the National Silver Convention at St. Louis in 1889 as a delegate and Solomon Spiegelberg the National Conference of Charities and Corrections in Baltimore.[62] In the early nineties Lehman Spiegelberg again represented the territory at the National Mining Congress in Montana while Abraham Staab attended the Western Interstate Wool Congress and Solomon Spiegelberg a Trans-Mississippi Commercial Congress.[63]

The strengthening of urban life in the eighties and nineties found the Santa Fe pattern repeated in many other towns where Jews lived. Henry N. Jaffa, already president of the Board of Trade that served as a quasi-government in Albuquerque, became the town's first mayor after its incorporation in 1885.[64] In 1890 Mike Mandell became the mayor of the city.[65] Neither of the mayors had been pioneer residents of the community, but they were persons well considered in commercial circles, active in town affairs, and not, apparently, highly controversial.

Elsewhere, Sigmund Lindauer became treasurer of Grants County in 1888.[66] Alex Gusdorf served on the Board of Immigration in 1883 as a representative of Taos County.[67] Appointments to economic conferences were legion. I. N. Cohen of Silver City and Alex Gusdorf attended a Mining and Industrial Exposition in 1883.[68] Louis Sulzbacher was sent to an American Forestry Congress in 1889.[69] In the nineties Albert Grunsfeld of Albuquerque and Samuel Eldodt of Rio Arriba County were frequently chosen for such duties.

The organization of new educational and service institutions in the territory also involved the energies of New Mexico's Jewish citizens. Charles Ilfeld served on the board of regents at the Normal School in Las Vegas after 1895 and Nathan Jaffa on the board at the New Mexico Military Institute in Roswell.[70] Marcus Brunswick became a member of the board of managers of the New Mexico Insane Asylum at Las Vegas and its director in 1897.[71] The above-cited examples indicate a deep and constructive involvement in the affairs of the communities in which the Jews lived and in the territory as a whole.

As in earlier periods of the territory's history, only an open attitude toward New Mexico's Jews could allow such a record to be compiled. Signs of that tolerance appeared even with respect to Jews on the world scene. As Europe moved into a new era of intolerance, it attracted the attention of New Mexican newspapers. In 1881 the *Santa Fe Weekly Democrat* found German anti-Jewish attitudes "one of the wonders of the enlightened age." The article expressed the sentiments that "in the great struggle for supremacy in every department of trade, science, literature and art, the contest should be open to all and if one outstrips all others, they should be subjects of admiration not envy." The Jews were good, law-abiding citizens, charitable and public spirited. The German complaint against them of being "shrewd and close traders," the paper found, "is surprising and ridiculous in the extreme. Nay more it savors of barbarism."[72]

Nevertheless, others found the success of the Jews disturbing. In 1886 Governor Edmund G. Ross removed Antonio Ortiz y Salazar from the office of territorial treasurer and replaced him with Bernard Seligman.[73] Writing to advise the governor out of his conceived sense of public duty, S.M. Ashenfelter of Las Cruces remarked, "The public comment has been made that there is entirely too much Jew at present in Santa Fe politics and among Santa Fe office holders." Ashenfelter did not trust Seligman.[74]

Ashenfelter was a figure of some political importance, an editor, and even a partner of Henry Lesinsky in the San Augustin Co., along with Joseph F. Bennett.[75] The governor, convinced that Seligman's appointment would enhance the value of public scrip, ignored Ashenfelter's advice.[76] But the existence of such attitudes among politically prominent persons who were themselves involved with Jews in business enterprises describes an atmosphere that bore a trace of the pollution of prejudice. One might add here the view held by William G. Ritch, the territorial secretary for many years, who found that "[the Jew's] religion is as intolerant as the Jesuit" in a community which had hardly expressed itself in terms of religious fervor.[77]

In general, though, anti-Semitism as a public issue was virtually invisible in New Mexico. Even Populism, which carried some nativist and anti-Semitic strains among its followers elsewhere, did not take that form in the New Mexico of the nineties. Discussing the political campaign of 1894, a leading student of the movement in the territory found no derogatory remarks about the Jews or the foreign born.[78] Moreover, Jews belonged in the ranks of the Populists. Sigmund Lindauer served as a delegate from Grant County at a meeting of the movement's leaders in Albuquerque in 1894.[79] New Mexico, with its heavily Spanish-speaking, Catholic population, did not provide good soil for some of the biases which the Populists may have shown elsewhere.[80]

❧

Slowly but surely the changes wrought by the railroad altered the fundamental conditions by which the sedentary mercantile capitalists had established themselves between the mid-1840s and 1880. As noted earlier, mercantile capitalism, according to business historians, rested on the ability to acquire scarce capital, the absence of efficient indirect lending institutions, and the necessity of hauling purchases long distances through sparsely watered or settled lands.[81] Specialized banking preceded the arrival of the railroad, but in the generation after 1880 it blossomed; over fifty banks received charters.[82] The increased liquidity of capital lessened generally the dependence for credit of the small producer upon the general merchant. The railroad sharply reduced the factors of distance and limited supply by the speed, safety, and quantity of goods that it could carry. The effect of these changes produced a more modern form of enterprise. Now the specialist entered the picture. Dependent on a sizable population and proximity to production in order to market efficiently, he could use the advantages of concentrated capital and division of labor to sell at a low price.[83] The general merchant had to adjust where the new factors came into play.

The effects of the changing economy can be measured partially by the evidence presented in Bradstreet's *Commercial Reports* of 1872 and 1897. In 1872 the nonspecialized general store clearly dominated the business scene. Of a total of 230 businesses listed for New Mexico, 161 were general stores, 70 percent. The *Report* for 1897 showed a sharply altered picture. The number of listings had risen to 1,616, a sign of the increasing search for credit sources. Of those, 412 were general stores, or about 25 percent. The number of general stores listed had risen about 150 percent, but the number of listings had risen over 600 percent. Clearly, the share of more specialized enterprises had grown enormously as compared with the general store, illustrating the principle expressed by the business historians.

The effects of specialization were most marked in the larger towns connected with the railroad. In 1872 Albuquerque, Santa Fe, and Las Vegas carried seventy-three listings in Bradstreet's *Report*. Of those, forty-eight were general stores, about 65 percent. In 1897 the 440 businesses listed in the three towns noted that forty-one were general stores, under 10 percent. The number of general stores in the three towns had declined sharply even as commerce expanded. Such enterprises still grew up in new areas and in smaller places, but in the towns heavily affected by the railroad they were rapidly disappearing.

As an important segment of the business community, the

Jews were deeply affected by the changes which occurred through
the rise of specialized business. In 1872 Bradstreet's *Report* for
the territory listed twenty-three out of twenty-seven Jewish-owned
enterprises as general stores, about 85 percent. By 1897 the new
Report offered the listings of seventy-six firms which were clearly
Jewish owned, of which forty-one were general stores, about 53
percent. The data for the three largest towns in 1897 reveal the
trend even more strongly. Of forty-five listed Jewish-owned firms,
fourteen were general stores, just under one-third.[84] The decline
of the dominance of the general store was important for the Jewish firms, if not quite as dramatic as it was for the business community as a whole.

The changes in the character of the Jewish-owned businesses
reflected the changing conditions. Rather than moving into totally new lines, Jewish businesses tended to break up into com-
ponents of what the generalized business had been. The shift
showed a concentration in dry goods establishments, clothing
stores, hardware, groceries, wool and hides, jewelers, and li-
quors. The wholesale as well as the retail trade were included in
many of the above varieties. Commodity distribution led the way,
but service delivery had entered the picture by the early twentieth
century. By 1903 real estate dealers, attorneys, and "capitalists"
had joined the ranks of occupations listed.[85]

The range of occupations engaged in by Jews did not, however, spread out as broadly as did the economy as a whole. The
largest new industry in Albuquerque was the railroad itself,
which introduced early on the construction of repair shops and
the labor force to man them.[86] Business directories and memoir
information show no direct employment of Jews in this segment
of the economy.

Trends in the value of the enterprises can be measured only
with caution. The partial data offered by credit reporting agencies
allow a tentative evaluation of this factor in Las Vegas in the first
generation after the coming of the railroad. In 1885 R. G. Dun's
Mercantile Agency reported the credit condition of fourteen Jewish firms rated (out of nineteen Jewish-owned listed and a total of

128 rated). In terms of estimated capital two firms were classified as C ($75,000 to $125,000), one rated D ($35,000 to $50,000), five received E ($20,000 to $35,000), two more received F ($10,000 to $20,000), two a G ($5,000 to $10,000), one an H ($3,000 to $5,000), and one an L (less than $1,000). Their credit worthiness was mostly good, the second grade of rating, compared to their capital position.[87]

In 1897 Bradstreet's *Commercial Reports* rated fifteen Jewish firms in Las Vegas. Although Dun and Bradstreet were then competing agencies and their rating keys were not exactly alike, some rough comparisons are possible. In the 1885 data, six out of the fourteen Jewish firms were capitalized at $20,000 or less. In 1897 twelve of fifteen rated businesses were in that category.[88] Fragmentary as that evidence is, a shift appeared to be developing that indicated a new pattern of growth. Of six new firms rated in 1897, all were in the $20,000 or less range of capitalization and four of the six were in specialized enterprises. Two firms which had existed in 1885 fell into lower categories, while the others remained constant or moved higher. Only two older firms, that of Charles Ilfeld and Friedman, Myer and Co., which had rated in the $75,000 to $125,000 class in 1885, rose in their capitalization in 1897 into the $150,000 to $200,000 class.[89]

The suggestion here is that specialization meant the creation of smaller, lower capitalized businesses than had grown up in the era prior to the coming of the railroad. In terms of economic status, the Jews in urban areas, at least, were beginning to move from the top stratum of wealth into a middle-level rank. That, in turn, raises the question of whether a less financially prominent community could maintain the high level of social and political visibility achieved by earlier generations of Jews.

The old successful pioneers also had to adjust to the changing economic environment. Charles Ilfeld moved to a much greater concentration in dealing with sheep and wool, undertook financing of inventories and credit of country stores through wholesaling, and adopted even more characteristics of commercial banking than before.[90] Parish, the historian of the Ilfeld

Company, viewed these moves as protective in nature, defenses against the threat of shrinking trade and greater competition.[91]

The appearance of the railroad and the effects of homesteading affected the place of real estate in the economy of New Mexico after 1880. Per capita valuation of property in that year for the United States stood at $870, while for New Mexico it was $410. By 1900 the national per capita valuation had risen to $1,165, but for New Mexico the figure had climbed to $1,374.[92]

The raising of livestock, cattle and sheep, had increased after 1870 as the railroad approached New Mexico. The value of this industry rose from $2,389,157 in that year to $31,727,400 in 1900.[93] Given the need for range land to practice this industry and the increase in homesteading, the desire to seek title and enclosure of land by fences introduced intrusions into traditional practices which resulted in hostility and violence even as the old dangers of conflict with the Indian declined.

As noted above, the importance of ranching certainly attracted the attention of some Jewish entrepreneurs. In Las Vegas, one of the major areas of growth for this industry, Charles Ilfeld became ever more heavily involved in it. His policies, however, continued to dictate that he not invest heavily in land since he required the rapid turnover of capital. Instead, he preferred at first to keep herds on private ranches supplemented by public range.[94] By the nineties, however, the size of his sheep operations and the need to collect them at central points led to some land purchases. Even these were temporary, and only in the twentieth century would specialization force Ilfeld to make substantial investments in ranches for his sheep operations.[95]

If for Ilfeld real estate practices changed slowly, in urban areas, town growth and real estate values led to some degree of speculation with an eye to land development. The most notable case among Jews in Santa Fe was the platting in 1881 of a downtown subdivision by the Spiegelbergs, possibly in expectation of a railroad boom. However, the lots were not sold.[96] In 1904 Abraham Staab also subdivided a property to sell.[97]

Beyond these two cases, the Jews of Santa Fe owned considerable property in the town. Representing something over one percent of the town's population in the mid-1880s, they held 7 percent of the property of the city, 12 percent of the commercial property downtown, and 30 percent of the downtown property.[98] That this land appears to have been heavily in Spiegelberg or Staab family hands makes it reasonable to assume that these two families had some land development in mind. Given their major interests in commerce and banking, however, their interest in land development opportunities seems fairly modest. In any case, Santa Fe did not undergo the land boom periods experienced in Albuquerque and Las Vegas with the appearance of the railroad.

➳

After 1880 new areas of New Mexico opened up to settlement. Such towns as Roswell and Clayton grew up in the eastern reaches of the territory, and Jewish families, even if they were few in number, made their mark in and on them. The number of new locations in which Jews lived expanded rapidly. In 1880 they were present in no fewer than sixteen places; in 1900 in at least thirty-five. Few places of any size had no Jewish inhabitants.

Unlike the towns attended by the rich banks of the Rio Grande and its tributaries and the decently watered pasturages of the north, in the east cattle and sheep range predominated and became the focal point for town building. Subsequently, agriculture also attracted attention in the Pecos River valley.

Roswell owed its formation primarily to grazing operations. The presence of the famous Chisum ranch inspired the establishment of a store by two Jewish families, the Jaffas and Pragers, possibly as early as 1884. In 1886 they were persuaded to move to the newly created town and opened Jaffa-Prager and Co., the first department store in the Pecos Valley, an economic landmark. Plains ranches as well as townspeople relied on them for supplies.[99] Important local figures, including the well-known Pat Garrett, provided land and helped build the structure to house the new business concern. In 1895, Jaffa-Prager sold part of its operations to the Joyce-Pruitt firm, but the most important part of the business remained heavily dedicated to its wool and sheep operations.[100]

Like the early Jewish newcomers to Las Vegas, rather than Santa Fe, the Jaffa-Prager families did not come to Roswell as their first stop in New Mexico. They had engaged in business in Trinidad, Colorado, and then in Las Vegas. Nor were they in the exclusive mold of the earlier German-Jewish immigrants. Nathan Jaffa was born in Germany, but William S. Prager was born in Pittsburgh. Their more substantial experience and better economic circumstances placed them in a good position to do well and to play an important part in the new community from the beginning.

As in earlier times, family ties proved important to the settlement process. Sidney Prager, Will's younger brother, came to Roswell shortly after his brother arrived, while Joseph J. Jaffa joined his elder brother in 1889. They too threw themselves into work and community affairs once they established themselves. One may speak of a family-based Jewish community centering around these two family focal points. The Jaffas and Pragers became the core of a Jewish congregation formed in 1903 with Nathan Jaffa taking the lead in religious matters.[101]

Both Nathan Jaffa and William Prager participated heavily in the creation of an institutional network for the new town. In 1891 the town elected a board of trustees, and Jaffa was one of those chosen to the board. The Jaffa-Prager store itself served as an informal center of operations. As early as 1889 the volunteer fire department met there, and Jaffa became its chief. Even the initial organization of the Roswell Masonic lodge took place in the store. In 1888 John W. Poe, Frank H. Lea, William J. Fountain, all local figures of importance, met with Will Prager to discuss the formation of a lodge. Shortly thereafter, Prager, who went to Las Vegas to study Masonic procedures, became the first master of Lodge No. 18. Jaffa was its third master.

The economic development of Roswell went hand-in-hand with Jaffa-Prager skills. In 1890 Roswell acquired its own bank.

Nathan Jaffa served as a vice-president and member of the board of directors. E. A. Cohoon, who founded the bank, noted that "Nathan Jaffa, W. E. Prager, John Poe, and Smith Lea [were] the men who were responsible for my coming to Roswell."[102] In 1900 Jaffa associated himself with the new Citizens Bank, where he served as cashier and on the board of directors. The new bank specialized in ranch and livestock loans.[103]

In his history of Roswell, James D. Shinkle states that "from 1890 to 1910, the most significant events in the development of the Pecos Valley centered about water or railroads."[104] On both issues, leadership rested with James J. Hagerman, who sparked the investment efforts. The Pragers and Jaffas contributed heavily to the coming of the railroad. A voluntary campaign by the town to offer a bonus for the rapid completion of the road in 1893–94 found the Jaffa-Prager Co. offering 500 acres of land; Sidney Prager, 120 acres; and Prager, Robertson and Cohoon, 50 acres.[105] The families had clearly done well and committed themselves to the continued development of the community that had become their home.

Whether the two families' economic interests ran beyond commerce and financial investment is not clear, although the above-noted businesses formed the cornerstone of their economic activity. Like creditors elsewhere, they sometimes received land as payment for commodities. The Leas apparently paid this way.[106] Perhaps the fact that their land donations appear as the largest contribution to aid the coming of the railroad indicates the secondary importance of landholding to them.

Unwittingly, Nathan Jaffa also made a contribution to water development in Roswell. His health problems inspired the need to drill for water that was less mineral in content than was first in use in the town. It was on the Jaffa home lot that such efforts in 1890 brought an artesian well home. People came from miles around to witness the phenomenon. The discovery of other wells soon followed, assuring the future of the town's development.[107]

Despite their small numbers, the Jewish population of Roswell formed a congregation in 1903.[108] Without a name and without the resources to afford a rabbi, concerned individuals nevertheless saw value in this minimal form of organization. Holiday services had probably long been performed under the leadership of Nathan Jaffa, who served as the acting reader for the congregation. Louis M. Prager recalled Jaffa's role as such at the Prager home when he was a child.[109] In 1907 Roswell's Jewish population totalled about forty-five persons.[110] Roswell's experience showed clearly that greater organization than had occurred at Santa Fe was indeed possible if the persons present were dedicated enough to carry on the activities.

Clayton, even more pointedly than Roswell, grew up as a railroad center for the shipment of cattle and wool as the roads crossed the endless plains of northeastern New Mexico. Before they came, the ranches of the whole area looked to Trinidad, Colorado, for shipment of their flocks and herds. The appearance of the Colorado and Southern line after 1885, however, led to the founding of Clayton in 1888. Cattle drives from as far as Roswell then came to use Clayton as the railroad loading point for their stock.

The Herzstein family settled there a few years later. The family migrated to the United States in the mid-eighties, and brothers established themselves first in Philadelphia and then in Mora County. Morris had set up a store in Liberty in 1888. After a tragic event in which the notorious Ketchum gang robbed and killed one brother, Levi, Morris left the area, initiated several ventures elsewhere, and finally settled in Clayton. Like the Jaffas and Pragers in Roswell, he was no novice at business. And like so many of his predecessors, his success led him to bring his nephew Simon west from Philadelphia in 1901. Three other brothers followed and opened new stores in town, forming a veritable clan of businesses.

How New Mexico was changing again becomes evident in Clayton. The original enterprise of Max Weil and Morris Herzstein had been a mercantile or general store. When it burned down, consuming an inventory valued at $100,000, Simon Herzstein opened a ready-to-wear clothing house—he was carrying Hart, Schaffner and Marx suits in 1905. Uncle Morris found it unbelievable that westerners would wear ready-made clothing, but Simon persisted. After the fire Morris turned to spending much time at his nearby ranch but also built a movie theater. Joe Herzstein concentrated his efforts on the marketing of pinto beans.[111] The diversification and specialization that was reaching New Mexico altered the traditional unidimensionality of the Jewish merchant—even in a small town.

In this era of expansion of cattle and sheep husbandry on the edge of the plains one finds atypical responses by Jewish settlers. Solomon Floersheim, who worked for Charles Ilfeld in the eighties as a collector, moved into storekeeping and then became a sheep rancher in the Springer area in 1893. He later added mercantile businesses to his work in Springer and Roy. All the enterprises achieved considerable success well into the twentieth century.[112]

Even in the eighties Jews lived in such isolated areas of New Mexico that they could appear as exotic creatures. Simon Vorenberg came to Mora in 1884 and worked for Lowenstein and Strauss, who, as Emma Vorenberg put it, "used to take . . . as clerks and salesmen, as many German-Jewish boys as it possibly could." In the late eighties he bought a general store in Cleveland, a few miles from Mora.[113] Only two non-Hispanic families lived there. When Simon married Theresa Harris in 1889 and brought her to Cleveland from her native Philadelphia, no one believed that the auburn-haired, hazel-eyed woman was Jewish and treated her as a great novelty. People came from miles around just to look at her.[114]

Nevertheless, under these conditions she remained a true "mother in Israel." She baked Sabbath bread and prayers were said at the table. Four children were born to the Vorenbergs in Cleveland, three aided by midwives, before they sold their store and returned to Mora.[115] The atmosphere in which the Vorenbergs lived as a result of their isolation and the dedication with which they maintained their beliefs and life-style present a picture of cultural survival which matches the success stories of the larger towns.

Perhaps even more unusual, however, was the elevation of Solomon Bibo to the governorship of Acoma pueblo in the eighties. The Bibos, as noted earlier, had traded with the Navajos in the seventies. Solomon, a younger brother of Nathan and Simon, followed them to New Mexico and eventually established trade relations with the Acomans, even learning Keres, their language. In the early eighties he became a licensed trader to the pueblo, and in 1884 he signed a thirty year grazing lease with Martin Valle, then its governor.[116]

Bibo's contract, which he sold to the Acoma Land and Cattle Co., incurred the wrath of Indian agent Pedro Sanchez and led to a suit to void the lease. But in 1888 the court decided against the right of the government to sue Bibo if the Indians did not wish it.[117] By that time—in 1885—Solomon had married Juana Valle, the granddaughter of Martin Valle. It was a clear sign of the goodwill he enjoyed within the pueblo, and in 1888 he was appointed governor, a position he held a number of times subsequently.[118]

The Bibos, in supporting Indians, found themselves caught in the midst of conflict between Hispanos and Indians over land claims in the mid-nineties. Simon and Solomon, settled at Cebolleta, were attacked in a circular which described them as "rich Jews [who] want to defraud us."[119] Since the broadside was the work of a priest named Julliard, the Bibos, alarmed, turned to Willi Spiegelberg, then already in New York, to seek help from the archbishop against such charges on the basis of the Spiegelbergs' long established relationship with the church.[120] No evidence of follow-up is known, but the anti-Semitism points up, as in the case of political activism by Jews in the eighties, the possibility of latent anti-Jewish feeling emerging as Jews became more openly prominent and extended the range of their interests.

In 1898 Solomon Bibo and his wife moved to San Francisco.

Nathan had gone there in 1884. Like Nathan, Solomon retained his holdings, sheep, and stores in New Mexico. In San Francisco he engaged in real estate ventures and opened a grocery store for imported foods. The latter enterprise was destroyed during the earthquake of 1906.[121] Nathan Bibo returned to New Mexico after the catastrophe.

In southwestern New Mexico, too, Jewish entrepreneurs moved in as the area opened up to settlement. Unlike the eastern tier of towns, there it was the lure of valuable minerals that sparked interest. That various ores, including copper and silver, existed in the region was well known in the Spanish and Mexican periods. Renewed interest in extracting them emerged after the Civil War, when the capacity of the miners to protect themselves against the Apaches or to gain military protection allowed Anglos to come to the area of what is now Silver City in some numbers. In 1870 the discovery of silver induced the intrepid to come.[122]

The first Jews in the area appeared at the time of the silver discovery. Henry Lesinsky, irresistibly drawn to mining ventures out of a youth of prospecting pursuits and even when he was a merchant at Las Cruces, came in the early seventies. Eventually, his major interest settled on the copper finds in the Clifton-Morenci area of eastern Arizona, but Silver City remained a base of operations.[123]

Others followed the more traditional paths of Jewish-owned enterprises. David Abraham had arrived in 1871 and opened a store. Unlike Lesinsky, Abraham rooted himself in Silver City, settled his family there, and became a pillar of the community. He also invested in mining and real estate, owned the well-known Billiard Saloon and by 1880 the Southern Hotel. He also built and ran an ice house. He is credited, in addition, with being one of the planters of shade trees.[124]

Other families arrived in the seventies and eighties. Isaac Cohen came from Jerusalem in 1872 and set up a two-story brick store with Morris Lesinsky, Henry's brother. By 1880 he was chairman of the County Commission and was elected to the Silver City town council.[125] Max Schutz came over from Las Cruces in 1877, and his brother Aaron followed in 1883. Along with the Abrahams, their lives entwined with the economic, political, and social life of the community.

In the nineties the old-timers began to pass from the scene. Isaac Cohen died in New York in 1893, and David Abraham passed away in 1894. Max Schutz, just past the turn of the century, noted in an advertisement, "I shall retire from business, if possible, on January 1 [1902]."[126] Newcomers, such as the Borenstein brothers, continued to arrive, but the period of the city's most rapid growth, which in the seventies and eighties had made it "the most flourishing of all the cities of New Mexico," had passed.[127]

Although the year 1900 did not spell the end of the changes introduced through the coming of the railroad, it serves as a guidepost indicating that the paths had become well marked. Mercantile capitalism had begun to be replaced by industrial capitalism, and the economic character of New Mexico bowed slowly before its power. The Jews, mostly in business, but like all others, had to comply with the new conditions tolerated by the shrinkage of isolation and spatial dimension, the arrival and demand for quantities of commodities heretofore unavailable, and the credit means available to receive and export them.

The growth of new urban centers and the concentration of population in them helped foster new institutions. For the Jews, the achievement of a new level of communal maturity resulted from their slowly growing, stable social base. Moderately disruptive of the old, the new conditions opened opportunities for social action in the changing environment. But unlike the spirit of the bold leap which characterized the arrival of the pioneer, newcomers moved along accustomed paths, adjusting to new markets, changing the internal character of their economic operations without affixing themselves to the railroad itself. Only in the newer, smaller communities did they still appear in their older mercantile role. Perhaps, as social scientists have suggested,

Jews found the large business enterprise, such as the railroad, a hostile or uncomfortable environment. As a result, they remained outside such organizations. The Jews seemed to be entering a period of more conservative development, where they were less prominent when compared with the earlier era.

The Era of Quiet
Change, 1900–40

$$\boxed{5}$$

From 1900 to 1940 the Jews of the world lived through a series of remarkable and traumatic changes. In the Russian empire, they endured a series of pogroms which captured the attention of the world. As subjects of the tsar they felt the disruption and stress of revolution and as Europeans, the terrible strains of World War I. In Central Europe they suffered, as did all others in the war years and beyond and then encountered the unprecedented hate and disruption of the rise of Nazism. The burden of anti-Semitism, expressed in physical violence, economic distress, and a sense of hopelessness, had already heavily affected the east European Jews in the eighties and nineties of the nineteenth century. They had reacted by emigrating in unprecedented numbers to the West and especially to the United States. That response continued, with interruptions, throughout the first forty years of the twentieth century.

Compared to these crises and turmoil, the life of the Jewish community in New Mexico appears serene—almost bucolic. Change did occur, but it was slow. The study of history, however, involves not only high drama and tragedy, but equally, the calmer, more mundane aspects of existence. The business of daily lives lived quietly appears as an evolutionary rather than a revolutionary process. In the history of a community one is as important as the other.

The slow change in the Jewish community mirrored change in New Mexico. While the new state did draw closer to the rest of the country, it still remained distinct, "a land apart," as Marc Simmons put it, from the national mainstream.[1] He attributed that separation to the continuing powerful presence of Hispano society. The "failure" of the latter to "melt" in the pot of national culture left the impression in many places that New Mexico was almost a foreign country.[2]

∼

One dimension of the relative calm of New Mexican Jewish history can be seen in population figures. As a result of events in Europe, American Jewry changed to a degree that might be called revolutionary. In the forty years included in this chapter Jewish numbers in America grew from one million to over four and three-quarters million.[3] By contrast the Jewish population in New Mexico increased quite modestly. Numbering between 400 and 500 in 1900, the Jewish community had expanded to 858 in 1917 and 1,160 in 1937, when censuses of Jews were taken.[4] Thus, while the number of Jews counted nationally nearly quintupled, in New Mexico they less than tripled.

Even more indicative of change from earlier periods was the slowdown in the rate of growth. Between 1860 and 1880 New Mexico's Jews had quadrupled, and from 1880 to 1900 they had doubled. During the next forty years the rate of increase less than tripled, most of that coming before 1920. Between 1920 and 1940 the rate of increase was only about 25 percent.

Within New Mexico the slowed rate of increase of the Jewish community matched growth conditions there. The territory of 1900 had 195,000 inhabitants, the state of 1940 had 532,000—an increase of about 170 percent. The growth rate of the Jewish population was about the same. Jews were measured as twenty-five hundredths of one percent of New Mexico's population in 1900 and twenty-seven hundredths of one percent in 1940.

The slowed growth rate of New Mexico's Jewish population reflected changes taking place within the local community as well as broader changes in the condition of the Jewish population of the Western world. It is important to consider that most of the increase of New Mexican Jewry to 1880 had come as a result of immigration. The young unmarried population could not reproduce itself. Between 1880 and 1900, the family had grown slowly as a social force in the community. But students of the subject have depicted birth rates among Jews as comparatively low. Among the German Jews generally that was already true in the 1880s.[5] Since New Mexico's Jews were heavily of this background, it may be assumed that births alone would not have greatly increased their numbers. Henceforth the low rate of natural increase and slowed immigration could account for the slackened rate of growth.

As noted earlier, the decline in rate of growth after 1900 occurred against the background of the greatest influx of Jewish immigrants that America had witnessed. While Jewish immigrants continued to arrive from Germany, that source of newcomers was small after 1880 as compared with emigrants from eastern European centers of Jewish population. Between 1885 and 1905 at the New York port of entry alone some 16,000 Jews arrived from Germany, but over 550,000 came from Russia.[6] This vast new immigration had little connection with New Mexico and the long-standing pattern of attraction through family and friends which had been so important in establishing New Mexican Jewry. Only a few east European Jews had ventured to New Mexico in the eighties and nineties. As late as 1930 only forty-nine foreign-born whites listed Yiddish, the spoken idiom of most east European Jews, as their mother tongue; in 1940 sixty did so. Of all Jews, foreign and native born, 100 knew Yiddish in 1940—less than 10 percent of the total.[7] The New Mexican Jewish community remained largely Germanic or native-born American in its ethnic background, even as the Jewish population on the national level became sharply less so.

The east European Jews, poorer than their German brethren upon arrival, without hinterland connections, stayed most often in the Northeast. They brought with them their own customs and languages, and their skills, which lay far more in manufacturing and trades than in commerce. These skills were more usable in the manufacturing centers of the Northeast than in the Southwest. The influx of such persons to the Southwest, therefore, was slow.

Meanwhile, the changes occurring within the New Mexico Jewish community continued to separate it slowly from that close tie to the Germanic homeland which had fueled its earlier existence. The percentage of native-born Jews in New Mexico grew. As noted earlier, they had reached over 40 percent by 1900. In 1910 virtual equality existed between native and foreign-born Jewish adults. Two-thirds of adult Jewish women were American born in 1910 and 40 percent of the males. Among the males, moreover, the foreign born represented an ever older portion of the population. Many had probably already brought to this country most of those persons whom they intended to bring. The native-born Jews had ever fewer ties with the Old World.

Some elements in this trend are visible in the numbers of immigrants declaring New Mexico as their destination from their port of entry. Between 1899 and 1910 only twenty-two indicated such intent.[8] Less than full data for the second decade of the century indicate a similarly low level of intention. One must also keep in mind that immigration, especially from Germany, underwent a major slowdown as World War I cut sharply into the flow. The entry of the United States into the war against Germany in 1917 halted emigration from there completely.

Conditions of immigration into America in the twenties and thirties continued to favor its diminution as a factor of Jewish growth. Although incoming numbers rose sharply in the early twenties, after 1924, when new restrictive immigration laws came into effect, they again fell off dramatically. In the early thirties the depression held the numbers to low levels seen only during World War I. Only in the later thirties, when the twin threats of Nazism and war arose, did the number of immigrants to New Mexico increase, again from Germanic Europe. Of course, direct foreign immigration to New Mexico was not the only source of newcomers. Older foreign-born immigrants with experiences elsewhere in the country still came, as did native-born American Jews.

The new circumstances of immigration reflected themselves in a slowly maturing population. The membership list of B'nai B'rith in Albuquerque indicates that between 1883 and 1900, 55 percent of the members were in their twenties and another 30 percent in their thirties. From 1900 to 1920, 49 percent were in their twenties and 45 percent in their thirties. From 1920 to 1936, 41 percent were in their twenties and 31 percent in their thirties. The remainder, members aged forty and above, however, had grown to 28 percent.[9] The day of New Mexico as a frontier particularly attractive to youth had come to an end—at least as far as its Jewish population was concerned.

❦

Modest population growth did not mean stagnation. The processes of change which had begun with the coming of the railroad continued to operate in New Mexico. One of the most notable trends was Albuquerque's increasing importance as the urban and commercial center of the state. Containing 6,238 persons in 1900, in 1940 it numbered 35,449—nearly a sixfold increase. However, it remained what it had started to be after 1880, a railroad-based town and a trade and distribution center for a limited hinterland.[10]

That Jews tended to live in towns rather than rural areas is axiomatic of their modern history; their economic activities dictated that pattern of residence. That rule also held true in New Mexico, and, as Albuquerque grew, an ever larger percentage of New Mexico's Jews formed part of the city's population. About 25 percent of them (120) resided there in 1900 and nearly 39 percent (450) did so in 1940. They represented about 1.9 percent of the city's population in 1900 and 1.2 percent in 1940.

Albuquerque's growth and the concentration of Jewish population within it placed the local Jewish community at the heart of New Mexican Jewry's development. Roughly equal to Las Vegas in size and complexity in 1900, by 1940 it stood alone in its diversity and capacity to provide the social and spiritual needs of a Jewish community. In terms of size and development, Congregation Albert was the state's leading Jewish institution.

Temple Albert itself was erected at Seventh and Gold streets, an imposing structure with a domed oriental cast. The laying of the cornerstone in 1899 was a notable event. The Masonic Grand Lodge of New Mexico performed the labor "with six Congregation Albert Masons serving as Grand Lodge officers." It was the first religious edifice in Albuquerque at which the Grand Lodge performed these duties.[11]

Given the relative slowdown in growth the congregation maintained itself well. There were thirty-four original members in 1897.[12] By 1900 the number of members and seatholders had risen to fifty.[13] A membership list for 1919 counts eighty-four members.[14] During the dark economic days of the depression, when dues became a heavy burden for some, the numbers declined; in 1934 there were only sixty-four members.[15]. By the early 1940s membership had again risen, and in 1944 the number was placed at eighty-seven.[16]

As with many successful organizations, Congregation Albert had the good fortune to have a cadre of dedicated leaders. Among the long-term early officers were presidents Henry N. Jaffa, 1897–1900, Berthold Spitz, 1902 and 1908–11, Alphonse Fleischer, 1912 and 1928–30 and as secretary 1899–1900; Samuel Neustadt, as secretary 1897–98, 1904–6 and as president in 1907, and Emil Uhlfelder as secretary from 1909 to 1912.[17] The leaders of the women's organization, the Ladies Benevolent Aid Society, are known in spotty fashion, but its presidents included the women of the best-known Jewish families of Albuquerque: Mrs. Alfred Grunsfeld, Mrs. Noa Ilfeld, Mrs. Henry Jaffa, Mrs. Louis Ilfeld, and Mrs. Seymour Lewinson. Mrs. Mike Mandell served from 1927 to 1934 and Mrs. Albert Stern from 1934 to 1939.[18] The service given by residents of long standing provided stability and valuable experience to the congregation.

The presence of an organized congregation with a recognized

religious leader added to the already known dimensions of Jewish participation in the wider community. Rabbi J. H. Kaplan joined with Christian clergy to seek the establishment of a nonsectarian charitable society to aid the impoverished sick in 1904.[19] A decade later Rabbi Moise Bergman served a number of terms as president of the Albuquerque Board of Charities.[20] The scholarly achievements of some of the rabbis brought them into contact with the growing institutions of higher learning as speakers and even as teachers. Rabbi Kaplan traveled to Roswell in 1905 to address an assemblage at the New Mexico Military Institute and at a Baptist church. In 1911 Rabbi Mendel Silber filled in for Dean C. E. Hodgin at the University of New Mexico's School of Education while the latter was abroad, taking over some administrative duties and teaching assignments.[21] New kinds of relations with other religious groups became possible. The Methodists were permitted to use the temple until their own church was built in 1904. Rabbis also took public stands on local issues, which, in their view, were for the good of the whole society. Thus, Rabbi Mendel Silber, in 1912, publicly supported the creation of a new high school in Albuquerque.[22]

The crystallization of the Jewish presence, however, also could raise new problems. Since the rabbi was the spiritual symbol of the Jewish community, unpopular positions taken by a rabbi could attract negative attention to Jews as a group. Rabbi Kaplan, who was a popular and dynamic person, joined with a Christian minister, F. E. Crawford, in 1906 to publish a small periodical named *The Barbarian*. The publication served as a gadfly for ethical awareness. In January 1907, Rabbi Kaplan, in response to a lynching, wrote an article which attacked the lynchers.[23]

An outcry erupted when the issue appeared. The *Albuquerque Morning Journal* considered the article "too dirty to be talked about in a decent newspaper."[24] Deluged by angry letters, some of which threatened violence to the rabbi, the paper condemned him as ignorant of the subject on which he wrote and of maligning nearly a third of America's population, that of the South.[25]

The Reverend Crawford defended his co-editor's motives, and Rabbi Kaplan published a letter, indicating that he intended to insult no one.[26]

Some members of the congregation responded quickly to the uproar. A special meeting called by twelve members on January 6, 1907, the same day the criticism appeared in the *Journal*, led to Rabbi Kaplan's resignation.[27] That opposition to him was less than universal can be seen from attempts to table the motion calling for his departure.[28] When it passed, furthermore, the congregation granted Kaplan three months salary and promised an additional three months pay if he had not found a permanent position by the end of the first three months.[29] It would appear that some of the congregation felt intimidated by the protests against the rabbi's stand.

Even in the late thirties the community could be disturbed by involvement in controversy. Rabbi A. L. Krohn, who served as rabbi at Temple Albert from 1931 to 1938, was active and highly visible in the general community. He taught courses on social work in the sociology department at the University of New Mexico, and contemporaries recall "that he was the only faculty member who could fill it [Rodey Hall, the largest classroom on campus] with students."[30] He was also president of the Bernalillo County School Board.

Rabbi Krohn became a strong advocate on behalf of the small, mostly Hispanic, farmers, who were in conflict with the Middle Rio Grande Conservancy District.[31] Such figures as Clinton Anderson, the future secretary of agriculture under President Truman, stood with the large landowners.[32] Senator Dennis Chavez, who described Krohn as a person who was "social minded, energetic, has the respect of the community and will treat everybody justly," sought to have him head the certification of work and direct relief in 1938 when the New Mexico WPA took over that function.[33]

In December 1937 a special meeting of Temple Albert's trustees instructed Krohn to desist. A special election in April 1938 on whether to retain him, gave Krohn a small majority, but he decided to withdraw.[34] Some of the congregation apparently still looked upon themselves as a small, isolated community, dependent on the goodwill of those in the larger community among whom they lived and unwilling to risk controversy. It is not without interest, although far from conclusive, to note that Clinton Anderson strongly supported relief efforts in Europe on behalf of the victims of Nazism.

The congregation managed to maintain itself financially during its early years but not always without difficulty. In January 1906, the trustees, under the leadership of Simon Stern and Julius Staab, found it necessary to appeal to city merchants to seek contributions in the East to aid the expenses of Temple Albert. In September the trustees proclaimed success and thanked both the above-named gentlemen and the Ladies Benevolent Society for their efforts.[35]

No doubt, expenses were high for the congregation relative to its size. In addition to the expenses of the temple, the congregation added a residence for the rabbi in the early years of the century. Salaries for rabbis were hardly munificent ($1,500 per annum during the first decade), and the frequent turnover may have reflected that condition. Special financial problems were solved by the capacity of the members to give. Disposition of pews in 1900 went "according to the amount subscribed" plus a 20 percent addition to the regular pew rental.[36]

Yet, the congregation was not poverty ridden in these early years and its membership even less so. In 1909 the finance committee reported a revenue of $2,700, which was, it concluded, "not a bad showing for a small number of Jews as we have in this city." If more were needed, those with children in the Sabbath school could be asked to increase their subscriptions. "It is safe to say," the report judged, "that none of our members are in such a shape that a dollar or two more or less a month of dues to this congregation would make any material difference to them."[37] Exceptional expenses, such as large repairs for the temple and improvements in the cemetery, were often met by the socials and bazaars organized by the Ladies Aid Society. In 1915 the mortgage of the temple was paid off.

After the prosperity of the twenties, the congregation, like the Jewish community as a whole and the population generally, felt the full effects of the depression which struck the country in 1929. Arrears in dues appeared as an increasing concern, along with requests for reduction of dues and resignations. The congregation found it necessary to put the parsonage up for sale in 1932. In 1933 President Seligman told the membership that "unless all outstanding dues are paid immediately and every member agrees to pay at least at the present rate of dues during the coming year . . . *the Congregation must quit.*"[38] In the late thirties conditions began to improve and the institution survived.

Slowly and quietly the Jewish population of Albuquerque began to display a growing complexity in its composition. In 1921 a second religious community announced its formal existence as Congregation B'nai Israel. The impetus for its origination lay in the desire for a more traditional practice of Judaism than offered at Temple Albert. The new congregation defined itself as Orthodox.[39]

The creation of the new congregation did not occur overnight. As early as 1919 an *Albuquerque Journal* item headlined "Orthodox Jews Will Observe Yom Kippur at the K. of P. Hall" invited all Jews to attend. M. S. Portman, a rabbi from St. Louis, was to conduct the services.[40] And even earlier, perhaps as early as 1915, the members of the future congregation, many of east European origin, had met to pray in private homes, hired halls, and even in the back of stores.[41] The members of the new congregation did not split off from Congregation Albert; they did not belong to it in the first place.[42]

Information on the early years of Congregation B'nai Israel is scarce. The lack of permanent quarters may have contributed to that. Its guiding committee included Ben Marcus, David Meyer, and Hyman Livingston. At its founding the congregation had seventeen members, and Isodor M. Freed served as shochet (ritual slaughterer) and teacher.[43] The congregation remained quite small and was, at times, on the brink of extinction in the twenties. By 1934, however, it began to achieve greater stability, renting quarters at 116½ West Central and inaugurating regular services and activities. Harry Levin, who arrived at that time, served as spiritual leader as well as Hebrew and Sunday School teacher.[44]

Also in 1934 the women of the congregation created a Ladies Auxiliary. Nineteen charter members led the way to organizing the social activities of the congregation, its religious school, and a variety of fund-raising activities. They managed to hold dances featuring such talent as the Duke Ellington and Paul Whiteman orchestras. By 1937 the auxiliary had purchased a lot at Coal and Cedar streets as a site for the future synagogue.[45]

In the course of the generation which passed from incorporation to the building of a synagogue, the congregation modified its practices. Dietary laws, the problems of separate seating for men and women, and other related matters presented obstacles difficult to solve in the atmosphere of Albuquerque.[46] Commenting on the state of traditional Judaism locally in 1923, Alphonse Fleischer of Temple Albert noted "the old line orthodox Jews are in the minority in Albuquerque, such as remain do not observe very closely the old Mosaic dietary laws and some of the extreme doctrine."[47] Despite Fleischer's evaluation, considerable differences of practice remained between the two congregations. In 1930 efforts by Temple Albert to broaden membership and reduce expenses in the difficult economic times led to an attempt at affiliation whereby the Orthodox might hold their own services in the temple vestry room, but it came to naught.[48]

At its inception in 1921, B'nai Israel was one-fifth the size of Temple Albert; in 1941 it was about half the size of the older Reform congregation. Perhaps the easing of observance and increasing east European numbers aided the congregation's growth. Early in 1941, after a generation of formal existence, B'nai Israel reached a cherished goal—construction began on the synagogue building. At that time the membership had reached about forty.[49] By then the congregation defined itself as Conservative rather than Orthodox.

cæ

Along with the development of local religious institutions, the first forty years of the twentieth century witnessed a strengthening of linkage between the Jews of New Mexico and the national as well as the international Jewish community. The process had begun, as we have seen, in the eighties in Albuquerque with the creation of B'nai B'rith. Ties with the outside world expanded after the turn of the century, inspired by the series of tragedies and difficulties encountered by the Jews of Europe. In addition, the process of local institutional growth linked those organizations with their national counterparts.

The plight of the Russian Jews attracted the attention of American Jews early in the century. The pogrom at Kishineff in 1903, followed several years later by a wave of similar anti-Jewish riots during the revolution of 1905, led to organized efforts to relieve their distress. Under the auspices of the National Committee for the Relief of Sufferers by Russian Massacres, the Albuquerque community contributed over $400 to the fund.[50] The Las Vegas Jewish community gave $265 to the same cause.[51] World War I and the revolutionary aftermath in Russia provided another shattering experience for the European Jews. In 1915 Albuquerque's Jews, led by Louis Ilfeld and Rabbi Moise Bergman, contributed to national campaigns to aid the victims.[52] Again in 1917, the same gentlemen, Mrs. David Weiller, and Mrs. Sol Benjamin formed a committee for the Jewish War Relief Fund in Albuquerque.[53]

The immediate postwar years, with civil war, hunger, and dislocation as their harvest, ensured continued appeals. But the tragedy of war also produced new opportunities to solve the problems of the Jews. The Balfour Declaration in 1917, with its promise of a Jewish homeland in Palestine, raised Zionism to a new level of attention and organization in the United States.

The creation of the Zionist Organization of America (ZOA) in 1918 gave the homeland movement a much stronger focus than it had had earlier. Historically, the issue of Zionism aroused considerable controversy among American Jews. Although no hard and fast lines can be drawn regarding attitudes, Reform Jews, who often looked upon themselves as a religious community and not a nation, tended to oppose Zionism, while Orthodox and Conservative elements looked to national community as a necessary core of Judaism.[54] The new status of the movement and the urgent needs of the European Jews eased differences, although it did not erase them. Julian Mack, a leading figure in the ZOA, conceded past difficulties in 1920, and he welcomed the new, friendlier tone, commenting, "Many Jews hitherto opposed to the movement have given us assurances of their support."[55]

By 1920 the ZOA reached Albuquerque. As the call came for funds to restore Palestine to the Jews, it was the members of the newly forming B'nai Israel who took the lead locally to organize the appeal. A committee to conduct the campaign included John Livingston, Ben Marcus, David Meyer, and M. M. Maisel—stalwarts in the Orthodox congregation.[56] Shortly afterwards, a newspaper report on a ZOA proclamation celebrating the redemption of Palestine noted that Hyman Livingston, another B'nai Israel founder, was president of the New Mexico district of the Zionist organization.[57]

National affiliation also came to New Mexico's religious institutions during the twenties. In 1923, in honor of its twenty-fifth anniversary, Temple Albert joined the Union of American Hebrew Congregations, which had been created in 1873 to represent all Jewish congregations, but managed to attract only the adherents of Reform Judaism.[58] The union followed the logic of its own development by creating national federations of temple brotherhoods, sisterhoods, and youth groups. Accordingly, the

temple's Ladies Aid and Benevolent Society affiliated with the
National Federation of Sisterhoods in 1923, further strengthening the linkage between New Mexican and national Jewish
institutions. [59]

&.

Another sign of the growing complexity of the New Mexico
Jewish community arose from generational developments. Although it posed no problem, distinctions between the pioneer
families and the newer arrivals created a minor degree of social
hierarchy. The financial and social position of the older established residents permitted them a primacy in the network of institutions. In Congregation Albert and B'nai B'rith it was their
presence which often set the tone on the boards of trustees. It was
their wives whose names appeared with great regularity on the
officers' lists of the women's organizations.

In part, their position may have been heightened by the new
era's historical consciousness. Histories containing laudatory biographies, special volumes depicting prominent families, were
part of a lore which distinguished past from newer arrivals. [60]
Their success, which permitted them to give large gifts, contributed to a sense of distinction. After his wife's death, Charles Ilfeld
gave the Normal University at Las Vegas a building and audito-
rium in her name. [61] Within the Albuquerque Jewish community
Alfred Grunsfeld willed $1,000 to Temple Albert upon his death
in 1921. [62]

To an extent, they became larger than life. During the depression, Jack Raynolds of Albquerque's First National Bank,
seeking to avoid a run on the bank, asked Louis Ilfeld for help.
With several thousand dollars in his hand, Ilfeld walked through
the queue and in plain view of the crowd, deposited the money
to his account. Many left the bank, reassured, upon seeing Ilfeld's action. [63] In Las Cruces, newer families attested to the feeling that although the Freudenthals were part of the general Jewish community, in a sense they stood apart as a result of their
longevity and success. [64] Long residence and success produced the

quality of *yikhus*, respect for lineage, that differentiated them from others.

ᔆᕈᕇ

As New Mexico's economic fortunes went, so went the Jewish population. In Albuquerque, the Jewish population grew as did the town itself. Where economic difficulties became chronic, however, Jewish communities declined. Las Vegas, which had the largest Jewish population of any place in the territory in 1900, offers the most important instance of such a downturn. Prosperity and optimism toward the future were high there in the eighties. But in the nineties, the town's problems began. The closing of Fort Union in 1891, the general financial panic of 1893, a decline in the price of wool, and the building of new rail lines which drew freight traffic to other areas all contributed to a worsening condition.[65]

Matters did not improve between 1900 and 1940. Las Vegas was still a passenger rail service center and suffered with the falling off of that traffic in the twenties as truck and automobile use increased. Further, the introduction of diesel locomotives withered the repair depot facilities located there.[66] On top of these woes agricultural depression struck Las Vegas in the twenties and grew even worse in the thirties.[67]

The process of decline did not occur evenly. The Jewish population of Las Vegas continued to grow in the first decade of the twentieth century. There were about 130 Jews there in 1900 and over 170 in 1910.[68] The effects, however, began to appear in the second decade. Comparisons of business directories for 1911 and 1921 indicate a heavy coincidence of firm names without significant change—a possible sign of stagnation.[69] Membership in the Montefiore Congregation offers another partial example of the leveling off. It had sixty-five members and twenty-two children in its school in 1900, fifty-five members and thirty children in 1907, and sixty-five members and twenty-two children in 1920.[70]

The real downturn in the Jewish community occurred in the

twenties and early thirties. By 1927 the Jewish population was estimated at eighty-six persons, down a third from the level of 1900.[71] By the early thirties, Montefiore Congregation had already lost its last known rabbi, David Bronstein, a sure sign of numerical and financial depletion.[72]

While Albuquerque expanded and Las Vegas declined, Santa Fe underwent another kind of transformation. The railroad's erasure of distance allowed numbers of visitors and published descriptions of the area to grow rapidly. Health, art, and archeology all became factors in forming a new image of the town and area which attracted scholars, artists, writers, and tourists.[73] In the second decade of the twentieth century, a national perception of Santa Fe as a place of unique cultural and physical environment became established.

By that time, the age of the pioneer German-Jewish merchants had passed. However, there had been among them those who appreciated the beauty and value of the artifacts and crafts of the living Indian culture in the midst of which they lived. Already in 1882, Jake Gold had established a business featuring Indian pottery and, to use the then-current term, curios. It may have been the first shop of its kind in Santa Fe.[74] Abe Spiegelberg, son of Solomon, who had lived in Santa Fe since he was a young lad, also became involved in collecting and selling Indian crafts and had a shop featuring such merchandise by the late nineteenth century.[75] In 1904 he wrote an article for tourists about Navajo blankets.[76] The older families, deeply rooted, showed great interest in the emerging institutions which reflected the new cultural interests. The Santa Fe membership of the Santa Fe Society of the Archeological Institute of America in the late teens included Mrs. Joseph Hersch, Leo Hersch, James L. Seligman, Solomon Spitz, and Abe Spiegelberg.[77]

Beyond those pioneers, interested newcomers arrived. Julius Gans left a law practice in Chicago and organized the Southwest Arts and Crafts Co. in 1915, which both manufactured and sold rugs and jewelry.[78] He may have been the first Jewish newcomer in Santa Fe to tap into the new interest and image of the town.

Not only Santa Feans found themselves attracted to the "aboriginal arts." Herman Schweizer, who became superintendent of Fred Harvey Co.'s News and Curio Department from 1901 until his death in 1943, has been called the "patriarch of the modern Indian crafts business." He was based in Albuquerque.[79]

In 1905, Rabbi Jacob Kaplan, writing on New Mexico for *The Jewish Encyclopedia*, estimated that Santa Fe had a Jewish population of about twenty-five.[80] But the new emerging condition of the city drew population as time passed. In 1927 there were about forty.[81] By 1940 there were seventy-five—approximately the same number as in 1880.[82]

Thus, unlike Las Vegas, Santa Fe did not descend into an economic abyss. Its comeback gradually attracted new population, including Jews. In 1912 Emil and Johanna Uhlfelder opened the White House, a dry goods and ready-to-wear store on the plaza. After Emil died, Johanna married Morris Blatt. In 1924, Blatt's daughter married Barnett Petchesky, a local shoe-store owner, and the fortunes of the two families merged. They did well enough to aid their relatives in Albuquerque, the Rosen-walds, and the Floersheims in Roy and Springer.[83]

Before the depression, other families such as the Lowitskis, Livingstons, and Yashvins arrived. And in the thirties came the Gustav Kahns and Martin Gardeskys, among others. Shoe stores, furniture, and pharmacies provided the basis for their livelihood. They never organized a congregation, but by 1936 they did create a chapter of B'nai B'rith.[84]

Other towns also exhibited a decline or leveling off in Jewish population. Roswell's Jews numbered forty-five in 1907 and eighteen in 1927. By 1940 their number had risen to forty, still below its 1907 level.[85] Silver City, with about thirty residents in 1900, had twelve in 1927 and twenty-six in 1940.[86] The smallest places, such as Elizabethtown and Cleveland, with single families or residents in 1900, appear to have had none in 1940.

Town building did not cease with the turn of the century. As new areas developed, Jews settled there. Like many Jewish settlers in the older eastern plains towns, they were not newcomers. Alex

Goldenberg had come to New Mexico in 1883, engaged in cattle ranching, unlike most Jews, in Doña Ana County, and even prospected in old Mexico before settling down to commerce at Liberty in Quay County. In 1901, he, Jacob Wertheim, his wife's brother, Alex Street, and Lee Smith pooled land they held to form the Tucumcari Townsite and Investment Co., creating the town of Tucumcari shortly after the railroad arrived.[87] Goldenberg continued the pattern of leadership in the development of the town witnessed earlier. He served as president of the board of education and as county commissioner. He was a prominent Mason both locally and in the state.[88]

The arrival of Joseph and Emma Vorenberg Wertheim in Carlsbad in 1916 exhibits a similar kind of career. After several years with a dry-goods store, he became a cotton broker and also opened an insurance agency. When he died in 1950, he was reputed to have been the wealthiest man in town in good deeds and received recognition for his generosity. St. Edward's Catholic Church said five masses for him, "a practice," church officials noted, "which we customarily follow for any deceased member of our Order."[89]

Joseph's brother, Herman, moved to Carlsbad in 1933, where he opened a furniture store. Herman's daughter, Betty Wertheim Dial and Joseph's daughter Jeanette Wertheim Sparks, married there. Arthur Kingston, Joseph's nephew, came to Carlsbad from Germany in the thirties after the rise of Hitler, left, and returned after World War II.[90] In effect an extended family pattern became the basis of a Jewish presence, which, while not large, was nevertheless stable. In the mid-thirties, at least another half dozen Jewish families lived there, forming the basis of a Jewish community.[91]

Las Cruces, while not new, underwent considerable change which brought growth to the town and region. The creation of Elephant Butte Dam in 1916 altered the economic character of the entire Mesilla Valley to its south. Considerable population increase followed. Doña Ana County contained 16,548 persons in 1920 and 30,411 in 1940.[92] Las Cruces itself, with less than 2,500 souls in 1900, counted 8,385 in 1939.[93]

While Jewish families in Las Cruces, as elsewhere, maintained stores, they also moved into the new commercialized agriculture that followed the opening of Elephant Butte. Louis E. Freudenthal, whose father, Phoebus, left the town at the turn of the century, studied agriculture at Cornell and followed a distinguished career in farming that included poultry and vegetable raising and possibly the earliest importation of pecan trees.[94] Similarly, Eugene Stern, with a merchant's career behind him, also moved into farming in 1928.[95]

Members of the small community, as elsewhere, displayed great energy outside of their basic economic activity. Samuel Klein, who followed his cousin, Joe Rosenfeld, to Las Cruces in the mid-twenties, served as mayor for many years, enjoying the support of the Hispanic population.[96] Louis Freudenthal's interests were legion, embracing Farm Bureau activities, organizing the Doña Ana County Taxpayers League in 1940, and participating heavily in the county's historical society.[97] Eugene Stern's philanthropy, even in the troubled depression era, included donations for all churches in the thirties, while he, with a small group of other persons, contributed heavily to keeping open the First National Bank of Doña Ana County in 1930.[98]

On the western side of the state, Gallup proved to be the scene of one of the more unusual Jewish communities. When Gustav Kahn decided to move there in 1914, it was a well-established town. The impetus for its development had been the arrival of the railroad in the early 1880s. Gallup became a trade center for an area from east of the Continental Divide to Arizona and for a hundred miles to the north and south of the tracks.[99] Agriculture, ranching, lumbering, the Navajo and Zuni Indian reservations, and coal mining formed the core of the region's economic activity. Indeed, coal for the railroad itself was an important element in Gallup's growth. In turn, the town serviced the needs of the mines.[100]

The Kahns found one Jewish family in town, that of Jacob Jacobson, who ran a dry-goods store. Their store handled the same line of merchandise. Gus Kahn added some young Jewish clerks and the family added two sons. They stayed until 1933, when the changes in locomotive fuel and hard times in the livestock industry brought what appeared to be a long-term decline to Gallup.[101]

Although there is evidence of Jewish merchants in Gallup in the 1880s and 1890s, some of the twentieth century residents stayed longer.[102] Sam Danoff had arrived in the Gallup area in 1911, an immigrant from Vilnius, Lithuania. He had deserted from the tsar's army in 1907 and had come to the United States.[103] Tuberculosis brought him to New Mexico. He worked first as a sheep herder and then became an Indian trader. With his brother Simon, he homesteaded land some eighteen miles from Gallup where they plied their trade with the Indians. For some years the place was called Danoffville. Around 1918 Danoff opened a store in Gallup, the ranch remaining in the care of his brother Louis and his family.[104] Louis Danoff and family left the ranch for Los Angeles, but Sam remained until 1946 when he retired to Albuquerque with his wife. Their son Isadore operated the Gallup store until 1967.[105]

In 1915, another east European Jew, Sam Moreel, arrived in Gallup. After a stint with a second-hand clothing store, he entered the junk and scrap metal business until his death in 1937 at the age of seventy-five. Born in Riga, Latvia, in about 1862, he had a family in St. Louis but came to New Mexico alone and remained so.[106] Something of a mystery, Moreel was well educated, had studied medicine at Heidelberg, written for a German-language paper in St. Louis, and was very well versed in Hebrew.[107] Walter Kahn, Gustav's son, who studied Hebrew with him, recalled, too, that his mentor had played chess by mail or telegraph with Albert Einstein. In 1928 or 1929, when crossing the country, Einstein stopped over in Gallup to meet him.[108]

There were too few families for a congregation in Gallup. Moreel's strong interest in Judaism, however, led him to draw Jewish families together once a month for social evenings and to conduct services at hired halls on the major holidays and in private homes on special occasions.[109] The Jews of Gallup, indeed, displayed an unusual capacity to provide Jewish services because of Moreel's skills and the interest of such families as the Kahns.

Even the smallest towns had their dramatic moments for the Jews present. In March 1916 Pancho Villa's raid at Columbus attracted national attention. The reasons for the Mexican guerrilla leader's incursion may have involved his need for supplies. He had apparently purchased supplies in times past from the Ravel brothers store, the largest in town.[110] During the raid Villa's men entered the store, captured one of the brothers, Arthur, while another, Louis, managed to hide under a pile of hides. During the skirmish between the American troops and the raiders, Arthur managed to escape. The Ravels suffered heavy losses from fire and looting, as did many others in town.[111] After 1921, the Ravels ranched and traded cattle in Mexico, opened a store for a time in Hachita, and when the crash destroyed the town in 1929, moved to Albuquerque.[112]

✍

Relations between Jewish and non-Jewish New Mexicans in the first forty years of the twentieth century, to judge by public events, remained benign. To some extent that distinguished New Mexico from other parts of the United States. For although America remained a most attractive dream and a safe haven for European Jews, it nevertheless became less comfortable for them in the late nineteenth and early twentieth centuries than it had been, with the exception of the Civil War years, in most of the nineteenth century.

The great changes in American life sparked by massive immigration, industrialization, urbanization, and a major foreign war demanded adjustments, which segments of the older, largely rural, and Protestant population sometimes found difficult to make. Religious, racial, and economic tensions emerged and found expression in nativist movements which understood their problems in terms of differences based on the above-noted factors. For some years after World War I, which produced a powerful patriotic impulse, such movements and attitudes created a hostile atmosphere toward Catholics, blacks, Jews, and foreigners. For American Jews, on balance, these stirrings were minor compared to the suffering of their counterparts in Europe, but they certainly aroused apprehension among a population keenly aware of what such hatreds meant in the Old World.

New Mexico's moderate growth and relative isolation, among other factors, insulated it from some of the newer expressions of discontent. It did not experience a tidal wave of immigrants, the rush of manufacture and urbanization, and the rapid appearance of new cultural milieux. There were changes, of course, but their tempo allowed considerable continuity with the past.

Attestations of good relations found frequent expression. Dr. Raphael Goldenstein, who became Temple Albert's rabbi in 1923, in studying the history of the congregation, found "that from the earliest days of this city [the relationship of] the Jew and Gentile has been a most cordial and helpful one."[113] That tone remained dominant. Catholic, Jew, and Protestant celebrated Brotherhood Day jointly in 1934 and again in 1939 under the auspices of the National Conference of Christians and Jews.[114]

The public response to the plight of the European Jews under Nazi domination characterized one dimension of the sympathy and goodwill of non-Jew toward Jew in New Mexico. In 1938 an appeal for aid under the auspices of the National Joint Distribution Committee for International Relief received strong affirmation in Albuquerque. Prominent New Mexicans, including The Very Reverend Douglas Matthews, dean of St. John's Episcopal Cathedral, John Simms, a former state supreme court justice, Clinton Anderson, and Gilberto Espinosa, voiced their support with radio talks over the station KGGM.[115] Cast in the form of a benefit day, all receipts from Albuquerque theaters for one day went toward the fund.[116] In all, some $5,000 was collected.

While the incentive for the campaign derived from a strong humanitarian impulse, evidence of appreciation for the place of Jews in New Mexico also emerged in some quarters. An editorial in the *Albuquerque Tribune,* lauding the public response, noted poignantly:

> *Albuquerqueans understand the debt they owe to minority groups, particularly to the Jewish people of this city and state. They have helped build the city, and the state. They have endured the hardships of pioneers and for many years have been a mainstay in our civic life. Through the years the Jewish people have contributed generously to the common causes. . . . They are generous and kindly. It is a privilege to be able to do something for those of their people who are suffering unspeakable indignities and hardships.*[117]

It was an affirmation of acceptance.

Yet, the rise of anti-Semitism nationally in the twenties could not be ignored. The outpourings of the *Dearborn Independent,* financed by Henry Ford, and the reemergence of the Ku Klux Klan moved into the consciousness of local Jews. The klan, which was anti-Catholic, anti-Jewish, antiblack, and antiforeigner and composed largely of white, native-born, Anglo-Saxon Protestants, exerted political influence and the threat of violence in many parts of the country.[118] But the klan did not do well in New Mexico. It claimed some anti-Catholic successes in Roswell, but in 1931 admitted, as a historian of the movement interpreted it, "that life was hard for a Protestant Anglo-Saxon organization, in a state whose population . . . was 80 per cent Catholic and a Jew was governor."[119]

An old Roswell klansman, who had been active during Reconstruction days in Louisiana and was also a Mason, explained his loyalty and belief in the organization. Above all he feared Catholicism and the papacy.[120] But he also feared the new immigration. Speaking to a Masonic gathering, he expounded,

> *I feel that this beautiful country of ours was never intended to be the world's common property, to be used as a dumping ground for the refuse of European nations but was reserved by our All-Wise Creator . . . as a splendid heritage for the Anglo-*

Saxon race, and in all probability for his favored people, the Jews.[121]

Untypically, the Jews escaped his direct censure. By the late twenties the klan had lost much of its appeal and was again restricted largely to the South.

As always, beneath the surface of benign relationship lay individual elements of hostility. Mary Austin, the novelist who lived in New Mexico for a time and in the late teens did some social research on a number of communities in the north, reported that in Taos County

> A type of Jew merchant drifted into the country who did much to keep it poor and unprogressive. They lie to the farmers, spreading tales about the probable price of wheat and what the government is likely to do about it . . . to enable them to buy more advantageously. They are accused of every sort of dishonesty, but in one way they have worked to advantage. As a reaction against the Jews small stores have sprung up in various placitas, owned and managed by Mexicans who taught themselves merchandizing rather than become victims of the hated Jews. There are, of course, individual Jews who are fairly honest, but their race has damned itself for generations in this country.[122]

It is difficult to distinguish, in this unpublished report, Mary Austin's views from her research findings. Few Jews had lived in Taos. Families such as the Gusdorfs were residents who had lived there since the 1870s and had achieved financial success and public recognition. Alexander Gusdorf acquired considerable land and, by the time Mary Austin was writing her report, was a banker.[123] One may surmise that his activities could have disturbed debtors. It is equally possible to picture a Jew (or anyone else) seeking to take advantage of a given economic situation for personal benefit. It is more difficult to know at what point a disliked Anglo became identified as a Jew to the Hispano. There is sufficient prejudice in Austin's statement to cloud the issue of how she felt and what her sources stated. One cannot deny categorically, however, that some degree of anti-Jewish feeling may well have existed.

∝❧∾

In partial counterbalance to Austin's views, individual Jews showed considerable concern for the Hispano poor in New Mexico. The depression struck New Mexico's Hispano and Anglo small farmers with special severity, placing many in a desperate position.[124] Governor Arthur Seligman, of old German-Jewish pioneer stock, labored hard to provide relief to the small farmers.[125] Indeed, Seligman aligned with such Republican progressives as Senator Bronson Cutting to introduce and revive industries in the state for the relief of the economically beleagured, to the dismay of Old Guard Republicans.[126] Louis Ilfeld, in Las Vegas, loaned villagers seeds and insect poisons. His interests were, of course, tied to the farmer, but not all merchants behaved in his manner.[127] It was also he who translated the rules for federal relief into Spanish.[128]

∝❧∾

Jews continued to participate in the political and public life of New Mexico between 1900 and 1940. Indeed, they attained higher positions than ever before. Yet the key fact of that participation rested heavily on the position of status achieved by the pioneer families of the nineteenth century or their descendants.

Nathan Jaffa is a case in point. When Theodore Roosevelt appointed George Curry governor in 1907, he allowed him a free hand in the choice of territorial officials. Curry, who resided in Roswell, related that "I had a long conference with Nathan Jaffa, a boyhood friend . . . to whom I offered the appointment of Secretary of the Territory . . . ." Jaffa, who had never sought public office, accepted, despite some initial reluctance.[129]

In 1909 Curry resigned to enter private business. Though he made no recommendations as to his successor, he recalled that "my personal preference was Nathan Jaffa."[130] Jaffa's fellow townsmen in Roswell concurred, petitioning the president "we venture to entertain the hope that [Curry's] successor will be a man equally qualified for the position. . . . We therefore respectfully recommend . . . the name of Hon. Nathan Jaffa, the present Secretary of the Territory."[131] Thomas B. Catron also viewed Jaffa's appointment with favor, but President Taft chose William J. Mills.[132] Clearly, the respect shown Jaffa was broad and deep. He continued to serve as secretary until 1912 when statehood came to New Mexico.

World War I provided an extraordinary occasion for public service with the mobilization of services to support the war effort. The old line Jewish families were prominent in these activities. The need to organize the food supply brought Arthur C. Ilfeld to the fore in the state's activities in this area.[133] Max Nordhaus, born in Germany, headed New Mexico's Liberty loan committee.[134] And women, too, played an important role in organizing food and social activities. The names of Mrs. Max Nordhaus and Mrs. Alfred Grunsfeld figured prominently in the Women's Auxiliary of the State Council of Defense.[135]

The highest position of all was attained by Arthur Seligman, the son of Bernard and Frances (Nusbaum) Seligman. Long interested in politics, even when running the Seligman Bros. store in Santa Fe, he served in various public offices, among them as mayor of Santa Fe and chairman of the Santa Fe county commissioners, and for many years as chairman of the Democratic county central committee, and the Democratic territorial and state committees. His appointments to various public boards were legion.[136] In 1930 he was elected governor of the state, and in 1932 he was reelected. He died in office in 1933.

Though clearly of Jewish parentage, Governor Seligman's religion at the time of his death is a matter of some debate. Frankie Lacker Seligman, the governor's wife, belonged to the Episcopal church, and the son born to them in 1898 was christened there.[137] An obituary described Seligman as "not a religious man in the way of church membership. . . . He was a contributor to Jewish and Catholic charities. . . ."[138] Upon his death, an Episcopal service for the dead was read at the House of Representatives. At the Fairview Cemetery, however, the Masonic ritual was performed.[139] Given the uncertainty of the governor's religious identity, it would be presumptuous to define it for him.[140] His family background and early life, however, place his career clearly within the framework of the history of the Jews of New Mexico.

Beyond the high level achievements of Jaffa and Seligman lay a host of lower appointed and elected office holders. Samuel Eldodt's term as state treasurer ended in 1901. On a different level, Jaffa himself served on the board of regents at the University of New Mexico, and Cecilio Rosenwald, the son of Emanuel of Las Vegas, on the board of the Insane Asylum at Las Vegas before 1920. Mrs. Herman C. Ilfeld served on the board of regents at New Mexico Normal University at Las Vegas, and Gerson Gusdorf at the New Mexico College of Agriculture and Mechanic Arts before 1931. Before 1920 Louis Ilfeld of Las Vegas served in the legislature and in the thirties was a regent at New Mexico Normal. Mrs. Max Nordhaus was vice-president of the State Board of Public Welfare in Albuquerque. Gerson Gusdorf of Taos and L. E. Freudenthal of Las Cruces served as members of county and state committees of the two major political parties.[141] In 1921 Berthold Spitz received appointment as postmaster in Albuquerque by President Harding.[142] S. S. Moise, an immigrant who developed the firm of Moise Bros. in Santa Rosa along with his brother, J. J. Moise, were both quite active in the political and public life of that area. Irwin S. Moise, the son of S. S. Moise, became a district judge in 1937 after practicing law in Tucumcari and working for the National Recovery Administration in Washington in the mid-thirties.[143] All of the names recalled the German-Jewish immigration of the nineteenth century and their descendants.

But some newcomers also received affirmation of public confidence. Reflecting the growth of professionals among the Jewish population, Harry S. Bowman, born in Colorado and a graduate in law from the University of Michigan, worked in legal and administrative capacities for Santa Fe County before his election as attorney general of New Mexico in 1921.[144] Abe L. Zinn from Gallup, also an attorney, served in the legislature in the late teens and became a justice of the state supreme court in the thirties.[145]

In the smaller towns, as in the late nineteenth century, the new arrivals continued to make their mark in local offices. In Tucumcari, Alex. D. Goldenberg served for a number of years on the board of education. His son, Max, was a Republican state committeeman in 1921.[146] In Clayton, Morris Herzstein was a councilman in 1916 and was chairman of the County Democratic Central Committee.[147]

Jews still assumed positions of status in social organizations. Arthur Prager was born in Colorado in 1890 and worked for public utilities from his youth. By 1919 he had become manager of Albuquerque Gas and Electric. Later, he became president of the Public Service Company of New Mexico. Before 1940 he had served at some time as president of the Albuquerque Chamber of Commerce, the Rotary Club, and the Albuquerque Country Club (membership was not closed to Jews). Prager belonged to Temple Albert, although his wife was not of the Jewish faith.[148]

Sidney Weil, born in Iowa in 1881 and by training knowledgeable in mining, came to Albuquerque in 1916. The lure of copper in Sandoval County brought him to New Mexico. He also became heavily involved in timber and coal operations. In 1922 he was elected to the city commission in Albuquerque and was, for a time, director of the Albuquerque Chamber of Commerce. He held life membership in Kiwanis in recognition of his service. Weil was a member of B'nai B'rith and of the Albuquerque Country Club. His wife, too, was apparently not of the Jewish faith.[149]

Newcomers, by their nature, did not gain or, perhaps, seek the public eye as much as the older established residents. But by the time the century moved into its second generation they began to achieve recognition in a political and public way. If they were by training a bit more professional, and, on the higher levels of status, more native born, then that fact merely reflected the changes occurring in New Mexico and among the Jewish population. Their performance indicates a continuing good relationship between New Mexico's Jewish and non-Jewish populations and an affirmation of individual respect.

〜

The economic life of New Mexican Jewry in the first forty years of the twentieth century, like the state itself, experienced growth, but only moderate change. The greatest development occurred in Albuquerque itself. There, the Jewish working population adjusted and adapted to the growth of the city, increasing in complexity but not experiencing any fundamental alteration of character.

By 1900 Albuquerque had already undergone some of the changes that resulted from the coming of the railroad. The railroad shops had become a major employer in the city. The city had 102 manufacturing establishments employing over 900 workers whose products reached a value of just under 1.9 million dollars.[150] There were wool-scouring mills, food-processing plants, and construction material factories, enterprises of a type, except for wool scouring, calculated to supply local needs.[151]

The population of the city had grown steadily by 1940 and so had the manufacturing sector of the economy of New Mexico. Nevertheless, two-thirds of the state's population was still defined as rural in that year. Even in Bernalillo County, where Albuquerque lay, the largest number of workers were still engaged in agriculture. Otherwise, except for the railroad, the largest employers in Bernalillo County were in construction and in the retail trade.[152] The changes since 1900 were not dramatic.

Using the membership lists of B'nai B'rith, which include about one-third or more of employed Jewish males in Albuquerque, one can get a sense of the changes in Jewish economic activity. Of seventy-seven members enrolled between 1883 and 1897, fifty-five called themselves merchants, fifteen clerks, and four traveling salesmen. The dominance of the traditional pattern of their economic activity had scarcely been affected by the appearance of the railroad, even if the form of the businesses themselves had begun to alter.

Those listed from 1898 to 1920 showed some greater differentiation. While over 70 percent of the 1883–97 contingent were merchants, 37 percent of the 1898–1920 group so designated themselves. But another 25 percent still were clerks or salesmen. Thus, over 60 percent of the new names added to B'nai B'rith membership remained in the most traditional of the occupations practiced by Jews in New Mexico. This share might also be enlarged if one included specialized forms of occupation still within commercial establishments, such as cashiers, bookkeepers, and managers. When one considers that many residents from the previous period still remained in the community, the change can hardly have been great. Most noticeable is the increase in professionals and in craftsmen.

The new members in B'nai B'rith between 1920 and 1940 indicate a pattern of occupational persistence. Merchants alone accounted for 47 percent of the new membership and clerks for 17 percent, nearly two-thirds of the total. Again, specialization accounts for the most significant change. Managers appeared as a signifcant category, and although not numerous, the number of professionals increased—lawyers, accountants, pharmacists. The entire list of members since 1883 included no railroad employees, and outside of a lone architect-engineer in 1920–40 and one carpenter, no other member of the construction industry appears. There were, however, shoemakers, tailors, and plumbers. One may speak of a broadening of economic activity in the white-collar area, but not in all areas of growth in Albuquerque. Viewed from the perspective of class attitude and activity, the Albuquerque Jewish population remained what it had been from its arrival in the mid-1840s—heavily middle class. The internal nature of business had changed but the centrality of business activity had not.

Albuquerque was peculiar in only one respect in the employment of its Jewish population. Studies of Jews in smaller cities during this period indicate over 57 percent in trade or commerce (Albuquerque was just under two-thirds), over 16 percent in manufacture (Albuquerque Jewry was virtually non-existent in this field) and over 16 percent in the professions and public service (Albuquerque was about 10 percent).[153] The greatest divergence lay in the area of manufacture.

The employment of Albuquerque's Jews resembled large cities of over 250,000 far less. In those places in 1900 about 60 percent engaged in manufacturing, 20 percent in trade, about 15 percent in clerical, public and personal service, and three percent in the professions.[154] In 1935 Detroit had about 54 percent in trade, 23 percent in manufacture, and 10 percent in professional and public service.[155] The greatest difference lay, again, in the area of manufacture.

Measured by the generational changes in large cities where the east European Jews settled, New Mexico's Jewish population changed slowly. In New York in one generation a population heavily involved as shop workers (in the clothing industry) gave way to another which was heavily middle class—either white collar or professional. For example, 60 percent of Jews in 1900 were in manufacturing and almost all were workers. In 1935, 60 percent of the Jewish children of working class fathers were in white collar occupations—either as proprietors or managers. The vehicle for change was a powerful drive for upward mobility expressed through education.[156] By contrast, New Mexico's Jews were already middle class at the outset and they remained so.

❧

The economic well-being of the Jewish community also experienced some change. In terms of its wealth, the general level probably dropped. Specialization undoubtedly contributed to that process up to 1925. A comparison of Bradstreet's ratings in 1897 and 1925 for Albuquerque, although based on the partial data of listings, indicates that the median of capitalization fell from the $20,000-$35,000 level in 1897 to $10,000-$20,000 in 1925—a period of reasonable growth and prosperity. Even more indicative of less favorable circumstances, however, was the condition of their credit ratings. While 90 percent of the businesses listed in 1897 received the highest grade of credit for the amount of capital valuation, in 1925, 63 percent received the second best grade of credit, and several held the third, or lowest grade of rating.[157] Many of the listings for 1925 were for businesses which had not existed in 1897, while a number of the listings which carried over were toward the higher end of the capital worth scale. New growth in smaller businesses continued as a trend from the late nineteenth century into the first quarter of the twentieth century.

Within the Jewish business community itself greater change took place after 1925 than before. Of course, many businesses which had existed in 1900 continued to exist in 1926 although not necessarily in their original form. Among these family businesses one finds the names of the Rosenwalds, the Mandell family, the Weinmans, and the Albuquerque Ilfelds. Even in 1935 one finds some continuity with the nineteenth century as well as additions which had appeared in the first generation of the twentieth century. Among those names one finds the Siegfried Kahns, the Weillers, the Benjamins, and the Lewinsons. Such families remained the core of continuity in the business community.

The continued population growth after 1900, however slowed, also meant the creation of new enterprises. Not surprisingly, the new enterprises rated by Bradstreet in 1925 tended to have lower capitalization than the older firms. Among them, too, one found some increasing diversity.

By 1926 the concentration of dry goods and clothing stores began to thin a bit. Jewelry stores and small department stores appeared in some number. And one could find second-hand goods, grocery, and furniture stores, and even a greenhouse among the new listings.[158]

Between 1926 and 1935 one finds fewer new businesses. These years included the depths of the depression as well as the time when population growth was slowest. Although the newcomers founded clothing, jewelry, and small department stores, there were also now shoe repair and tailor shops, feed stores, and several financial enterprises.[159] By 1940, the pace of growth had picked up. And again, although new clothing stores appeared, there were also new furniture stores, Indian curio shops, and drugstores.[160] The core of Jewish trade in 1940 still lay in dry goods, clothing, and department stores, despite a dilution of that branch of trade through a slow expansion into other lines of merchandise.

🙰

Changes also occurred regarding women in the economy. In 1900 Jewish women in New Mexico did not work in the market-place. With few exceptions that had been the case throughout their history in the territory. They ran the home and bore and raised the children in accord with the values of their economic class. Where congregations and sisterhoods existed, they devoted their energies to those organizations. One can conjecture that the relatively high economic position of the Jews may have made women's participation in work outside the home unnecessary. There were, after all, plenty of male relatives and growing boys to be incorporated into the existing enterprises.

By 1910, however, business directories show a small number of Jewish women employed as clerks, teachers, and stenographers. Such work indicates some level of education and training and an intent to work. The growing presence of educational institutions, the spread of technology such as the typewriter, and economic specialization and less affluence may well account for their entry into the work place.

The level of involvement, to judge by the directories, changed little by the mid-twenties. By the mid-thirties, however, listings of working women had quadrupled and had become much more diverse. In 1935 Jewish women were public servants, nurses, and proprietors, as well as teachers and clerks. In 1940 their numbers continued to rise.[161]

While working women still amounted to less than 10 percent

of the male Jewish working population, the increase nevertheless represented a distinct change of economic and social participation. Some of it is attributable to educational training and made possible by economic specialization. How much of a role the depression itself played in making work a necessity is difficult to measure on the basis of existing information.

All in all, the changes introduced by the appearance of the railroad cast an ever-broadening, but slow-moving shadow in the first forty years of the twentieth century. New Mexico's Jews were affected by its presence and continued to adapt to the economic changes the railroad caused directly and indirectly. The trend toward specialization of business appeared particularly strong in Albuquerque, but also occurred elsewhere. At the same time, wherever new towns began, patterns of settlement visible in new towns in earlier times repeated themselves.

The economic fortunes of the Jewish community largely followed the general progression of New Mexico's economy. Where the railroad or other basic factors, such as world agricultural prices or the depression, dictated decline, Jewish businessmen either altered their enterprises to adapt to the new conditions or suffered the consequences and went elsewhere or out of business. Las Vegas and Santa Fe are prime examples of severe decline and altered and rejuvenated activity in these places by Jewish businessmen.

Mostly, retail businesses owned by Jews continued to grow in the direction of specialization as branches of activity once contained within the general store. A few moved into the hides, wool, and agricultural fields. With Albuquerque increasingly the center of Jewish population of the whole state, however, the relatively small urban specialized shop characterized the major business activity of the Jew. This represents no great change of direction and the observer of 1900 in New Mexico would have easily recognized the Jewish business community of 1940.

Yet the changes did alter the economic position of the Jewish community. It seems safe to say that it no longer enjoyed the same degree of economic visibility apparent in the nineteenth century. The enterprises were smaller and less prominent as the period moved on.

The internal changes within business practice itself also affected the occupational character of the community. More persons specialized within the business. Managers and accountants became more common and reflected the growth of professionalization. The result is a picture of a more complex internal structure in business itself, even if the businesses involved the handling of the same general products as in earlier times.

Jewish occupational activity also broadened in other ways. While the growth of the Jewish community was modest, its increasing Americanization and its greater exposure to the educational system, both through local development and an altered pattern of immigration, witnessed an increase of participation in the professions. Women, too, partially as a result of changing attitudes toward work and as a result of economic necessity, increasingly entered the ranks of the employed as teachers, secretaries, nurses, and proprietors. It was an evolution, not a revolution, with the greatest change appearing in the time of the Great Depression.

The growth of Jewish religious and sociopolitical institutions was somewhat more dramatic. Albuquerque's Jews in particular responded to the greater complexity of their population and reflected the greater range of options open to Jews within the context of American Jewish life. The fate of the Jews of the world also found its echo in new organizations and collective efforts barely begun by 1900.

In their ethnic and occupational makeup, New Mexico's Jews probably differed more from the vast majority of American Jews in 1940 than it did in 1900. Minimally affected by the vast immigration from eastern Europe, marginally touched by manufacture, and far removed from many of the class, religious, and ideological distinctions that marked American Jewish life in the first forty years of the century, New Mexico's Jews still represented a relatively narrow part of the spectrum of expression that characterized American Jewish life between 1900 and 1940. They more resembled their own forefathers of New Mexico. There were not many Orthodox Jews, Hassidim, socialists, anarchists, or trade unionists, and only a few tailors. The relatively static continuity of their experience seems to suggest that the adventurousness which had marked the nineteenth century had passed—at least for the moment.

The Explosive Era, 1940–80

From 1940 to 1980 New Mexico experienced changes in its history as great in their own way as those produced by the coming of the Spaniards, the Americans, and the railroad. The impetus for the changes, as in earlier times, came from outside. World War II, which spread throughout the world after 1939 and finally engulfed the United States, initiated the drama. As a consequence of the war, New Mexico became an important stage for military preparations.

The changes brought about directly by the war, however, did not stand alone. At the end of the conflict, as one scholar put it, "the West had become a barometer of American life," innovative, aggressive, and a leading area of growth.[1] That change was the result of many factors: improved transportation and communication, available resources—material and environmental, and the expectation of a better life.

&

The wave of change swelled as war loomed on the horizon. The excellent weather and the abundance of open space offered advantages for aviation which attracted the attention of the federal government. In 1940 Kirtland Field in Albuquerque became a service center for military aircraft and in 1942 a training center. Eventually, it became a major military base.[2] After Pearl Harbor, White Sands developed as a gunnery and bombing range for the air force. In 1943 the isolated area of Los Alamos became the site for the highly secret research to develop the atomic bomb.[3] In the space of three years New Mexico had become a focal point for some of the most important research and training facilities and projects in the nation.

Many of the developments begun under the pressures of war, however, did not disappear once the conflict had ended. Not only did many of the newly created installations become permanent, but some which had already existed, such as the Veterans Administration hospital, grew rapidly in conjunction with them. Along with the new federal installations, other institutions grew, adding to the scientific and professional community of the state and the city of Albuquerque. The present-day Lovelace Medical Center, a small organization of specialty medicine before World War II, expanded by leaps and bounds and developed a considerable research arm.[4] The University of New Mexico added law and medical schools, offering in-state professional degrees for students for the first time, and adding considerable numbers of new faculty. During this period of general growth, the university added specialists in every branch of learning. Such developments continued to break down the relative isolation of New Mexico while adding a highly educated segment to the growing population.

The federal investment in New Mexico also produced its own economic environment. New population produced a greater local market for products. Manufacture itself, under the stimulus of new needs and a new skilled population, became more important.[5] By 1960, in addition to the consumer and construction services required by the new population, employment had been stimulated in electronics, aircraft-related industry, and scientific and engineering services.[6]

ᘡ

Los Alamos provides an example of how war and postwar events could provide a continuum of development for the state and nation as a whole, but also specifically for the Jewish community. Most of the early Jewish working residents of Los Alamos were connected with research projects dedicated to the making of the atomic bomb. Sabbath services were already being conducted there in 1944 by the personnel of the highly secret base themselves in Hebrew.[7] About 110 persons attended the Passover seder in 1945. An account of wartime Los Alamos confirms the strong feelings of the many Jewish scientific and technical personnel about the fate of their families, friends, and co-religionists in Europe.[8] The secrecy which surrounded the whole base brought the Jewish population there the appellation of "the invisible congregation."[9] Rabbi Solomon Starrels of Temple Albert and Rabbi Harvey Wessel of Ft. Sumner visited there between 1944 and 1946 at which time, with the war's end and the transfer of many personnel, what existed of a congregation disbanded.

At that time a more permanent community came into existence. Since a sizable number of Jews continued to work and live there, services and other activities did not end. In 1948 branches of B'nai B'rith and Hadassah, a Zionist women's group, were formed, and in 1954 a cover organization called the Los Alamos Jewish Center came into existence.[10] Rabbi Abraham Shinedling of Albuquerque served the group every other week in the mid-fifties.[11] Thus, the war and postwar needs of the national government combined and allowed the creation of a wholly new community of Jews.

Neither the facility nor the Jewish community within the new town proved short-lived. In the early eighties an active community continued to exist. Some seventy families supported the Los Alamos Jewish Center, which Rabbi Leonard Helman of Santa Fe visited several times a month to aid with services and the teaching of the children.[12]

∽

One of the most impressive dimensions of change in the postwar era was numerical increase. New Mexico grew from a population of 532,000 to 1.3 million—two and one-half times in forty years. That increase pales beside the growth data on the

Jews. In 1937 there were 1,160 in New Mexico; in 1980 there were 7,155.[13] That increase was over sixfold.

The relative rate of Jewish growth was not a smooth process. In the first generation of the period there was even a decline. In the second generation, however, the growth of the Jewish population was quite heavy. Table 1 depicts this trend:

Table 1:   Jewish Population Growth in New Mexico, 1937–81

Year	No. of Jews	Total Population	Percentage
1937	1,179	531,818 (1940)	0.22
1955	1,500	781,000	0.19
1961	2,700	951,023	0.28
1970	3,645	1,006,000	0.36
1981[14]	7,155	1,300,000	0.55

Far more impressive than the growth of the state was the remarkable expansion of Albuquerque. Containing some 35,000 residents in 1940, in 1980 it numbered 330,000, nearly a tenfold increase. Again the growth of the Jewish population was even more impressive. With a community of 450 in 1940, it had rocketed to 6,500 in 1980—a fourteenfold increase.[15] While New Mexico generally became more urban than before as a result of this growth, the effect of it in the Jewish community was even greater. In 1940, 39 percent of the Jewish population lived in Albuquerque; in 1980, close to 90 percent of the state's Jewish population lived there.

❧

Postwar America experienced powerful social impulses and changes. Some of them, such as the maturation of the social security system and American notions of retirement, changed living patterns for the older population. Others, growing directly out of the war, such as the GI Bill of Rights, enabled unprecedented numbers of Americans to attend institutions of higher education. Strong social causes, such as the civil rights movement among minorities, led them to act on their own behalf with new energy and expectations. Women, partially in conjunction

Table 2: Educational Attainment of Jews in Albuquerque, by Age, 1981

Age	Grad. or Profess.	Undergrad. College	High School	Tech. School	Elem. School
60+	20%	31%	41.6%	3.6%	3.6%
50–59	34	42	18	6.5	—
40–49	47	41	8.3	2.5	—
30–39	55	38	3.5	2.6	—

with that movement, moved to define themselves anew with equal vigor. All of these facets of change reflected themselves in New Mexico and within its Jewish population.

The creation of new institutions within the Jewish community even brought a change in what the community knew about itself. To perform its work satisfactorily, the Albuquerque Jewish Welfare Fund (AJWF), which later became the Jewish Community Council of Albuquerque (JCCA), periodically collected information about the Jewish population, and the census became part of the life of Albuquerque Jewry.

One dimension of change appeared in the educational level of the population. Whether one considers the influx of highly schooled newcomers or trends within the already settled population, the results end up the same. The pursuit and acquisition of high-level education became increasingly common among Albuquerque's Jews. Based on the JCCA census of 1981, Table 2 lays out the increases in level of formal education acquired by those thirty or older.[16]

What had happened is clear. The older the individual, the more likely it was that he or she ended formal education with high school. Even in that eldest group, which would have ended its formal education in the 1950s, half had exposure to higher education (that is, undergraduate or graduate college). In the youngest category (age 30–39) the rate of those who acquired some level of higher education reached 93 percent. By 1981 it was difficult to imagine how a higher rate of achievement could be possible.

Table 3:   Occupational Distribution of the Jewish Population
            in Albuquerque, 1955–84

Occupation	1955	1965	1981–84[18]
Professionals	16.1%	21.4%	38.4%
Technicians	9.1	6.4	4.6
Subtotal	25.2	27.8	43.0
Managers	15.5	12.8	10.5
Sales	12.3	9.3	8.9
Proprietors	40.1	29.5	20.8

What had occurred in Albuquerque was impressive even by comparison with other areas. In 1960 the city claimed the highest number of Ph.D.s per capita in the United States.[17] When Albuquerque's Jewish population is measured against other locales, such as New York and Chicago, a much higher proportion of those with graduate education and a lower proportion of those with only high school experience appears in the New Mexico metropolis.[19]

The far-reaching changes in education level were reflected directly in the way Albuquerque's Jews earned their livelihood. Only a partial picture can be created with the imperfect data available, but an impression of the changes in the major occupational categories emerges in Table 3 by combining the congregational membership lists of Congregations Albert and B'nai Israel for specified dates supplemented by business directory data.

There was a marked movement upward in the percentage of professionals. They became the major category of occupational activity by the early eighties. This change was accompanied by a decline in the old merchant or proprietor category and in the share of managerial and sales personnel as parts of the whole. It spelled an important change in the economic character of the Jewish community in Albuquerque, although not in terms of class or status. Manual labor and crafts were quite minor categories at any date.

Table 4: Educational Attainment of Jews in Albuquerque by Age
and Sex, 1981

	Women			Men		
Age	Grad.	Coll.	H.S.	Grad.	Coll.	H.S.
61+	11%	35%	50%	25%	36%	32%
51–60	18	43	30	47	40	12
41–50	29	58	10	61	29	9
31–40	47	38	5	64	32	3

The changes among women were even more marked than
for men. Table 4 compares education levels attained by both
genders.[20]

The youngest age group of women with graduate-level education increased fourfold over the oldest, while the men more
than doubled. Between the oldest and youngest categories of both
sexes, those who had no more than high school experience
dropped tenfold, but in 1981 the two groups were nearly equal.
Each successive age category of women had moved closer to the
level of education achieved by the men. A veritable revolution
had taken place in the postwar years.

The rise in the level of education among the women led
directly to changes in their employment and occupations. As for
women generally, the number of Jewish women in the work place
rose dramatically. Of those between the ages of twenty-one and
thirty, 62 percent engaged in full-time employment, as did 42
percent of those between the ages of thirty-one and forty. In the
latter age group another 28 percent worked part time during the
years when child bearing and rearing were high. Among those
forty-one and fifty in age, 50 percent engaged in full-time work.[21]
Not many of their mothers had worked outside the home in 1940;
their grandmothers might well have been astonished at the
change.

The occupations in which they worked also indicate the
scope of the change. Most marked was their entry into the profes-

sions. The JCCA census of 1981 showed only one Jewish female attorney over the age of fifty in Albuquerque but eight below that age. Four female medical doctors practiced, all under forty, and a sizable number of professors, psychologists, and scientists, all under fifty. There were four accountants, speech therapists, and artists over the age of fifty and twenty-eight under fifty.[22]

Another marked change in the Jewish community in postwar New Mexico was the sharp rise in the size of its retired population. That trend was part of a general phenomenon of American life that took place with the development of pension funds and the expansion of social security benefits during and after the war. A new attitude toward retirement accompanied the greater means available to retirees. Retirement, as one writer put, became a "consumable commodity," a natural and desirable process.[23]

The West did very well in attracting its share of this older population. A mild climate and the greater ease of transportation—both automobile and air, made the region attractive and accessible. New Mexico may not have experienced the rate of growth in its elderly that characterized Arizona or California, but the new visibility of retirees as a distinct segment of the population was unmistakable.

A Jewish Welfare Fund survey conducted in 1966 begins to tell the story of numbers. The 713 families who responded to the questionnaire accounted for a possible 2,366 persons, including 940 children. Individuals over sixty-five numbered 120 or about 5 percent.[24] In the early eighties, another investigation reported those over age sixty at 29.6 percent of a random sample.[25] Although no statistically accurate comparison between the two surveys can be made (among other issues, they do not use the same age parameters), it seems reasonable nevertheless to assume that the increase in numbers of older Jews was considerable.

This trend can be examined also through the data of the 1981 JCCA census. How long the eldest portion of the population lived in Albuquerque gives us a partial clue to the growth of this segment of the community. The 267 persons aged sixty or over revealed the following picture in terms of residential longevity.

Table 5: Length of Residence in Albuquerque of Jews Aged 60
or Over, 1981

Yrs.	0–10	11–20	21–30	31–40	41+
Nos.	130	34	36	44	23
	(48.6%)	(12.7%)	(13.4%)	(16.4%)	(8.6%)

In the seventies alone virtually as many newcomers of late middle and retirement age arrived as already lived here.

New community development also reflected New Mexico's growing attractiveness for the elderly. In the early 1960s developers began to build homes on the mesa west of the Rio Grande and at the north end of Albuquerque. The Amrep Corporation advertised its product mainly in the Midwest and on the East Coast. By 1977, some 5,000 mostly middle-income retirees lived in the new community of Rio Rancho.[26]

Retirees of the Jewish faith also came. Some joined the older congregations across the river in Albuquerque, but in time, they began to organize themselves closer to home. The distance involved was inconvenient for some, and there were enough persons to create a social club in 1974.[27] In 1976 fourteen charter families created the Rio Rancho Jewish Center. Using bingo, raffles, and dinners to raise funds the congregation purchased a building in 1978 and managed to pay off the mortagage by 1981.[28]

One result of the new attitude toward retirement and the increased numbers of elderly was the creation of organizations and institutions dedicated specifically to their needs. Far more than in the older, rural America and at a time when benefits to them were quite limited, the retired became a distinct class, living separately from the younger generation. The extended family ceded ground to the new organizations designed exclusively for the elders.

Recognition of this new state of affairs occurred also among the Jewish population of New Mexico, particularly in Albuquerque. By 1959, the Welfare Fund, with the aid of the National Council of Jewish Women, organized the Silvertones to enable persons over sixty to meet, socialize, and help others.[29] Looking to the future in a private effort, some members of the Welfare Fund, led by David Specter, created the Albuquerque Home for the Jewish Aged, Inc., and shortly thereafter purchased land on Wyoming Blvd. to realize their purpose.[30] In time, the Welfare Fund contributed regularly toward the land purchase, and in 1967 the home merged with the fund.[31] However, a study of the feasibility to build and maintain a home for the Jewish aged suggested that it was simply prohibitive at that time and should be considered as a long-term goal.[32] In the late seventies, through the creation of a separate corporation, the Jewish community participated in the creation of Shalom House, a residence for the well elderly of all faiths. It was perhaps the first stage toward a community solution for care of the elderly Jewish population in New Mexico.

Intermarriage, as in earlier times, remained a fact of life in the postwar years. The factor of an overwhelmingly male Jewish population so prevalent in the nineteenth century had eased considerably over time as the Jewish population grew and the balance between males and females evened out with the growing number of families and progeny. After World War II, the stream of families provided greater choice of mates for those seeking Jewish spouses.

Increased availability of mates of the same religion did not alter the fact that the Jewish population was still relatively small or that the relative openness of society still produced intermarriage. In fact, these latter two conditions point to rising rates of intermarriage.[33] Lack of data for the prewar era, however, makes long-term comparisons difficult. But in the early eighties about one-third of married Jews who lived in Albuquerque had intermarried, a much higher figure than in areas of heavy Jewish population, such as New York, Chicago, or Miami.[34]

New conditions, however, altered the old oft-held assumption that intermarriage invariably worked against the continuity of Jewish existence. Tolerant attitudes in the postwar United States toward such unions and religious identity in general combined with attitudes which encouraged Jews to maintain their identity, spouses to convert to Judaism, and children quite frequently to be raised as Jews. The census materials on Albuquerque's Jews gathered in 1981 described a situation in which younger couples converted less than older ones, but, of those who did, the balance in favor of Judaism was considerable. [35]

〰

After World War II the Jewish community continued to take on an increasingly American character by virtue of birthplace. In the early eighties about 90 percent were native born. [36] The evidence also showed a heavy migration from other parts of the country to New Mexico, particularly from the mid-Atlantic and eastern north-central states. [37] More than a third (37.4 percent) of Brigitte Goldstein's random sample had been in Albuquerque for less than ten years and another 28.9 percent from ten to nineteen years, together representing two-thirds of her total sample. [38] If being a native-born American had become commonplace for the Jew, birth in New Mexico itself still remained a condition of only a minority in this period of rapid internal migration.

The changed condition of world and American Jewry also reflected itself locally. The heavy Germanic background of the early twentieth century had gradually given way by 1940 to a more indigenous population, although the rise of Nazism had induced a spurt of immigration from Germanic Europe in the thirties. Goldstein's sample, which found 10.5 percent foreign born in all, limited western European immigration to 5.4 percent of the total, which was presumably largely Germanic. [39] Twelve percent of their fathers and 11 percent of their mothers were western European. [40] The informal survey of over a thousand Jews in Albuquerque in 1981 also found 10 percent, or 109 persons, foreign born, forty-two from Germanic Europe, about forty per cent, and of those, all had migrated to the United States in the thirties. [41]

While there were relatively few new arrivals in the postwar period from eastern and southeastern Europe, the heavy immigration to New Mexico from the eastern United States altered the background character of New Mexican Jewry. While a little over 4 percent were direct immigrants from eastern and southeastern Europe, over 34 percent of the fathers and 30 percent of the mothers of Goldstein's respondents were of this background.[42] Two-thirds of all grandparents in her sample were born in that part of the world.[43] The Germanic background had been clearly outdistanced by the eastern and southeastern European strain, even if increases in the native born remained the major dimension of change.

The change could be seen in the linguistic background of the New Mexican community. In 1940, as noted earlier, under 10 percent of New Mexico's Jews claimed some knowledge of Yiddish. Goldstein's sample in the early eighties revealed over 25 percent who claimed a good understanding and another 38 percent with a poor understanding. Speaking, reading, and writing skills were far lower.[44] The lower level of skills claimed implies eastern European background at least one generation removed.

Such changes in background, even in the face of the heavy Americanization of New Mexican Jewry, produced feelings which reflected themselves in a broadened range of Jewish life. In the sixties, for example, a Yiddish Club existed for a time, composed of native speakers, others less fluent, and those who sought to learn the language.[45] In 1966 it even produced plays by Scholem Aleichem, the best known of east European writers, in Yiddish![46] These played several nights to packed houses in the Old Town Studio. Nostalgia and the sense of loss of Yiddish culture obliterated by the Holocaust contributed, no doubt, to such expression, but it could not have happened in prewar Albuquerque.

Traces of the east European Jewish experience carried by native-born American newcomers from the East continued to appear in the seventies. In the middle of the decade an effort was made to establish a Scholem Aleichem Folkschule.[47] With its roots in Yiddish and its outlook culturally secular, the institution lasted into the eighties and drew some like-minded persons into its orbit. It also drew opposition from more religiously oriented elements of the Jewish population.[48] In the last analysis, however, it would appear that such movements were too far removed from the existing native-born cultural and social base of the Jewish community to gain wide and deep support.

〰

The changes in New Mexico which grew out of America's involvement in World War II formed only one dimension of what affected New Mexican Jewry. World War II was both the setting for and the prologue to events of a magnitude for Jews unmatched since ancient times. The plight of central European Jews in the late thirties, drastic as it was, paled beside the Holocaust itself and the aftermath of the war which was so important in the creation of the state of Israel in 1948. It fell upon American Jews, relatively well off and safe, to provide material sustenance and rescue for their co-religionists in Europe. Beyond that, the scope of the problem, if it was to be dealt with at all, placed it in the hands of governments.

The demands upon the resources of American Jews, under these circumstances, became heavy. To deliver aid and support, moreover, required an organizational structure that could do the job. Such organizations grew out of already existing forms which had evolved over the troubled years of the twentieth century. Beyond the aid delivered by governments, American Jews had to support the transfer of Jews out of the displaced persons camps in Europe in which they lived following their release from concentration camps to new lives mainly in Israel and the United States. The American Jews had to consider the absorption and resettlement of hundreds of thousands of persons, involving economic support, job placement and training, and the heavy burden of social adjustment.[49]

To meet the challenges raised by the problems of world Jewry as well as the growing complexity of local Jewish life, the institutional framework of New Mexican Jewry underwent considerable elaboration in the postwar period. In 1948 the Albuquerque Jewish Welfare Fund was incorporated "to collect donations . . . and to distribute or use the same for the benefit of Jewish welfare and philanthropic causes, locally, nationally, or internationally." It was to seek cooperation among Jewish organizations in Albuquerque and the state of New Mexico. The new organization reflected the mood of the Jews based on their experiences of the recent past and their fears for the future by the statement that funds were to be granted to meet "any emergency of a catastrophic nature."[50] In 1972, as noted earlier, its name was changed to the Jewish Community Council of Albuquerque (JCCA). Unlike earlier congregational organizations, the new structure sought to appeal to all Jews—those unaffiliated with congregations and those who belonged. That Albuquerque had such an organization reflected the growing size of the community and the concern of all Jews with the fate of their brethren elsewhere.

One measure of how important the fate of the sorely afflicted Jews of the Old World was to them can be seen from the level of support given to them by American Jews. From 1939 to 1970 the central agencies of the Jewish population raised about 4.2 billion dollars.[51] The United Jewish Appeal (UJA), the major organization for providing support for Jews outside the United States, received almost 2.4 billion dollars, well over half of the total collected.[52]

New Mexico's Jews responded to the new international circumstances as did American Jews elsewhere. The plight of the European Jews and the fate of the state of Israel took first place in their attentions as a matter of communal concern. A sampling of the allocation reports of the AJWF and its JCCA successor indicate the prominence of that interest in financial terms. In 1957–58, out of a total of $63,000 allocated for all purposes, $41,000 went to the UJA (about 65 percent). In 1960, $47,000 out of $73,000 dollars (about 64 percent) took the same path. The UJA's share fell to 56 percent in 1965 ($44,000 out of $78,000) and by 1970 it had slackened to 50 percent ($46,000 out of $92,000).[53] In 1982 the JCCA continued to allot over 50 percent of its annual fund drive after administrative costs to the UJA.[54]

Annual-fund raising drives became a way of life for many of New Mexico's Jews. Those who gave did so out of their sense of obligation—some gladly, some with resignation. Nor was it easy to gather the sums needed. Lewis R. Sutin wrote to Welfare Fund contributors in 1953 with a sense of nostalgia, "If we had one family who would give $10,000.00, it would be considered 'a little lower than the Angels'." He added, "Albuquerque had such families in the past. . . ."[55] The relative wealth of the pioneer period was not forthcoming or, perhaps, available in the early postwar period.

But if the extraordinary postwar situation was not enough, emergencies indicated how much further the local Jewish population would go to support their causes. The passions and fears aroused by the outbreak of Arab-Israeli warfare in 1967 led the community to raise "twice as much for the Emergency Fund as we raise in the regular campaigns."[56] And again in 1973, when the news from the Yom Kippur War appeared grim, the call by the JCCA for emergency funds drew a 47 percent response rate as compared with the 32 percent reponse rate for the regular annual campaign. Whereas the regular campaign took in roughly $145,000, the emergency campaign of the same year amassed $192,000.[57]

The Jewish community's level of concern with the fate of Israel could rise or fall with the ebb and flow of dramatic events, but the general interest remained high and constant. In the sixties one finds discussions about which banks were purchasing Israeli bonds.[58] As did American Jews elsewhere, the JCCA kept informed of the attitudes and voting records of New Mexico's congressional delegates on Middle East issues and informed them of their own views.[59] The institutional presence of the Jewish community by the 1970s was clear and open in its stand.

The strong feelings of American Jews toward the existence and safety of Israel drew them into the public arena as a community as never before in their modern history. However, many other issues affecting Jews, other minorities, and all American society also emerged in the postwar world. The social turmoil of the sixties and seventies, a time of frank and buoyant activism, served to draw Jews ever more out of their communal anonymity. They began to respond as a community to issues where previously only local organizations and individuals had spoken up.

By 1967 the board of the AJWF was discussing how the Jewish community could aid blacks by making on-the-job training available and how to deal with discrimination in housing.[60] The wanderlust which seized American youth in the sixties attracted many persons to and through New Mexico. A report in January 1968 noted that the AJWF had aided 184 transients. Many had received a night's lodging and food and some even aid for transportation. Liaison with agencies to aid unmarried mothers, aid for Jews and non-Jews to enter Jewish hospitals, and dealing with Jewish runaways "because we have always said, we will be responsible for our own" all presented parts of the social scene of the period.[61]

Nevertheless, involved persons still felt that these efforts fell below what the Jewish community should do. In 1967 Michael Sutin, the president of the board of the AJWF, sounded his dissatisfaction with the fact that no position had been taken on fair housing, religious observances in the public schools, or Sunday closing laws. He even noted that there were reservations regarding participation in political action programs in support of Israel.[62] Fears of too much limelight and the possibility of hostile reactions did not die easily.

How much that mood had changed in the seventies can be seen in how the community moved into discussion of controversial issues. The increased openness of the Jewish community had even attracted newspaper attention by 1980. An Albuquerque journalist found the cause in the newcomers from midwestern and eastern centers who were a generation away from their European origins and whose experience in large cities where a Jewish milieu had existed and accustomed them to practice their heritage openly.[63] "Instead of fading quietly into a many-hued western sunset," the author noted, ". . . [they] were maintaining and asserting their identity . . . adding a vibrant element to the city's increasingly cosmopolitan mix."[64] The process of increasing political visibility had obviously begun earlier, but the newcomers undoubtedly reenforced, broadened, and hastened it. Moreover, they added to it cultural and intellectual dimensions.

The framework of open expression usually lay within the Jewish institutions, although at times the forms of expression included moving beyond the boundaries of the Jewish community. One can only give examples. In 1952 some of the members of Temple Albert created a Men's Club to stimulate Jewish religious activities and promote a spirit of comradeship with the general community. Membership was not limited to the congregation.[65] The Men's Club provided an open forum for discussion with knowledgable citizens normally at Sunday morning breakfasts.[66] In the early eighties a reporter characterized the meetings as "a kind of substitute New England–type town meeting . . . all very civilized . . . a way to meet people and be informed with lox and bagels."[67]

In 1964 Temple Albert established a Social Action Committee to relate Judaism's principles to world problems and to stimulate individual commitment by congregants on contemporary issues.[68] Over the years it sponsored programs on nuclear disarmament, dialogues between Catholics and Jews, discussions on abortion, and on First Amendment and Central American issues.[69] The Social Action Committee served as a vehicle for letter-writing campaigns on such matters as the condition of Soviet Jewry, aid to Israel, and prayer in public schools.[70] It sent representatives to the Religious Coalition for Abortion Rights. On the issue of abortion, the JCCA endorsed and became a sponsoring organization for a local chapter of the Religious Coalition for Abortion Rights in 1978. Regardless of one's position, it was clear by 1980 that Jewish institutions were committing themselves openly on matters of great controversy as never before.

The University of New Mexico also served as a focal point of new activity. In the 1940s the growing number of Jewish students led to the creation of a branch of Hillel. Growth and organization proved slow; the organization was chartered in the sixties when the Jewish student population stood at around four hundred.[71]

Supported by B'nai B'rith with some help from the AJWF, and counseled by Jewish faculty members, the organization purchased a house near campus in 1972. Zoning problems involved with parking led to the sale of the property after a short time. At that time some fifty Jewish students were dues-paying members. Student apathy and feelings that anti-Semitic attitudes may have been involved contributed to the modest results for Hillel.[72] The organization survived the seventies weakly. Nevertheless, its presence was another sign of the growing breadth of Jewish activities.

ᕇᕗ

The foundations of Albuquerque's Jewish congregational life did not change after 1940. Temple Albert and Congregation B'nai Israel, which received a permanent home in 1941, remained the twin focal points of Jewish religious activity. However, both expanded greatly together with the increase in Jewish population, and the variety and scope of their programs grew accordingly.

The need to keep facilities and programs up with congregational membership led to frequent residential additions and changes. B'nai Israel added to its building in the 1950s and in the same decade purchased land for a new synagogue at Washington Street and Indian School Road. In 1969 ground was broken for that structure in which the congregation is still housed.[73]

By the end of the forties, Temple Albert faced a similar problem. A new temple opened on Lead Avenue in 1951. It remained adequate for only a few years. By the late 1950s additions had to be made, and in the 1970s the congregation began a search for land for a new temple. In the early eighties the land purchase at Natalie and Louisiana Boulevard set the stage for the third site for Temple Albert since its formation and the second since World War II. The new temple was dedicated in 1984.[74]

The physical structures followed numerical growth. Temple Albert had 87 members in 1944.[75] By 1953, 172 families belonged and in 1958, about 250.[76] In the early 1980s the congregation claimed over 460 family memberships.[77]

B'nai Israel's growth experiences were similar. The membership of 40 in 1941 had swelled to 175 when Rabbi Isaac Celnik became its spiritual leader in 1971.[78] In 1980 there were over 400 family memberships.[79]

New forms of religious organization emerged. In 1973 a Chavurat Hamidbar (Fellowship of the Desert), an independent family-oriented group emphasizing Jewish education and discussion in members' homes, took root.[80] University of New Mexico faculty members played an important role in this venture.

✑

The loss of its traditional isolation affected New Mexico in more than economic ways. Far more than ever before national moods and issues became translated into matters of local concern and interaction with forces that represented those issues on a broad platform. As individual citizens, New Mexico's Jews concerned themselves with the common issues that affected all other citizens. But as issues which touched the already activated Jewish community in particular became part of the greater consciousness of the broader population, reactions and outcomes appeared which showed clearly that New Mexico had moved closer to the mainstream of American life.

How local and broader issues could come together for New Mexico's Jews may be illustrated by an incident which occurred at the end of our history in the early eighties. In 1983 a controversy erupted at New Mexico State University at Las Cruces which reflected the changing state of affairs. It centered around the student yearbook, *The Swastika*, which employed the old

Indian symbol as its logo and had done so for many years before
the Nazi era in Germany.

Not that the issue was totally new. The use of the symbol had
come under scrutiny in the late thirties and during World War
II. In 1940 an editorial in the *Roundup*, the student newspaper,
had pointed out that some Indian tribes in New Mexico and Arizona had dropped the symbol out of their resentment of the Na-
zis.[81] Indeed, during the war years its use disappeared from the
yearbook's pages and from ROTC uniforms and band instru-
ments, although the name remained in existence.[82] And in 1972,
the Anti-Defamation League of B'nai B'rith (ADL) sought unsuc-
cessfully to have the name changed. This effort was apparently
met with some hostility.[83]

The controversy broke into the open over a photograph in
the 1982 edition of the yearbook. It depicted the swastika on students dressed in Nazi-like uniforms.[84] The news editor of the
Roundup, a Jewish student named Paula Steinbach who was also
active in the Hillel group on campus, called for an end to its use.

Students rallied to both sides of the issue. Supporters for the
status quo invoked arguments of "we had it first" and its place as
a hallowed tradition. Those opposed argued to its negative effect
as a Nazi symbol and the harm it would do the university. As
news of the affair spread throughout the state and outside authorities, including the governor, became involved, the issues of student democracy and rights were invoked.

Before the affair ended, a range of feeling about Jews had
been expressed which indicated a broad spectrum of attitudes.
Letters to newspapers raised the issue of Jews feeling sorry for
themselves; Jews were castigated, particularly those who had survived the Holocaust; a sculpture on campus by the noted Jewish
artist Sol Lewitt was defaced, and Paula Steinbach was tempo-
rarily dismissed as news editor. Israel's treatment of Palestinian
Arabs came up for criticism. In short, a variety of feelings relating
to Jews one could expect to hear in every part of the United States
came to light on the university's problem.

Opponents of the swastika's use also had their day. In a minority, they presented arguments depicting the narrowness of viewpoint of the symbol's defenders, their lack of sensitivity toward the feelings of Jewish students, and, again, the harm done to the university's image. Faculty members, students, and interested outsiders were all involved in urging discontinuation of its use.

In the end, Governor Anaya asked the board of regents to cease using the symbol. His will was carried out by the board, although not unanimously.

This action, which coincided with the end of the use of the Confederate flag at the University of Mississippi and, a few years earlier, the use of Indian dress as symbols at the University of Oklahoma and Stanford University, represented stands by students of minority groups, black and Indian, to uphold their dignity. In this sense, the Jewish students and those who joined them in the conflict at Las Cruces were reflecting national moods among minorities and those sympathetic to them rather than a purely local mood.

The event also revealed some differences between the local Jewish community and the Jewish students at the university. In seeking support for the students, the ADL turned to the town's Jewish community. However, the ADL encountered apprehension among the Jewish townfolk about what they considered national involvement in a local matter.[85] They preferred the matter to be contained rather than opened up. Perhaps they feared that crystallization of the issue into sharply drawn sides would draw hostility to them and cost them the comfort of being a known quantity of neighbors and local residents rather than Jews. Besides, the older residents were probably quite aware of the traditional meaning of the symbol and willing to regard its presence in that light. Whatever the students thought, the local community had its own interests and perspectives. Some of the town's Jewish residents, however, took the side of the students in letters to editors.[86]

Other evidence of entrance into New Mexico of national and local expressions of anti-Jewish feeling also appeared from time to time. Already in 1963 Michael Sutin, New Mexico's representative of the Anti-Defamation League, possessed a considerable collection of mailings of hate literature and local contacts for such materials existed in Albuquerque, Santa Fe, and Farmington.[87] The use of swastikas to deface Jewish institutions became known to New Mexico's Jews. Rio Rancho's Jewish Center in 1979 and Congregation B'nai Israel in Albuquerque in 1982 both experienced such incidents.[88] It was an unmistakable sign of the influence of ideologies created elsewhere finding echoes in New Mexico.

~

Postwar international events, the civil rights movement, and old Hispano grievances, all silhouetted against the war in Vietnam, produced their own environment in New Mexico in the sixties. Reies Tijerina, a Texas-born Hispano of Christian fundamentalist background, emerged in the decade as a dramatic figure, seeking to right wrongs perpetrated against the "Indo-Hispano" population of New Mexico. These grievances included land grant losses and various forms of discrimination against Spanish-speaking citizens.[89]

Tijerina's study of his subject matter and the nature of the times combined to provide him with his orientation toward the unrest of the decade. He saw comparisons, as did others, between dispossessed land grant heirs and the peoples in underdeveloped societies and parallels between the struggles of the blacks for liberation and equality and the condition of the Hispanos in New Mexico.[90] In 1966 his Alianza movement launched a campaign of direct action, the highlights of which were the occupation of the Echo Campground in the Carson National Forest in northern New Mexico and a raid on the courthouse in Tierra Amarilla in 1967. These events produced a widespread reaction, pro and con, to Tijerina.

At that time, his fame, or notoriety, drew him to the attention of far-flung elements of the civil rights movement and the

New Left. He became Martin Luther King's choice to head a Poor People's March in New Mexico.[91] While attending the New Politics convention in Chicago in 1967, Tijerina also established contact with black Muslims.[92]

After his return from Chicago, Tijerina, in a talk at St. John's College in Santa Fe, revealed some of his ideas to the middle-class, Anglo audience. To depict group relationships in New Mexico he used a scale of race age in which the Spanish-American was four and a half years old, the Anglos twenty-five years old, and the Jews, sixty. His point involved the naiveté of the first as compared to the others, who had, as land speculators, undone the Spanish-American. "Thomas B. Catron," he asserted, "I am told he was a Jew, it takes a well developed race to do what they did to us, but we will not have our rights tampered with."[93] The *Albuquerque Journal* reported that Tijerina's remarks "brought on a stunned silence in the meeting room."[94]

That Tijerina blamed Anglos for the loss of Hispano land grants was well known. What was not clear, however, was his reason for distinguishing between Anglos and Jews and his erroneous identification of Catron as a Jew. Tijerina's intellectual journey to his views on race and Jews are part of his biography and go beyond the scope of this volume. It should also be noted that he subsequently denied that he was critical of Jews, denied knowing any Jews in New Mexico and stated "there are some good Jews and some bad ones."[95] In the mid-seventies he even courted the Jewish community for a time in the name of minority issues. At Tijerina's invitation Rabbi Celnik of B'nai Israel participated in a program devoted to that subject.[96] However, Tijerina did not drop his erroneous facts or his views.

Tijerina's statements, insofar as the Jewish community was concerned, produced no overt reaction. When the Poor People's March took place in May 1968, a Catholic priest, Fr. Luis Jaramillo, criticized the whole Jewish community for lack of interest in the campaign because of Tijerina's leadership.[97] However, Mrs. Palmyra Andrews, chair of the food and lodging committee, responded to the charge, noting, "We have had a very gratifying response from all segments of the Albuquerque community and that certainly includes the Jewish community."[98]

The Alianza remained alive, but the radicalism of the late sixties faded. Tijerina remained, but the limelight he had enjoyed dimmed and localized as the years passed and the war ended. Jewish institutions, it appears, continued not to respond directly to his views.[99] That Tijerina had condemned the behavior of Jews and others by racial definition seems undeniable, but the impact of his opinions may well have been more harmful to his cause than helpful to him. Knowledgable persons have expressed the opinion that his views cost him some measure of his credibility.[100] Insofar as Tijerina latched on to an indigenous element of anti-Semitism, his attitude could only be disturbing to Jews. The effects of his attitude, however, appear to have been inconsequential in the short term.

An extraordinary development in the seventies, at least for Anglo Jews, was the emergence of knowledge of a crypto-Jewish presence in New Mexico. Still in the early stages of research at the time of writing, one must ask why this phenomenon emerged then and what it had come to mean by 1980. If the signs of crypto-Judaism's existence are correct, and much points to their accuracy, then why in a century and a third since American law arrived in New Mexico did not crypto-Jews reveal themselves?

Answers can only be tentative at this point. One must bear in mind that only a few crypto-Jews came forth to reveal their identity. Clemente Carmona suggested that his education and contact with Anglo Jews in California, along with his own yearnings, helped remove the traditional barriers and brought him to an Albuquerque congregation.[101] It would appear, then, that education and awareness of and contact with the outside world changed the old basic conditions. Contact with Anglo Jews made possible what was unavailable or marginally available in earlier times.

If some of the old isolation between Hispano and Anglo was breaking down, however, much continued to exist. Traditional Hispano ways and society still carried much weight. For the crypto-Jews, revealing themselves involved significant problems. The generations of secrecy had produced psychological barriers which made the open practice of Judaism strange to them. Their religious practices had evolved a long way from the normative Judaism of contemporary American Jews. And if that were not enough, their deep cultural and economic ties with Hispanic society could be endangered by open allegiance to an outside community. Fear of ostracism and economic retribution remained.[102]

On the other hand, new currents present among the younger generation of Hispanos affected their crypto-Jewish counterparts deeply. Faced with problems of heightened awareness of ethnic and civil rights issues and the weakening of such older institutions as the family, the core of the transmission process of crypto-Judaism, they had to confront difficult choices. To be a Jew and a Hispano appeared to one informant to be contradictory. To identify herself as a Jew entailed dropping her identity as a Chicana. Asked why she could not be both, she replied, "When is a Hispanic not a Hispanic? When you're a Jew. Then, all of a sudden, you're not Hispanic any more. Suddenly you're Sephardic. And you don't 'belong' any more."[103] And Carmona, responding to questions about the problems of the younger crypto-Jewish generation under the pressure of peers, school, and media, noted the reluctance to be different from either the Hispanic or the American culture.[104]

In all likelihood, there are far more Hispanos with some measure of Jewish heritage who are Christians than there are those who still consider themselves Jews. How their awareness of a Jewish past affects them and their relationship to the Anglo-Jewish community is difficult to evaluate. However, it is primarily a consideration of Hispano identity and only secondarily related to Anglo Jews. At the close of the period under discussion, that is, up to 1980, one could not define the problem as a major factor of Hispano-Jewish relations in New Mexico.

From the perspective of Anglo Jews, the immediate effect of a crypto-Jewish emergence was small. Few such persons made their way into existing congregations. Those aware of their presence either welcomed them or had doubts about their qualifications as Jews. The rabbis of the leading congregations worked with them as they made their way into the milieu of the modern American Jew.

The probability that there were more of them still extant carried a certain sense of potential. Nevertheless, the burden of action lay on the crypto-Jews to make themselves known, and outside of a number of interested persons with amateur or professional research interests, New Mexico's Jewish institutional leaders did not seek them out.

～

Although Albuquerque was the center of growth in the postwar era, other towns also exhibited new vitality. Las Cruces, with the continuing agricultural development of the Mesilla Valley, the creation of the White Sands Proving Ground, and the growth of New Mexico State University, received an opportunity to expand as a local center. While such old-line families as the Freudenthals provided a thread of continuity with the pioneer past and Joseph Rosenfeld and Eugene Stern with the early twentieth century, newcomers contributed heavily to the creation of a Jewish presence.

In the early forties thirty-four persons made up the Jewish population of the town.[105] At that point observant Jews from Las Cruces attended services in El Paso. Mark Wechter, who moved to Las Cruces in 1948 from El Paso, recalled seeing the Samuel Klein family at services there.[106] Eugene Stern had done the same with his children.[107] By 1961, the number of Jews had reached a hundred.[108] By that time the combined efforts of Jews in the business and professional community, White Sands, and the university faculty had created a local congregation (1955), and a Jewish religious school predated its appearance by two years.[109]

In the early 1960s the congregation resolved to build a temple. The thirty-five to forty families, with the heavy support of Eugene Stern, and aided by El Paso's Jewish community, built Temple Beth El.[110] By 1966 Las Cruces hired its first part-time rabbi and came of age as a religious community.[111]

In Santa Fe, too, a Jewish population which had begun a numerical comeback and the start of institutionalization before the war, continued to strengthen after the war ended. In 1953 some fifteen Jewish families founded the Santa Fe Jewish temple, which took the name of Beth Shalom in 1969.[112] By 1964 the congregation had between forty-five and fifty members with an estimated twenty-five to thirty unaffiliated families.[113] By that time a sisterhood had been created. Growth was rapid thereafter; a 1981 membership list included 192 families of whom 180 lived in town or close to it.[114] The congregational growth was a communal expression of general growth. From the seventy-five Jews estimated in Santa Fe in 1940, the numbers had expanded to 135 in 1961, to 260 in 1973, and reached 300 by 1980.[115]

The maturation of the congregation took place gradually. The early rabbis, dating from the late fifties, tended to be retired, and stayed only a brief time. Bar mitzvahs were still often prepared for in Albuquerque.[116] Rabbi Shinedling, a retired rabbi in Albuquerque, frequently prepared Santa Fe youth for the rite of passage and performed part-time ministerial services between more permanent rabbis in the sixties. After a stint of several years by Rabbi Samuel Markowitz into the early seventies, Beth Shalom achieved stability with the appointment of Rabbi Leonard Helman in 1974.

When the community established itself formally in 1953, the economic makeup of the Jewish population reflected a strong core of family businesses. Well-established firms clustered their activities around clothing and furnishings, shoes, furniture, pharmacies, and some services, such as laundries and home repairs.[117] The numerical core appeared geared to the needs of the permanent population of Santa Fe rather than the tourist trade.

Even in 1964 the basic character of the community had not

changed a great deal. Such older families as the Picks, Kahns, Petcheskys, and Bells continued to run their businesses as they had earlier. About 64 percent of the identified Jews belonged to such proprietorial families in 1953. In 1964, they still accounted for 60 percent of identified Jews.[118] Professionals amounted to 21 percent of this population in 1953 and 16 percent in 1964. Perhaps the greatest sign of change came in state government employment—7 percent in 1953 and 14 percent in 1964.

When searching for a rabbi in 1973, Robert Burman, the correspondent to the Rabbinical Placement Commission, described the state of the Jewish population in Santa Fe. He saw the community growing rapidly. Young people were arriving. It was a variegated population "composed of descendants of old-time settlers of European immigrants and of relative newcomers from the larger American cities."[119] How much more complex the character of the population was becoming can be seen in 1975 when the High Holidays required one Reform and one Orthodox service.[120] The leadership of the congregation viewed the body as not wealthy, its members living heavily on fixed incomes.[121]

By 1981, however, much greater change had occurred in the economic composition of the Santa Fe Jewish community. Based on the known occupations of Beth Shalom's membership in 1981, over one-third engaged in professions including law, medicine, mental health, science at Los Alamos, and teaching.[122] Over 12 percent were employed by the state, and a fair number of them were also professionals by training. In 1964 it was difficult to measure the number of retired persons in the Jewish community, but in the 1981 population they accounted for about 15 percent of those identified. In accord with the altered character of Santa Fe, one also found Jewish artists, craftsmen, and artisans, about 6 percent. Thus, over half the population engaged in work or in retirement was outside the commercial world that had dominated the economic activity of the Jewish community in the past.

Between 1964 and 1981 the older sorts of business enterprises, which had so long supported the Jewish population, diminished in number, although they did not disappear. Newcomers created new kinds of enterprises, among them restaurants, motels, architecture and engineering agencies, solar equipment and printing firms, building supply houses, and financial consultancies. However, the percentage of Jewish persons engaged in business in Santa Fe declined, making up about one-third of the total Jewish population.

In effect, the Jewish population of Santa Fe in the generation ending in the early eighties underwent a change like that experienced in Albuquerque, but reflecting the character of the city. The population became professionalized, and the city attracted retirees and persons interested in the arts, scientists working at Los Alamos, and those who sought employment in the state's capital. It was a highly educated and cosmopolitan community. Yet, the older element did not disappear. One still encountered the names of the earlier twentieth century and the memories and monuments of the more distant past, the Staab house and the Spitz clock, as well as the Kahn Shoe Store and The Guarantee.

Roswell grew at a rate after World War II matched in rapidity only by its growth in the late nineteenth and early twentieth centuries. The war led to the creation of Roswell Army Air Field in 1941, which became Walker Air Force Base in 1948. In 1940 the town had a population of 13,482. By 1960 it had grown to 39,593. The closing of the air force base in 1967 proved a shock. The population fell to 33,908 in 1970, but by 1980, it was back up to 39,676.

Roswell's Jewish population, never large, had declined from the early twentieth century to 1940, at which time it was placed at twenty-three persons.[123] In 1981, twenty-five members, many of them families, belonged to the congregation.[124]. The community included residents of long standing. Sam Stolaroff had come in 1911, opened a general store which operated into the post–World War II era, and still belonged to the congregation in 1981. Ben Ginsberg, on contract from Baldwin Piano Co., came in 1917 to sell pianos and also belonged to the congregation in 1981.[125] There were even descendants of the earliest pioneer Jewish families, the Pragers, in town, although the latter no longer adhered to Judaism.

Despite meager numbers, the Jews of Roswell had sought to identify themselves as a religious community early in the century. A newspaper article in 1904 had described the Jewish congregation of Roswell, organized in 1903, and its hopes for a building and a rabbi.[126] The growth commensurate with such hopes did not come. The new expansion after World War II, however, brought Jews, both civilian and military, who contributed to the realization of the intentions of the early pioneer families. In the early fifties, ten prominent members of the community purchased an empty church building and formed Temple B'nai Israel.[127] The presence of Jewish military personnel from the base swelled the numbers attending services. However, the closing of the air base in 1967 affected the Jewish community adversely, as it did all Roswell. Nevertheless, in 1981 the congregation continued to exist, it had its temple, and the population was growing, even though still without a rabbi.

⚬

Quantitative descriptions made possible by the growth of institutions, the use of computers, and the development of social science techniques of measurement became characteristic of much historical description in the postwar era. Despite the value of such data and the results derived from them, some dimension of human, individual, and qualitative measurement becomes lost if such description alone exists. Amid statistics, how does one appreciate the value of the thirty-year career of a Rabbi David Shor as rabbi of Albuquerque's Temple Albert? The city expressed its appreciation by proclaiming November 30, 1973, as "Rabbi David Shor Day."[128] How does one convey the passionate concern of Rana Adler for the newly arriving refugee families in early years after World War II? But one can only mention such anecdotal highlights.

And the historian who discusses the growing sense of historical consciousness in the community cannot ignore those who expressed that feeling through their labors. To mention only those who have passed away, one must note Rabbi Floyd Fierman, late of El Paso, whose decades of research almost single-handedly created and sustained an interest in the history of the pioneer Jewish families in the Southwest, but mainly in New Mexico. Rabbi Abraham Shinedling, who retired to Albuquerque, was indefatigable in his efforts to collect and preserve materials of existing old-line families from all corners of the state.

On a narrower scale, but reflecting in equal measure their growing sense of historical consciousness, several persons have made valuable contributions. Milton Taichert of Las Vegas, who arrived there early in the century, served as a gentle guardian of the community's documentary possessions and gracefully informed new generations of the history of that community. Israel Carmel, of Albuquerque's Temple Albert, carefully collected materials related to the history of his institution and the community. Within recent years, a New Mexico Jewish Historical Society has even come into existence.

⟩

This historical consciousness accompanied a growing sense of belonging among New Mexico's Jews. Despite considerable new growth, the threads of continuity strengthened as generations stayed. The Albuquerque Seligmans, the extensive Minces and Nordhaus family connections, the Freudenthals of Las Cruces provide examples which go deep into New Mexico's Jewish Anglo past. Second-generation connections exist in a number which can only be described as stable and strong. Congregation walls are replete with commemorative evidence of gifts and bequests which speak to that continuity.

While a sense of belonging formed one dimension of a diminishing alienation, New Mexico's loss of isolation allowed newcomers to fit in with relative ease compared to the past. They could not have the sense of remoteness that the older periods of New Mexico's history conveyed. Geographic isolation is so much reduced compared to the prewar period, and so much less than in the nineteenth century, that a sense of belonging and involvement comes much sooner. Newcomers are not as new and different in their culture as were the young immigrants of the nineteenth century recently departed from family and foreign homeland. One stretches to find differences of attitude between easterners arriving in Rio Rancho in the seventies and their counterparts in Albuquerque who settled here a decade earlier. Arriving professionals, even if at an early stage in their careers, have their training in hand and have accepted prearranged positions or practices. Such circumstances alone induce a degree of confidence and assurance greater than was possible in earlier times.

In the broader picture, awareness of the history of the Jews since World War II has left less room for the contemporary Jew to be silent. Institutional and numerical growth and the public response of Jews to issues affecting them and the general community show both a feeling of confidence in their capacity to express themselves as well as a feeling of the necessity to do so. Obligated to speak out as never before on their own behalf, Jews attracted more open response and, at times, more hostility to themselves than before. But they also acted with a greater sense of themselves as citizens, human beings, and Jews.

Epilogue

By measure of numerical growth, the history of New Mexico and that of its Jewish population have gone hand in hand. When growth was slow, the Jewish population grew slowly, when growth was rapid, the Jewish population followed suit. It is also clear that Jewish numbers increased modestly compared to the growth of the general population. One may infer with equal modesty that from the point of view of the Jews their New Mexico experience has been a favorable one.

For the most part, New Mexico's Jewish population grew as a result of immigration. The westward movement of the German-Jewish immigrants in the nineteenth century brought them almost everywhere in the United States, and their arrival in New Mexico was part of that pattern. In the twentieth century the migration of Jews from Germany fell off, became sporadic, and disappeared completely with World War II. The great east European migration of Jews to the United States of the late nineteenth and early twentieth centuries did not affect New Mexico directly; those Jews did not go there in significant numbers.

As a partial result of increasingly limited foreign immigration, the character of New Mexico's Jewish population changed. Between the turn of the twentieth century and World War II Jewish numbers grew slowly, resting on a low rate of natural increase and a reduced flow of immigration. The population gradually evolved into an assimilated New Mexico-and American-born one. After World War II, a renewed heavy influx produced unprecedented growth, consisting primarily of American-born Jews, the descendants of east European immigrants.

Given this history, one may ask whether the Jewish population of New Mexico can be a self-sustaining one or must continue to rely on immigration for a healthy communal existence. Even in the slow growth era of 1900 to 1940 there was little sign of any impending disappearance. The Jewish population of New Mexico in 1980 was, of course, much larger and better balanced in terms of gender than the old male-dominated pioneer population of the nineteenth century. Marriage within the group had become far more possible. The Jewish population also became more varied in its economic composition than its nineteenth-century predecessor. The community of 1980 was far better organized and capable of meeting the needs of its members as Jews than ever before. On this basis it would seem better able to hold its own than ever before. Thus, a modestly optimistic prognosis appears with regard to the permanence and viability of the community.

The prospects for that permanence, however, also contain some problems. While New Mexico's environment, both economic and natural, has attracted increasing numbers of Jews, it is still not clear to what degree the economic and social character of the state's Jewry commits them to generational continuity of residence. For example, the growing number of retirees attracted to New Mexico may contribute much to the enrichment of the Jewish community and the state in the present, but such a population, by its very nature, does not add to the progeny of the next generation.

The increased professionalization of the Jewish working population in an atmosphere of high value and status for the professions would also appear to justify a favorable future for Jews in New Mexico. But the skills of the professionals allow them considerable mobility, perhaps even more than for the old sedentary merchants who built their businesses over a lifetime and often sought to turn them over to their children. The generational pattern of residence for the professional, then, may depend on the kind of skills needed in the state. While doctors and attorneys may reasonably count on a need for their services, atomic scientists may have far less certainty. Their presence will rest on the continuing interest of the federal government. The availability of resources for research and teaching may determine whether Jewish or any other faculty will be attracted to come or stay at New Mexico institutions of higher learning.

On the other hand, the growing size, complexity and diversity of the Jewish community have made the state far more attractive as a place to settle or stay than it has been in the past for Jews concerned with their identity. It is possible to maintain a stronger level of commitment to Jewish life if one is so inclined than ever before in the past. Whether that all adds up to a self-sustaining Jewish community in the long run is still in question, but it is more likely than ever before. However, if the population proves to be of a single generation, then the most permanent aspects of the community's existence might be the institutions it created and a smaller static resident population.

In a historical sense, the economic experience of the Jews in New Mexico has been a favorable one. In the pioneer period preceding the railroad they came largely to engage in commerce and in the free-wheeling enterprise that characterized the American frontier experience. The prosperity which attended the development of a capitalist economy and the linking of New Mexico to the East formed the economic milieu in which the Jewish population worked and lived. Their skills and employment coincided with the larger dynamics driving the economy. In many ways, it proved the most prosperous period for the Jews in economic terms.

The railroad's appearance altered the relationship of New Mexico to the national economy. It changed and partially destroyed the economic conditions and rules which had held sway in New Mexico, obliging the population engaged in commerce to adjust its practices. Between 1880 and 1940 the economic condition of the Jewish working population declined somewhat relative to what it had been earlier. Not that it was thrown into poverty. Commerce, as practiced by individuals or families, simply could not hold to the same high economic level as before. The Jews in New Mexico were affected by the new presence of large-scale organizations, but not linked to them, remaining largely individual entrepreneurs.

After 1940, economic conditions again changed sharply. The role of the federal government in fostering its own needs placed a new emphasis on the economy of New Mexico, at the base of which lay a need for highly professional skills. The growth of state institutions and many aspects of the discovery of the West by the rest of the country led in the same direction. The Jewish working population reflected these changes. It had adjusted, largely through immigration and training, to a more favorable position than it had enjoyed between 1880 and 1940. It did not achieve this position, though, through the kind of proprietorship that had characterized the pioneer period, but to a much larger degree than before through service in such fields as health care, the law, education, research, and government employment. In comparative terms, the pioneer period still was the one in which Jews did best economically, but after 1940 they were again a part of the leading forces driving the economy of New Mexico.

The Jews of New Mexico have also undergone an evolution as a social and religious community in terms of their identity. The pioneers came to New Mexico as individuals or family members. Before 1880 they created no formal institutions for themselves. Priorities of individual or family welfare, paucity of numbers, and the absence of certain social factors, such as the nuclear family, all contributed to that condition.

Growing numbers and changes in the social composition of the Jewish population after the 1880s led to the creation of Jewish organizations around which a sizable portion of Jews grouped themselves. Jews now openly practiced their religion as congregations and engaged in social functions as Jews but still behaved as nondenominational individual citizens in their relations with the general community.

After World War II the new factors in the life of American Jewry, such as consciousness of the Holocaust, the existence of Israel, and the general issues of civil rights in the United States, produced a new atmosphere. Although Jews still behaved as individuals on many issues, a new sense of danger and confidence produced an atmosphere in which the Jewish community began to speak out on general issues. This became the case increasingly in New Mexico. Just as Catholics, Hispanos, blacks, Protestant fundamentalists, and others spoke out on issues they considered important to their interests, so too did the Jews through their own institutions. Where in an earlier day individual equality and worth had been a major measurement for all, now group expression became an important part of the picture.

Beyond issues of communal stability and individual well-being, lies the question of the historic place of the Jews in the development of the territory and state. As an important part of early economic Americanization, they drew Hispano farmers into the modern world as they linked them into a broader economy involving forts and reservations in the Southwest, as well as international markets in wool and other agricultural products. In their newer preponderance as professionals, they still act as agents of modernization in education, health care, and scientific research. In this sense, they have played a vital role in the modernization carried through by the Anglos.

From the beginnings of their settlement they participated in the urban growth of the area by their residence and economic activity. Within the towns the Jews appeared as a cosmopolitan and service-oriented element. Their self-interest as merchants and their need and desire to be part of the general community led them to take part in every civic activity that added cultural and social dimension to their place of settlement. Their means and education, within the context of an open society, permitted their participation. Although they generally did not seek public office at first, by the 1880s they began to do so and have continued to follow that path throughout the period covered by this study.

Over time, too, there has been a slow cumulative dimension to the history of the Jews in New Mexico. For some purposes, history serves as a legitimizer of presence. The cultures of the Indian, the oldest residents, and the Hispanicized population, the next oldest, have characterized a great deal of what New Mexico is and stands for by their longevity. The Anglo, from this perspective, is the newcomer. The Jew, as part of the Anglo cultural world, shares this position.

Insofar as the Jew is separate from the Christian Anglo, however, his position requires its own legitimation. The growing historical awareness of Anglo and Jew in New Mexico has produced a sense of belonging which grows with historical depth. Harvey Fergusson's Jewish merchant hero in *The Conquest of Don Pedro*, by fact of his literary existence, exemplifies an image based on historical experience which says the Jews had something to do with the making of this place as it now is and that they belong to it. Their lives have intertwined with the history of New Mexico. They lie buried in its soil, and they are part of the human lore that provides a psychological archeology of place. New Mexico has enough unique identity to make such matters important.

When the historian singles out one group in society for examination, the effort to find differences and uniqueness receives the balance of attention. Anglos in general and Jewish Anglos in particular presented an unusual preponderance of the population engaged in commerce within the economic and social context of nineteenth-century New Mexican society. In contemporary New Mexico, the Jewish population may still appear unusual in the level of education achieved within the group and their participation in the professions.

Viewed from a national perspective, however, New Mexico itself appears unusual. The relatively small component of manufacturing in the economy and the great size of federal involvement, whether in research or military facilities or in Indian affairs, are indicators of this. The unusual character of the size and place of the Hispano population differentiates New Mexico from other parts of the United States. Further, one might note the socioeconomic characteristics of pueblo Indians, Hispanos, and blacks as being unusual when viewed from the perspective of the national population. Indeed, one might ask if any minority is a microcosm of the socioeconomic composition of the whole?

Beyond uniqueness there are larger questions of commonality. As individuals, Jews and others in New Mexico found common ground in the openness of a democratic society, common ground in business associations, and common need for mutual respect. New Mexico is as distinctly pluralistic as any part of the United States. The success of the Jews in New Mexico, however, has its base ultimately in their acceptance of the common ground of general American values and their commitment to participate in the broader economic and social processes at work in society. Nevertheless, they never denied their identity and, as they have grown more secure, they have strengthened it. Given the increased internal and public strength of that communal identity in a group which separated itself from Anglo society in a most minimal way, the Jews' history in New Mexico exemplifies the conjuncture of fruitful coexistence among the universal elements of American society and the unique social organism of a minority community. To my way of thinking, it has been to the benefit of all.

Notes

ABBREVIATIONS

AJA, American Jewish Archives, Cincinnati

AJWF, Albuquerque Jewish Welfare Fund

AJYB, *American Jewish Year Book*

IOBB, International Order of B'nai B'rith

JCCA, Jewish Community Council of Albuquerque

NMHR, *New Mexico Historical Review*

TANM, *Territorial Archives of New Mexico*

INTRODUCTION

1. A recent doctoral dissertation uses these criteria to establish religious identity. See Blaine P. Lamb, "Jewish Pioneers in Arizona, 1850–1920," Ph. D. diss., Arizona State University, Tempe, Arizona, 1982, pp. 3–4.

CHAPTER 1

1. Floyd S. Fierman, "Jewish Pioneering in the Southwest: A Record of the Freudenthal-Lesinsky-Solomon Families," *Arizona and the West* 2, no. 1 (Spring 1960): 55–56.

2. "Letter of Fay F. Blake to Dr. Jacob R. Marcus," September 29, 1976, Carrasco-Sanchez Family, AJA, Cincinnati.

3. Ibid.

4. Ibid. The same qualm was expressed to this author in discussion with a descendant of such a family in 1984.

5. Herbert E. Bolton, "Defensive Spanish Expansion and the Significance of the Borderlands," in *Bolton and the Spanish Borderlands*, John F. Bannon, ed. (Norman, 1974), pp. 44–45.

6. Herbert E. Bolton, "The Mission as a Frontier Institution in the Spanish American Colonies," ibid., p. 189.

7. Herbert E. Bolton, "Defensive Spanish Colonization," ibid., p. 44.

8. France V. Scholes, "Church and State in New Mexico, 1610–1650," *NMHR* 12, no. 1 (January 1937): 103.

9. Max L. Moorhead, *New Mexico's Royal Road: Trade and Travel on the Chihuahua Trail* (Norman, 1958), p. 28.

10. Oakah L. Jones, Jr., *Los Paisanos: Spanish Settlers on the Northern Frontier of New Spain* (Norman, 1979), p. 28.

11. Ibid., p. 119.

12. Fray Angélico Chávez, *Origins of New Mexico Families* (Santa Fe, 1954), p. xi; Jones, *Los Paisanos*, p. 119.

13. Chávez, ibid., p. xii.

14. Jones, *Los Paisanos*, p. 130.

15. See Richard E. Greenleaf, *The Mexican Inquisition of the Sixteenth Century* (Albuquerque, 1969), pp. 2–3; Seymour B. Liebman, *The Jews in New Spain: Faith, Flame and the Inquisition* (Coral Gables, 1970), p. 16.

16. Liebman, *The Jews in New Spain*, p. 17.

17. Martin A. Cohen, "Introduction," *The Jewish Experience in Latin America*, v. 1 (New York, 1971), pp. xxxix–xl.

18. Cited in Liebman, *The Jews in New Spain*, p. 42.

19. Martin A. Cohen, "Some Misconceptions About the Crypto-Jews in Colonial Mexico," *American Jewish Historical Quarterly* 61, no. 4 (1972): 280–81.

20. Paul J. Hauben, *The Spanish Inquisition* (New York, 1969), p. 11.

21. Stanley M. Hordes, "The Inquisition as Economic and Political Agent: The Campaign of the Mexican Holy Office Against the Crypto-Jews in the Mid-Seventeeth Century," *The Americas* 39, no. 1 (July 1982): 24–25.

22. Cohen, "Some Misconceptions," p. 280.

23. Ibid., pp. 289–91.

24. Ibid., pp. 292–93.

25. Liebman, *The Jews in New Spain*, pp. 183–84.

26. H. P. Salomon, review of *The Jews in New Spain, American Jewish Historical Quarterly* 62, no. 2 (December 1972): 191.

27. Liebman, *The Jews in New Spain*, pp. 185–86, 216.

28. Cohen, "Some Misconceptions," p. 286.

29. Liebman, *The Jews in New Spain*, pp. 291, 297.

30. Cohen, "Some Misconceptions," p. 287.

31. Liebman, *The Jews in New Spain*, pp. 149–50.

32. Ibid., pp. 151–82; Greenleaf, *The Mexican Inquisition*, pp. 168–71.

33. Liebman, *The Jews in New Spain*, pp. 291–92.

34. Ibid., p. 294.

35. Jones, *Los Paisanos*, p. 33.

36. Liebman, *The Jews in New Spain*, pp. 80–81.

37. George P. Hammond, "Don Juan de Oñate and the Founding of New Mexico," *NMHR* 1, no.1 (January 1926): 51–52.

38. France V. Scholes, "Troublous Times in New Mexico, 1659–1670," *NMHR* 12, no.4 (October 1937): 429–45.

39. Ibid., pp. 447–48.

40. Scholes, "Troublous Times," *NMHR* 15, no.4 (October 1940): 410, 412–13.

41. Scholes, "Troublous Times," *NMHR* 16, no.3 (July 1941): 326.

42. Richard E. Greenleaf, "The Inquisition in Eighteenth-Century New Mexico," *NMHR* 60, no.1 (January 1985): 57.

43. Chávez, *Origins*, p. 35. Present-day descendants of crypto-Jews still consider López de Mendizabal a Marrano. See David S. Nidel, "Modern Descendants of Conversos in New Mexico," *Western States Jewish Historical Quarterly* 16, no.3 (April 1984): 257.

44. Chávez, ibid., pp. 35–37.

45. Liebman, *The Jews in New Spain*, p. 297; Cohen, "Some Misconceptions," p. 287.

46. Interview with Fay F. Blake, Albuquerque, 1987.

47. Tomas Atencio and Stanley M. Hordes, "The Sephardic Legacy in New Mexico: A Prospectus," Albuquerque, 1987, p. 9.

48. Ibid., p. 11.

49. See Chapter 6, pp. 194–96.

50. Fay F. Blake, "Signs of Secret Judaism in New Mexico," Albuquerque, unpublished manuscript in her possession, p. 2.

51. Nidel, "Modern Descendants," pp. 261–62.

52. Blake, "Secret Judaism," pp. 4–5.

53. Ibid., p. 7.

54. Nidel, "Modern Descendants," pp. 255, 259.

55. This was related to the author by the individual concerned.

56. Nidel, "Modern Descendants," p. 250.

57. Ibid., pp. 252, 254.

58. Richard G. Santos, "Chicanos of Jewish Descent in Texas," *Western States Jewish Historical Quarterly* 15, no.4 (July 1983): 329–30, 333. See also Carlos Montalvo Larralde, "Chicano Jews in South Texas," Ph. D. diss., UCLA, 1978.

59. *Albuquerque Journal*, July 27, 1986, Section C, p. 1.

60. Atencio and Hordes, "The Sephardic Legacy in New Mexico," p. 22.

61. Mary Austin, "Social Survey of Taos County, New Mexico," 1919, p. 9. Microfilm. Special Collections, Zimmerman Library, University of New Mexico. This item is reproduced by permission of The Huntington Library, San Marino, California. AU543.

62. Victor Valle, "The Exodus of New Mexico's 'Hidden Jews,'" *Los Angeles Times*, Part VI, July 15, 1988, p. 34, citing National Public Radio broadcast, "Search for the Buried Past: the Hidden Jews of New Mexico."

63. Fray Angélico Chávez, *My Penitente Land: Reflections on Spanish New Mexico* (Albuquerque, 1966), p. 35.

CHAPTER 2

1. John Rowzee Peyton, *A Virginian In New Mexico*. Time: 1773 (Santa Fe, 1967), p. 21. The editor of Peyton's letters has his doubts about their truthfulness. F. W. Hodge, "A Virginian in New Mexico in 1773–1774," *NMHR* 4, no.3 (July 1929): 239, 254–55.

2. Fray Angélico Chávez, "New Names in New Mexico, 1820–1850," *El Palacio* 64, no.9–10 (September, October 1957): 315.

3. Fray Angélico Chávez, "New Names"—conclusion, *El Palacio* 64, no.11–12 (November–December 1957): 373.

4. *New York Times*, December 24, 1880, p. 2. Some secondary accounts describe Speyers's death as a suicide, a result of his financial reverses on Black Friday in 1869. Such a conclusion seems unlikely considering that his death took place eleven years later as a result of cancer.

5. James Josiah Webb, *Adventures in the Santa Fe Trade 1844–1847*, Ralph P. Bieber, ed. (Glendale, Calif., 1931), p. 54. Richard Salazar, of the New Mexico State Archives, notes that the earliest reference to Speyers is his manifesto of November 8, 1843. Fur Traders-Extranjeros, #9, New Mexico State Records Center and Archives.

6. A. Wislizenus, M.D., *Memoir of a Tour to Northern Mexico* (Washington, 1848), p. 5[26].

7. The editor of Webb's memoirs described Speyers as "a Prussian Jew." That description became fixed in the secondary literature. Webb, *Adventures*, pp. 29, 189, 262.

8. Wislizenus, *Memoir*, p. 5[26].

9. *New York Times*, December 24, 1880, p.2.

10. In a conversation between the author and Dr. Jacob R. Marcus in 1983, the latter was certain that Speyers was a Jew and noted that Jews in New York who converted frequently did so at St. Marks. William J. Parish muses about but does not establish a documentary connection between Speyers and the similarly named banking house of Frankfort, which had a branch in New York. "The German Jew and the Commercial Revolution in Territorial New Mexico 1850–1900," *NMHR* 35, no.1 (January 1960): 3. This New York Spier (the spelling varies) is classed by Alex D. Goode (Cimonce, pseud.) among a series of important Jewish families "who did not wish to be known as Jews." "A History of Jewish Economic Life from 1830 to 1860 in the United States," Hebrew Union College, Cincinnati, 1933, p.37. See also the ambiguity expressed about Speyers's Jewishness in Samuel Walker McCall, "Their Eminent Part," *For the Honor of the Nation* (New York, 1939), pp. 163–67.

11. Parish, "German Jew," p. 3.

12. Webb, *Adventures*, p. 1.

13. Interviews with Leitensdorfer's father, John Eugene Leitensdorfer, a well-known figure in Missouri, indicate that he was born in the Tyrol, was "sent to college, for the purpose of being educated in the Romish church," left school, and later, in the Near East, "made a formal renunciation of christianity" in favor of Islam and "circumcised himself in the presence of the faithful" to show his good faith. He is described as one who "can utter the Hebrew words of worship almost exactly like a rabbi," Latin prayers "after the manner and in the tone of the capuchins," and "pronounce the religious sentences of the musselman in Arabic with the earnestness of a mufti." John Francis McDermott, "The Remarkable Life and Adventures of John Eugene Leitensdorfer," *Bulletin of the Missouri Historical Society* 15 (January 1959): 106–11.

14. Lehman Spiegelberg, "Commerce of Santa Fe," 1884, p. 1, Histories, AJA, Cincinnati.

15. George A. Spiegelberg, a grandson of Solomon Jacob, argued for the year 1841. See Parish, "German Jew," p. 143.

16. Robert E. Levinson, "American Jews in the West," *Western Historical Quarterly* 5, no. 3 (July 1974): 285–86.

17. Nathan Glazer, "Social Characteristics of American Jews, 1654–1954," *AJYB* 56 (1955): 9. The census takers were too hasty in their exclusion of Oklahoma. Jews had settled there in the early seventies and had engaged in trade since the later sixties. See Henry J. Tobias, *The Jews in Oklahoma* (Norman, 1980), p. 12.

18. Harry S. Linfield, *The Jews in the United States, 1927: A Study of Their Number and Distribution* (New York, 1929), pp. 89–90.

19. Abraham J. Karp, "What's American About American Jewish History: The Religious Scene," *American Jewish Historical Quarterly* 52, no. 4 (June 1963): 289–90.

20. Levinson, "American Jews," p. 285; Harold I. Sharfman, *Jews on the Frontier*, foreword by Ray Allen Billington (Chicago, 1977), p. x; Max J. Kohler, "Some Jewish Factors in the Settlement of the West," *Publications of the American Jewish Historical Society* 16 (1907): 23.

21. Rudolf Glanz, "The Immigration of German Jews Up to 1880," *YIVO Annual of Jewish Social Science* 2–3 (New York, 1947/ 1948): 85; Eric E. Hirshler, "Jews from Germany in the United States," *Jews From Germany in the United States*, Eric E. Hirshler, ed. (New York, 1955), pp. 34–35.

22. Selma Stern-Taeubler, "The Motivation of the German-Jewish Emigration to America in the Post-Mendelssohnian Era," *Essays in American Jewish History* (American Jewish Archives, 1958), pp. 251–52.

23. Ibid., p. 253.

24. Ibid., pp. 255–57.

25. U.S. Congress, Senate. Reports of the Immigration Commission, *Emigration Conditions in Europe* v. 12, pp. 6–11. 61st Congress, 3rd Session, Senate Document 748 (Washington, 1911).

26. Glanz, "Immigration of German Jews," p. 85; Linfield, *Jews, 1927*, p. 66.

27. Glanz, ibid.; Marcus Lee Hansen, *The Atlantic Migration 1607–1860* (Cambridge, Mass., 1941), p. 140.

28. H. S. Linfield, *Statistics of Jews and Jewish Organizations: Historical Review of Ten Censuses 1850–1937* (New York, 1939), pp. 10–12.

29. Hirshler, "Jews from Germany," p. 38. See also Rudolf Glanz, "Notes on Early Jewish Peddling in America," *Jewish Social Studies* 7, no.2 (April 1945): 127.

30. Adolf E. Schroeder, "The Survival of German Traditions in Missouri," Gerhard K. Friesen and Walter Schatzberg, eds., *The German Contribution to the Building of the Americas* (Hanover, N.H., 1977), pp. 291–92.

31. Ibid., p. 298.

32. *The Seventh Census of the United States: 1850* (Washington, 1853), p. 996; Secretary of the Interior, *Population of the United States in 1860; The Eighth Census* (Washington, 1864), p. xxiv. My calculation comes from a comparison of the total German immigration against the total American population and the German immigration to New Mexico against the total population of the territory. See also Richard R. Greer, "Origins of the Foreign-Born Population of New Mexico During the Territorial Period," *NMHR* 17, no.4 (October 1942): 282.

33. *The Seventh Census of the United States: 1850,* p. xxxvi; Greer, ibid., pp. 282–83.

34. Floyd S. Fierman, "Merchant-Bankers of Early Santa Fe, 1844–1893," *Southwestern Studies* 1 (El Paso, 1964), p. 11.

35. Floyd S. Fierman, "The Staabs of Santa Fe: Pioneer Merchants in New Mexico Territory," *Rio Grande History* 13 (Las Cruces, 1983): 2, 6.

36. Freudenthal Family Papers, Family Correspondence, July 11, 1869. Rio Grande Historical Collection, New Mexico State University Library, Las Cruces.

37. Glanz, "Immigration of German Jews," p. 92.

38. Isaac M. Wise, *Reminiscences,* trans. and ed., David Philipson (Cincinnati, 1945), 2nd ed., p. 38.

39. Lewis E. Atherton, *The Frontier Merchant in Mid-America* (Columbia, Mo., 1971), pp. 45–47.

40. Parish, "German Jew," p. 5.

41. Max L. Moorhead, *New Mexico's Royal Road* (Norman, 1958), pp. 49–51.

42. Ibid., pp. 58–59.

43. Ibid., pp. 62–63.

44. Ibid., p. 75.

45. Ibid., pp. 65–66.

46. Fierman, "Merchant-Bankers," pp. 4–5.

47. Howard R. Lamar, *The Far Southwest 1846–1912: A Territorial History* (New York, 1970), pp. 66–67, 70–71, 107.

48. Fierman, "Merchant-Bankers," pp. 11–12.

49. Parish, "German Jew," pp. 10–11.

50. Robert W. Frazer, "Purveyors of Flour to the Army: Department of New Mexico, 1849–1861," *NMHR* 47, no. 3 (July 1972): 213.

51. Ibid., pp. 225–26.

52. Ibid., p. 227.

53. Parish, "German Jew," pp. 2, 9.

54. Ibid., p. 4.

55. Charles F. Coan, *History of New Mexico* (Chicago, 1925), v. 1, p. 360.

56. Waddy Thompson, *Recollections of Mexico* (New York, 1846), pp. 229–30; Moorhead, *Royal Road*, p. 82.

57. U.S. Senate, 62d Congress, 2d Session, *Occupation of Mexican Territory*, Document No. 896 (Washington, 1912), p. 70.

58. Blaine P. Lamb, "Fifty-Four Years on the Southwest Frontier: Nathan Benjamin Appel in New Mexico, Arizona, and Southern California," *Western States Jewish Historical Quarterly* 16, no. 2 (January 1984): 125.

59. Ibid., pp. 125–26.

60. Office of Indian Affairs, *The Official Correspondence of James S. Calhoun*, Annie H. Abel, ed. (Washington, 1915), p. 264.

61. The National Archives, *Population Schedules of the Eighth Census of the United States, 1860: New Mexico*, v. 2 (Washington, 1967), roll 714, p. 37. Microfilm.

62. Ibid., p. 31

63. Ibid., v. 1, p. 6.

64. Ibid., p. 46.

65. John C. Rives, *Appendix to the Congressional Globe for the First Session, Thirty-Second Congress*. New Series, v. 25 (Washington, 1852), p. 327.

66. Territory of New Mexico vs. James H. Carelton, New Mexico State Records Center and Archives, Santa Fe.

67. *Correspondence of Calhoun*, p. 381.

68. Ibid., pp. 198–99.

69. John M. Kingsbury Correspondence, 1858–1860, February 6, 1859, DeGolyer Library and Fikes Hall of Special Collections, South-

ern Methodist University. The records of county licenses show that Selig Weinheim obtained licenses as a merchant between 1855 and 1860 in Santa Fe County. He does not appear in the 1860 census. TANM, County Licenses, 1851–95, Santa Fe County, roll 51, frs. 628, 631, 638, 641, 644, 647.

70. Kingsbury Correspondence, ibid., March 5, 1859.

71. Franz Huning, *Trader on the Santa Fe Trail: Memoirs of Franz Huning* (Albuquerque, 1973), p. 58.

72. Bernalillo County District Court Records, Civil Case #350, New Mexico State Records Center and Archives, Santa Fe.

73. The National Archives, *Population Schedules of the Seventh Census of the United States,* 1850: New Mexico (Washington, 1963), roll 468, pp. 345–46. Microfilm.

74. Ibid., p. 347.

75. Ibid., pp. 339–74.

76. Ibid.

77. Parish, using an unspecified time period, estimated that German Jews "constituted, perhaps, more than three-fourths of the German immigrants of the Territory. . . ." *The Charles Ilfeld Company* (Cambridge, Mass., 1961), p. 7. Given the 1850 census figure of 229 German-born persons, that would bring the number of Jews in New Mexico to about 170. In the 1860 census, German-born residents of New Mexico totalled 569 (excluding Poland), which would have brought the Jewish population to roughly 425. Since Parish uses only nine merchants for his table in 1849 and twenty-five in 1859, there is a twenty-fold difference between his figures for merchants and his assumption of totals. Parish, "German Jew," p. 15. Neither occupational distribution nor family size could account for such a discrepancy. The smaller numbers used by Parish himself and those of the present study appear far more realistic.

78. Parish, "German Jew," p. 15.

79. Ibid.

80. TANM, County Licenses, rolls 49–52, 1851–95.

81. *The Occident and American Jewish Advocate* (Philadelphia) 6 (October 1848): 317; 13, no. 156 (March 1856): 2.

82. *The American Israelite* 28, no. 13 (September 23, 1881): 10.

83. Fierman, "Merchant-Bankers," pp. 12–14.

84. *The American Israelite* (September 23, 1881): 10.

85. See, for instance, the negative attitude expressed by Henry Lesinsky, who arrived in New Mexico in 1859, *Letters Written by Henry Lesinsky to His Son* (New York, 1924), pp. 21–22, 45.

86. "Copie Book Emanuel Rosenwald," Emanuel Rosenwald Collection no. 220, June 20, 1860, Special Collections, Zimmerman Library, University of New Mexico.

87. Kingsbury, February 6, 1859, February 20, 1859, DeGolyer Library and Fikes Hall of Special Collections, Southern Methodist University.

88. Ibid., February 6, 1859.

89. Ralph P. Bieber, "The Papers of James J. Webb, Santa Fe Merchant, 1844–1861," *Washington University Studies* 11 (1923–24): 184, 301.

90. Ibid., pp. 287, 292, 294.

91. Ibid., p. 299.

92. An unidentified business ledger notes a bill for Goldstein and Spiegelberg in 1848. They may have been partners briefly. Economic Records, "Unidentified Business Ledger, 1848–49." New Mexico State Records Center and Archives, Santa Fe.

93. Floyd S. Fierman, "The Frontier Career of Charles Clever," *El Palacio* 85, no. 4 (Winter 1979–80): 3.

94. Howard R. Lamar, "Political Patterns in New Mexico and Utah Territories 1850–1900," *Utah Historical Quarterly* 28, no. 4 (October 1960): 366.

95. Fierman, "Merchant-Bankers," p. 11.

96. Fierman, "Clever," pp. 3–4.

97. Executive Record Book no. 1, New Mexico State Records Center and Archives, Santa Fe.

98. Lamar, *The Far Southwest*, p. 88.

99. Davis Yancey Thomas, *A History of Military Government in Newly Acquired Territory of the United States* (New York, 1904), pp. 115–16.

100. Manuel Alvarez Papers, New Mexico State Records Center and Archives, Santa Fe.

101. Jacqueline D. Meketa, *Louis Felsenthal: Citizen-Soldier of Territorial New Mexico* (Albuquerque, 1982), p. 17.

102. The National Archives, *State Department Territorial Papers*, *New Mexico*, July 16, 1851 (Washington, 1954), roll 1, p. 116. Microfilm.

103. LaMoine "Red" Langston, *A History of Masonry in New Mexico* (Roswell, n.d., [1977?]), p. 137.

104. James F. Meline, *Two Thousand Miles on Horseback, Santa Fe and Back* (Albuquerque, 1966), p. 192.

105. Flora Spiegelberg, Collection no.18, Special Collections, Zimmerman Library, University of New Mexico.

106. Floyd S. Fierman, *Guts and Ruts* (New York, 1985), p. 24.

107. Lansing B. Bloom, ed., "Historical Society Minutes, 1859–1863," *NMHR* 18, no.3 (July 1943): 262, 277, 287.

108. Ibid., pp. 255–56.

109. Ibid., p. 247.

110. Ibid.

111. Ibid., p. 257.

112. Burt Noggle, "Anglo Observers of the Southwest Borderlands, 1825–1890: The Rise of a Concept," *Arizona and the West* 1, no.2 (Summer 1959): 109, 113, 122–23.

113. William J. Parish, "German Jew" (concluded), *NMHR* 35, no.2 (April 1960): 131.

CHAPTER 3

1. Martin H. Hall, *Sibley's New Mexican Campaign* (Austin, 1960), p. 32.

2. Ibid., pp. 6–13, 53, 122–23.

3. Ibid., pp. 54–55.

4. Lesinsky, *Letters Written by Henry Lesinsky*, pp. 43–44.

5. Hall, *Sibley's Campaign*, p. 166.

6. Ibid.; Ray C. Colton, *The Civil War in the Western Territories* (Norman, 1959), p. 40.

7. Fierman, "Merchant-Bankers," p. 24.

8. Flora Spiegelberg, "General Sibley in Santa Fe, New Mexico," Collection no.18, Special Collections, Zimmerman Library, University of New Mexico; Colton, *Civil War*, p. 40.

9. Flora Spiegelberg, ibid.

10. N. M. State Records Center, *TANM*, roll 25, folders 78–79, 133–134, 172–173.

11. Amberg and Elsberg, "Bill on Confederacy," New Mexico State Records Center and Archives, Santa Fe.

12. Flora Spiegelberg, "General Sibley"; H. H. Bancroft found

the claims unpaid. *History of Arizona and New Mexico* (San Francisco, 1889), p. 719.

13. Meketa, *Louis Felsenthal*, pp. 27–28.

14. The figures for 1870 and 1880 are based on the *Population Schedules* of the ninth and tenth censuses of 1870 and 1880 respectively.

15. *AJYB*, 1914–1915, v.16, p. 370.

16. See Sidney Jocknick, *Early Days on the Western Slope of Colorado* (Denver, 1913), p. 236; David Lavender, *The Big Divide* (New York, 1948), pp. 94, 144.

17. Linfield, *Jews in the United States, 1927*, pp. 89–90.

18. Meline, *Two Thousand Miles on Horseback*, pp. 168–69.

19. William A. Bell, *New Tracks in North America* (New York, 1870), p. 151.

20. Lansing B. Bloom, ed., "Bourke on the Southwest, VII," *NMHR* 10, no.4 (October 1935): 303.

21. The paragraphs on birthplace, marriage, and children are based on the *Population Schedules* of 1870 and 1880.

22. *The Israelite* 19, no.5 (August 2, 1872): 5.

23. Jewish Circumcision Record, p. 10, DeGolyer Library and Fikes Hall of Special Collections, Southern Methodist University. An article by Marjorie Hornbein, "Dr. John Elsner, A Colorado Pioneer," in the *Western States Jewish Historical Quarterly* 13, no.4 (July 1981): 296 cites a copy of the document cited by HJT.

24. *Die Deborah* (October 12, 1877): 2.

25. *Die Deborah* (September 14, 1877): 2.

26. *The American Israelite* (November 6, 1874): 6.

27. Ibid.

28. *Die Deborah* (September 14, 1877): 2.

29. *Die Deborah* (November 9, 1877): 2.

30. Terry J. Lehmann, "Santa Fe and Albuquerque 1870–1890: Contrast and Conflict in the Development of Two Southwestern Towns," Ph. D. diss., Indiana University, 1974, p. 50.

31. *Die Deborah* (October 12, 1877): 2.

32. Ibid.

33. Floyd S. Fierman, "Nathan Bibo's Reminiscences of Early New Mexico," *El Palacio* 69, no.1 (Spring 1962): 49.

34. See Paul Horgan, *The Centuries of Santa Fe* (New York, 1956), pp. 227–75. The chapter entitled "The German Bride, 1870"

coincides in most instances with Flora Spiegelberg's notes in the Flora Spiegelberg Collection in the Special Collections at the University of New Mexico and at the AJA, Cincinnati. Horgan does not identify her in his work and introduces some curious liberties. The date of her arrival was 1875, not 1870. Although educated in Europe, she was an American. Moreover an artist's sketch of what one is supposed to assume is the Spiegelberg house is clearly the Staab mansion. Michael L. Lawson's "Flora Langermann Spiegelberg: Grand Lady of Santa Fe," *Western States Jewish Historical Quarterly* 8, no.4 (July 1976): 291–308 is based largely on the same materials.

35. David T. Bailey, "Stratification and Ethnic Differentiation in Santa Fe, 1860 and 1870," Ph.D. diss., University of Texas, Austin, 1975, pp. 103–4.

36. Ibid.

37. The figures on the Jews result from my compilations based on the *Population Schedules* of 1860 and 1870 compared with Bailey's results.

38. Bailey, "Stratification," p. 104.

39. Ibid.

40. Ibid., p. 105.

41. Ibid.

42. The key to the rating system defined Aa as "very large means, and the highest grade of credit;" AaA as "large means, and the highest grade of credit;" A as "a house fully established, with large capital, and of undoubted business character, ability and credit." *Bradstreet's Commercial Reports* 30 (January 6, 1872, New York).

43. Lehmann, "Santa Fe and Albuquerque," pp. 22–23.

44. The National Archives, Records of the Office of the Comptroller of the Currency, Record Gp. 101, "Selected Documents Relating to the Second National Bank of New Mexico, charter No. 2024." Microfilm (Washington, 1961).

45. Lehmann, "Santa Fe and Albuquerque," p. 25.

46. Cited in letter from Colonel Dudley to Edw. P. Smith, Commissioner of Indian Affairs, January 26, 1874. Bureau of Indian Affairs, Letters and Documents Relating to the Bibo and Spiegelberg Families, Record Gp. 75, AJA, Cincinnati.

47. Ralph E. Twitchell, *Leading Facts of New Mexican History* (Cedar Rapids, Iowa, 1917), v.5, pp. 258–59.

48. Parish, *Charles Ilfeld*, p. 8.

49. Ibid., p. 35.

50. Ralph E. Twitchell, *Old Santa Fe: The Story of New Mexico's Ancient Capital* (Chicago, 1925), pp. 479–80.

51. Floyd S. Fierman, "The Staabs of Santa Fe: Pioneer Merchants in New Mexico Territory," *Rio Grande History* 13 (1983): 14.

52. Ibid.

53. Roman L. Latimer, "Spiegelberg Brothers: Bankers and Merchants to New Mexico Territory," *Numismatic Scrapbook Magazine* 38, no. 432 (February 1972): 121. Pictures of the scrip are included in the article.

54. Correspondence between William J. Parish and Paul A. F. Walter, then president of the First National Bank of Santa Fe, concurred that the practice existed, though it declined after banks became established in New Mexico. William J. Parish Papers, Archive no. 276, Box IV, Folder 1, July 8, 1953, July 22, 1953, Special Collections, Zimmerman Library, University of New Mexico.

55. Errett Van Cleave, "Credit on the Santa Fe Trail: Business Pioneering in Pueblo Regions," *Credit and Financial Management* 41 (October 1939): 17.

56. Twitchell, *New Mexican History*, v. 5, p. 258.

57. The other seven were Ceran St. Vrain, John Greiner, Antonio Jose Otero, Charles P. Clever, Ambrosio Armijo, Jose Manuel Gallegos, and Felipe Delgado. Ibid.

58. George B. Anderson, *History of New Mexico*, v. 1 (Los Angeles, 1907), p. 412.

59. Other stockholders included Felipe Chaves, Belen; Telesfor Jaramillo, Los Lunas; Ambrosio Armijo, Albuquerque; and Jose Manuel Gallegos, Charles P. Clever, and Adolph Guttmann of Santa Fe. See Latimer, "Spiegelberg Brothers," p. 120. The Spiegelberg bank stockholders included two persons who had participated in the 1863 attempt to create a bank. See note 57.

60. Fierman, "Merchant-Bankers," p. 32.

61. Elkins to Northrup and Chick, April 29, 1872. First National Bank of Santa Fe, Letter Books, v. 3, pp. 434–35, Archive no. 177, Special Collections, Zimmerman Library, University of New Mexico.

62. William J. Parish Papers. Transcription of organization papers of the Second National Bank, Box IV, Notebook 2, Archive no. 276, Special Collections, Zimmerman Library, University of New Mexico.

63. Twitchell, *New Mexican History*, v.5, p. 234; Anderson, *History of New Mexico*, v.1, p. 415.

64. Lamar, *Far Southwest*, p. 139.

65. See Chapter 3, pp. 62–63.

66. Victor Westphall, *Thomas Benton Catron and His Era* (Tucson, 1973), p. 72.

67. Fierman, *Guts and Ruts*, pp. 10–11.

68. Darlis A. Miller, *The California Column in New Mexico* (Albuquerque, 1982), pp. 66–67.

69. Parish, *Charles Ilfeld*, pp. 84–86.

70. Westphall, *Catron*, p. 34.

71. Miller, *California Column*, pp. 51–52; Lesinsky, *Letters Written by Henry Lesinsky*, pp. 48–54.

72. Miller, ibid., p. 131.

73. *Daily New Mexican*, March 22, 1872, p. 4.

74. Fierman, *Guts and Ruts*, p. 11.

75. Sheldon H. Dike, "The Territorial Post Offices of New Mexico," *NMHR* 34, no.1 (January 1959): n. p.; (continued) 34, no. 3 (July 1959): n. p.

76. Robert W. Frazer, *Forts of the West* (Norman, 1965), pp. xiv–xv.

77. Edward H. Spicer, *A Short History of the Indians of the United States* (New York, 1969), p. 96.

78. Ibid., pp. 196–97.

79. Frank McNitt, *The Indian Traders* (Norman, 1962), pp. 46–47.

80. Ibid., p. 47.

81. Ibid., p. 46.

82. Ibid., p. 109.

83. Ibid., p. 110. McNitt ranks the Seligmans and Charles Ilfeld lower.

84. See *Annual Reports of the Commissioner of Indian Affairs to the Secretary of the Interior* for the years 1874–1879, Washington.

85. *Fifth Annual Report of the Board of Indian Commissioners to the President of the United States, 1873* (Washington, 1874), pp. 16, 18.

86. *Annual Report of the Commissioner of Indian Affairs to the Secretary of the Interior for the Year 1876* (Washington, 1876), pp. 156–57, 162–63. The volume of beef cattle sales and the price relate to beef on the hoof and the price was to be figured net, about 50 percent of the gross weight being taken as tare.

87. Lynn I. Perrigo, *Gateway to Glorieta: A History of Las Vegas, New Mexico* (Boulder, Colo., 1982), p. 3.

88. F. Stanley, *Fort Union (New Mexico)* (n. p., 1953), p. 73.

89. Coan, *History of New Mexico*, v.1, p. 399.

90. R. H. McKay, *Little Pills* (Pittsburg, Kan., 1918), p. 20.

91. *TANM*, rolls 49–52. County Licenses.

92. Fierman, *Guts and Ruts*, pp. 89–96.

93. Parish, *Charles Ilfeld*, pp. 7–21.

94. Lee Scott Theisen, ed., "Frank W. Angel's Notes on New Mexico Territory, 1878," *Arizona and the West* 18, no.4 (Winter 1976): 365–66.

95. See Chapter 3, p. 67.

96. Parish, *Charles Ilfeld*, p. 23.

97. New Mexico Supreme Court Records, 1872, no.7, New Mexico State Records Center and Archives, Santa Fe; United States Bankruptcy Proceedings, 1872, New Mexico State Records Center and Archives, Santa Fe.

98. Spiegelberg Bros., "Bad Accounts, 1881," Jewish Merchants, New Mexico State Records Center and Archives, Santa Fe.

99. R. G. Dun and Co., *Western Territory*, v.1, p. 175. Baker Library, Harvard Graduate School of Business. Cited with permission of Dun and Bradstreet.

100. *TANM*, roll 51, County Licenses.

101. "Charles Ilfeld Autobiography," William C. Ilfeld Collection, p. 1, New Mexico State Records Center and Archives, Santa Fe.

102. Rosenwald Family Collection, "Las Vegas, N. M., May 12, 1910," dictated by Emanuel Rosenwald, pp. 2–6, AJA, Cincinnati.

103. Rosenwald Family Collection, "Contracts," AJA, Cincinnati.

104. Fierman, "Jewish Pioneering," pp. 54–71.

105. Floyd S. Fierman, "Nathan Bibo's Reminiscences of Early New Mexico," *El Palacio* 68, no.4 (Winter 1961): 235–36.

106. Ibid., pp. 249–50.

107. Ibid., pp. 250–52.

108. Floyd S. Fierman, "Nathan Bibo's Reminiscences of Early New Mexico, *El Palacio* 69, no.1 (Spring 1962): 49.

109. Ibid.

110. Fierman, "Nathan Bibo's Reminiscences," *El Palacio* 68, no.4:234.

111. Fierman, "Nathan Bibo's Reminiscences," *El Palacio* 69, no.1:55.

112. Floyd S. Fierman, "The Triangle and the Tetragrammaton: A Note on the Cathedral at Santa Fe," *NMHR* 37, no.4 (October 1962): 313–14; Flora Spiegelberg, "Tribute to Archbishop Lamy of New Mexico," *El Palacio* 36, no.3–4 (January 1934): 23–24.

113. Lawson, "Flora Spiegelberg," p. 298.

114. Fanny Goldstein, "Sixty years Ago on the Santa Fe Trail," *The Jewish Advocate* (November 22, 1935).

115. Fierman, "Triangle," p. 318.

116. Ibid., pp. 312–13.

117. Lawson, "Flora Spiegelberg," p. 299.

118. Paul Horgan, *Lamy of Santa Fe: His Life and Times* (New York, 1975), p. 391.

119. Letter to author from Ted Schuyler, Los Lunas, New Mexico, December 20, 1983.

120. William A. Keleher, *The Fabulous Frontier* (Santa Fe, 1945), pp. 132–33. Keleher cites his source in this later printing, p. 155, 1982. Dr. Edward Staab, Abraham's son, noted that loans were made but denied that such a negotiation took place. Fierman, "Triangle," p. 312. Staab's granddaughter, Elizabeth Nordhaus Minces, notes that Staab was posthumously honored in 1967 for his role in the building of the cathedral at the Annual Conference of Christians and Jews. She noted her grandfather's loans and destruction of the notes due and states that the inscription over the arch was put up out of gratitude by the archbishop. "The Family: Early Days in New Mexico," pp. 9–10, Albuquerque, New Mexico, August 1980. In possession of John Feldman, Albuquerque.

121. Fierman, "Triangle," pp. 313–14.

122. Sister Blandina Segale, *At the End of the Santa Fe Trail* (Columbus, Ohio, 1932), pp. 108–9.

123. Ibid., p. 109.

124. Langston, *A History of Masonry in New Mexico*, pp. 174–75.

125. Anderson, *History of New Mexico*, v.1, p. 495.

126. Abraham I. Shinedling (with Milton Taichert), "The Las Vegas, N. M. Congregation (the Montefiore Congregation) and the Jewish Community of Las Vegas, N. M.," pp. 18–19, Histories, AJA, Cincinnati.

127. Louis E. Freudenthal, comp., A Century of Freemasonry at Las Cruces, 1867–1967 (n. p., 1967), pp. 7, 13.

128. Anderson, History of New Mexico, v. 1, p. 496.

129. Rev. Clifton M. Henderson and Jean Woodburn Henderson, comps., "Directory and Maps of the Masonic Cemetery, 1876–1979," p. 4, Special Collections, Zimmerman Library, University of New Mexico.

130. Lehmann, "Santa Fe and Albuquerque," p. 49.

131. Centennial Celebration, Santa Fe, New Mexico, July 4, 1876 (Santa Fe, 1876), pp. 55, 64.

132. National Archives, Interior Department Territorial Papers, New Mexico, 1851–1914 (Washington, 1962), roll 1, August 11, 1877, folders. 73–74.

133. Lehmann, "Santa Fe and Albuquerque," p. 51.

134. Ibid., p. 54.

135. San Miguel District Court Records, Criminal Folder no. 231a, New Mexico State Records Center and Archives, Santa Fe.

136. Ibid., no. 333, August 12, 1870.

137. Ibid., no. 434.

138. See Herbert Hoover, "History of the Republican Party in New Mexico, 1867–1912," Ph.D. diss., University of Oklahoma, 1966, pp. 59–62.

139. Lamar, Far Southwest, p. 147.

140. Ibid., pp. 146–47; Lehmann, "Santa Fe and Albuquerque," p. 45.

141. Fierman, "The Staabs," p. 9.

142. Westphall, Catron, pp. 94–95.

143. Lehmann, "Santa Fe and Albuquerque," p. 45.

144. Ibid., p. 37.

145. Ibid., p. 41.

146. Westphall, Catron, pp. 102–3.

147. Simeon H. Newman, III, "The Santa Fe Ring: A Letter to the New York Sun," Arizona and the West 12, no. 3 (Autumn 1970): 273–74, 285–86.

148. Lamar, Far Southwest, p. 135.

149. Fierman, "The Career of Clever," El Palacio 85, no. 4 (Winter 1979–80): 3–5.

150. Calvin Horn, New Mexico's Troubled Years (Albuquerque, 1963), pp. 118–19.

151. Cited in Fierman, "The Career of Clever," pp. 34–35.

152. State Department Territorial Papers, Roll 3, p. 150.

153. Bureau of Indian Affairs, Letters and Documents Relating to the Bibo and Spiegelberg Families, Record Group 75, December 22, 1873, AJA, Cincinnati.

154. Ibid., May 18, 1870.

155. F. Stanley, *Ciudad Santa Fe, Territorial Days, 1846–1912* (Pampa, Texas, 1965), p. 268.

156. See Chapter 3, note 59.

157. Van Cleave, "Credit," p. 16.

158. See Chapter 3, pp. 78–79.

159. Robert J. Rosenbaum, *Mexicano Resistance in the Southwest* (Austin, 1981), p. 5.

160. Ibid., pp. 10–17.

CHAPTER 4

1. *Interior Department Territorial Papers, New Mexico, 1851–1914* (Washington, 1962), National Archives, roll 1, folder. 394.

2. Ibid., folders 394–95.

3. Ibid., folders 398, 400.

4. U.S. Bureau of the Census, *Fourteenth Census of the United States: 1920, Population*, v.1 (Washington, 1921), p. 20.

5. Ibid.

6. Population Schedules for the tenth and twelfth censuses, New Mexico, 1880, 1900. There may have been as many as 220 in 1880 and 500 in 1900. How much uncertainty there was in estimates can be seen from the information offered by the *American Jewish Year Book* (*AJYB*). The first volume appeared in 1899 and offered the figure of 2,000 for the number of Jews in New Mexico, v.1, p. 284. A year later, the *AJYB* revised its estimate downward to 1,500, v.2, 1900–1901, p. 624. The third volume displayed some frustration, noting that estimates ranged between 500 and 1,500, v.3, 1901–2, p. 143.

7. U.S. Census Office, *Twelfth Census of the United States Taken in the Year 1900, Population*, v.1 (Washington, 1901), pp. 271–74.

8. R. G. Dun, *Mercantile Agency Reference Book 67* (January 1885, New York).

9. Department of the Interior, Census Office, *Compendium of the Tenth Census* (June 1, 1880), Part I, rev. ed., Washington 1885, p. 394;

U.S. Census Office, *Twelfth Census of the United States, Population* v. 1, p. 274.

10. Bernice Ann Rebord, "A Social History of Albuquerque, 1880–1885," M. A. thesis, University of New Mexico, 1947, pp. 55–65, 89–92.

11. Deborah Dash Moore, *B'nai B'rith and the Challenge of Ethnic Leadership* (Albany, 1981), p. 33.

12. Ibid., p. 251.

13. Compiled from B'nai B'rith Lodge No. 336 Registration Book of Membership, 1883–1936, Box No. 2311, AJA, Cincinnati.

14. Ibid.

15. IOBB, Albuquerque Lodge No. 336, Minute Book, 1883–98, p. 7, Box x-81, AJA, Cincinnati.

16. Ibid., p. 133.

17. B'nai B'rith Cemetery Association, Albuquerque, New Mexico, Box 681, AJA, Cincinnati.

18. IOBB, Albuquerque Lodge No. 336, Minute Book, 1883–98, pp. 28, 37, 39.

19. Ibid., pp. 48, 78.

20. Ibid., p. 184.

21. Ibid., p. 63.

22. Ibid., p. 32.

23. Ibid., pp. 48, 51.

24. Ibid., p. 77.

25. Ibid., February 26, 1896, p. 175.

26. Ibid., pp. 282, 285.

27. Ibid., p. 288.

28. Ibid., p. 312.

29. Gunther Rothenberg, comp., *Congregation Albert 1897–1972* (Albuquerque, 1972), p. 18.

30. Congregation Albert, Albuquerque, N.M. Minute Book, 1897–1913, pp. 2–3, AJA, Cincinnati.

31. Ibid.

32. Ibid.

33. *AJYB*, 1900–1901, v.2, p. 234.

34. Cited in *The American Israelite* 31, no.6 (October 17, 1884): 7.

35. Document in possession of Milton Taichert, Las Vegas, New Mexico.

36. *Constitution and By-Laws of Congregation Montefiore*, Las Vegas, New Mexico, 1886. In possession of Milton Taichert, Las Vegas.

37. Milton W. Callon, "Chanukah Comes to Las Vegas," *Denver Westerners Monthly Roundup* 26, no.9–10 (September-October 1970): 303.

38. Congregation Montefiore, Las Vegas, Miscellaneous Records 1880–1964, AJA, Cincinnati.

39. The *AJYB* for 1907–8 cites 1887 as the date of the organization's founding, v.9, p. 258, while v.2 of 1900–1901 uses October 2, 1895, p. 324. The By-Laws are included in the minute ledger of the society in the possession of Milton Taichert, Las Vegas, p. 206.

40. Hebrew Ladies Benevolent Society Minutes, Milton Taichert, Las Vegas.

41. Interview with Milton Taichert, Las Vegas, August 14, 1986.

42. Lehmann, "Santa Fe and Albuquerque," pp. 198–237.

43. L. Spiegelberg, "Commerce of Santa Fe," p. 4, Histories, AJA, Cincinnati.

44. Lawson, "Flora Spiegelberg," p. 305.

45. Fierman, "The Staabs," pp. 21–22.

46. *Santa Fe New Mexican*, January 6, 1913, p. 3.

47. *The American Israelite* 32, no.23 (December 4, 1885): 1.

48. Ibid.

49. *Albuquerque Morning Journal*, February 27, 1884, p.[4].

50. Congregation Montefiore, Las Vegas, Miscellaneous Records 1880–1964, By-Laws, 1886, p. 13, AJA, Cincinnati.

51. Sulzbacher went to Kansas City and served as counsel to the Atchison, Topeka and Santa Fe Railroad. In 1900 he became a justice of the Supreme Court of Puerto Rico and served until 1904. He then became a federal judge in the District Court of the Western District of the Indian Territory. See Oscar Kraines, "Louis Sulzbacher: Justice of the Supreme Court of Puerto Rico, 1900–1904," *Jewish Social Studies* 13, no.2 (April 1951): 127–28.

52. A more detailed analysis of the context of generational change can be found in Henry J. Tobias and Charles E. Woodhouse, "New York Investment Bankers and New Mexico Merchants: Group Formation and Elite Status Among German-Jewish Businessmen," *NMHR* 65, no. 1 (January 1990): 21–48.

53. *Interior Department Territorial Papers, New Mexico, 1851–1914*, roll 1, folder 423; William S. Speer, ed., *The Encyclope-*

dia of the New West (Marshall, Texas, 1881), pp. 36–37.

54. Ibid., roll 1, folder 717.

55. Ibid., roll 2, folder 109.

56. Ibid., roll 1, folder 272; P. A. F. W. [Paul A. F. Walter], "Arthur Seligman," *NMHR* 8, no.4 (October 1933): 306–7.

57. T. B. Catron to Sulzbacher, August 3, 1892, "Letter Books" v.5, pp. 183–84, Catron Collection, Special Collections, Zimmerman Library, University of New Mexico.

58. T. B. Catron to Messrs. Ilfeld Bros., Albuquerque, September 11, 1892, "Letter Books" v.5, p. 338.

59. Herbert H. Lang, "The New Mexico Bureau of Immigration, 1880–1912," *NMHR* 51, no.3 (July 1976): 197.

60. *Interior Department Territorial Papers*, roll 1, folders 348, 833.

61. Lang, "Bureau of Immigration," p. 202.

62. *Interior Department Territorial Papers*, roll 2, folders 21, 59.

63. Ibid., folders 145, 158, 246.

64. Marc Simmons, *Albuquerque* (Albuquerque, 1982), pp. 232–33; Lehmann, "Santa Fe and Albuquerque," pp. 175–76.

65. C. O'Conor Roberts, *Albuquerque City Directory and Business Guide for 1896* (Albuquerque, 1896), p. 73.

66. *Interior Department Territorial Papers*, roll 1, folders 567, 866.

67. Ibid., folder 744.

68. Ibid., folder 723.

69. Ibid., roll 2, folder 9.

70. Ibid., folders 372, 575.

71. Ibid., folder 576.

72. *Santa Fe Weekly Democrat*, January 13, 1881, p. 2.

73. Lamar, *The Far Southwest*, pp. 180–81.

74. N. M. State Records Center, *TANM*, "Edmund G. Ross, 1885–1889, Letters Received," December 22, 1886, roll 101, folder 518.

75. Miller, *California Column*, p. 57; *Interior Department Territorial Papers*, New Mexico, "Articles of Incorporation," roll 1, folder 2.

76. Karen D. Shane, "Edmund G. Ross: Governor of New Mexico, 1885–1889," M. A. thesis, University of New Mexico, 1983, pp. 56–57.

77. Cited in Lehmann, "Santa Fe and Albuquerque," p. 50.

78. Robert W. Larson, *New Mexico Populism: A Study of Radical Protest in a Western Territory* (Boulder, Colo., 1974), p. 108.

79. Ibid., p. 87.

80. Ibid., p. 178.

81. Parish, *Ilfeld*, p. 35.

82. Anderson, *History of New Mexico*, v. 1, p. 435.

83. Parish, *Ilfeld*, pp. 35, 82.

84. The data for these paragraphs are derived from Bradstreet's *Commercial Reports* 30 (January 6, 1872) and 116 (January 1897), New York.

85. *New Mexico Business Directory including El Paso, Texas, 1903–4* (Denver, 1903).

86. Jim F. Heath, "A Study of the Influence of the Atchison, Topeka, and Santa Fe Railroad Upon the Economy of New Mexico 1878 to 1900," M. A. thesis, University of New Mexico, 1955, p. 65.

87. *The Mercantile Agency Reference Book* 67 (January 1885), R. G. Dun and Co. Students of the credit agencies have commented on the differing standards of reliability they applied to Jews and some other hyphenate Americans. One scholar notes that "This presumption of dishonesty, mismanagement, and likely failure, and a creditor's need for extreme vigilance often followed the Irish or Jewish shopkeeper even after he attained some permanence in an economy with a high rate of small business attrition." See David Gerber, "Ethnics, Enterprise, and Middle Class Formation: Using the D & B Collection for Research in Ethnic History," *Immigration History Newsletter* 12, no. 1 (May 1980): 3.

88. *Bradstreet's Commercial Reports* 116 (January 1897), New York.

89. Ibid.

90. Parish, *Ilfeld*, p. 110.

91. Ibid., p. 111.

92. Cited in Heath, "AT&SF," p. 73.

93. Ibid., pp. 100–101.

94. Parish, *Ilfeld*, p. 172.

95. Ibid., pp. 172–73.

96. Linda Tigges, "Land Use Patterns in Santa Fe, 1885–86," p. 19, unpublished article courtesy of the author.

97. Ibid.

98. Ibid., p. 3.

99. V. H. Whitlock (Ol' Waddy), *Cowboy Life on the Llano Estacada* (Norman, 1970), p. 182.

100. James D. Shinkle, *Reminiscences of Roswell Pioneers* (Roswell, N.M., 1966), pp. 200–201.

101. See Chapter 4, pp. 127–28.

102. "Roswell was 'Pearl of the Pecos'—1880," *Old Timers' Review* 4, no.1 (1982): 7.

103. James D. Shinkle, *Fifty Years of Roswell History—1867–1917* (Roswell, N.M., 1964), p. 171.

104. Ibid., p. 184.

105. Ibid., pp. 187–88.

106. Louis Prager, "My Memories of Roswell, 1903–1978," tape, Chaves County Historical Museum, Roswell, N.M.

107. Shinkle, *Fifty Years of Roswell*, pp. 124–25.

108. *AJYB*, 1907–8, v.9, p. 258.

109. Interview with Louis M. Prager, Roswell, N.M., August 8, 1986.

110. *AJYB*, 1907–8, v.9, p. 258.

111. Mrs. Harry Thompson, et al., *Clayton, the Friendly Town in Union County, New Mexico* (Denver, 1962), pp. 40–45.

112. Carl Floersheim, "Biography of Solomon Floersheim," Biographies file, 1959, AJA, Cincinnati.

113. Emma Vorenberg [Mrs. Joseph] Wertheim, "Memoirs, 1861–1965," pp. 1–2, Biography file, AJA, Cincinnati.

114. Ibid., p. 2.

115. Ibid., pp. 2–4.

116. Sandra Lea Rollins, "Jewish Indian Chief," *Western States Jewish Historical Quarterly* 1, no.4 (July 1969): 156–60.

117. Ibid., p. 160. See also Floyd S. Fierman, *The Impact of the Frontier on a Jewish Family: The Bibos* (El Paso, 1961), pp. 14–16.

118. Rollins, ibid., pp. 161–62; Fierman, ibid., pp. 15–16.

119. Fierman, ibid., pp. 17–18.

120. Ibid., p. 18.

121. Interview of Leroy Bibo and Mrs. Max Weiss, children of Solomon Bibo, February 21, 1969, conducted by Dr. N. B. Stern, AJA, Cincinnati.

122. Conrad K. Naegle, "The History of Silver City, New Mexico,

1870–1886," M.A. thesis, University of New Mexico, 1943, pp. 2–20.

123. Lesinsky, *Letters Written by Henry Lesinsky*, pp. 47–49; Fierman, "Jewish Pioneering in the Southwest," pp. 60–61.

124. Silver City Public Library, Biographical folder, David Abraham. Silver City, N.M.

125. Silver City Public Library, Biographical folder, I. N. Cohen, Silver City, N.M.

126. Silver City Public Library, Biographical folder, Max Schutz, Silver City, N.M.

127. Twitchell, *New Mexican History*, v. 3, p. 260.

CHAPTER 5

1. Marc Simmons, *New Mexico: A History* (New York, 1977), p. 163.

2. Ibid., pp. 163–64.

3. *AJYB*, 1899–1900, v 1, p 284; *AJYB*, 1941–42, v.43, p. 657.

4. *AJYB*, 1939–40, v.41, p. 186.

5. Nathan Glazer, "Social Characteristics of American Jews," *AJYB*, 1955, v.56, p. 24.

6. *AJYB*, 1914–15, v.16, p. 346.

7. Bureau of the Census, *Sixteenth Census of the United States, 1940: Mother Tongue* (Washington, 1943), p. 21.

8. U.S. Congress, Senate, Reports of the Immigration Commission, *Statistical Review of Immigration*, v.20, p. 326. 61st Congress, 3rd Session, Senate Document 756 (Washington, 1911).

9. B'nai B'rith Lodge No. 336, Albuquerque, Registration Book of Membership, 1883–1936, AJA, Cincinnati.

10. Howard N. Rabinowitz, "Albuquerque: City At A Crossroads," *Sunbelt Cities: Politics and Growth Since World War II* (Austin, Texas, 1983), p. 256; Ralph L. Edgel, "Manufacturing in New Mexico," *New Mexico Business* 5, no.12 (December 1952): 13.

11. Israel C. Carmel, "Laying of Cornerstone, Congregation Albert Synagogue by the Most Worshipful Grand Lodge Ancient Free and Accepted Masons of New Mexico, Albuquerque, New Mexico, September 3,1899," pp. 12–13. Paper presented May 13, 1978, in possession of HJT.

12. *Albuquerque Herald*, January 14, 1923, p. 2.

13. *AJYB*, 1900–1901, v.2, p. 324.

14. Temple Albert Archives, "Membership list, July 1, 1919," Diamond Anniversary, Box 1, Albuquerque.

15. *Congregation Albert*, p. 32.

16. Ibid., p. 35.

17. Ibid., pp. 58–59.

18. Ibid., p. 60.

19. *Albuquerque Morning Journal*, January 27, 1904, p. 8; November 11, 1905, p. 5.

20. *Congregation Albert*, p. 26.

21. *Albuquerque Morning Journal*, March 24, 1911, p. [6].

22. Ibid., November 28, 1912, p. 6.

23. *Congregation Albert*, p. 22.

24. *Albuquerque Morning Journal*, January 6, 1907, p. 5.

25. Ibid.

26. Ibid., January 8, 1907, p. 8; January 27, 1907, p. 7.

27. Congregation Albert, Albuquerque, N.M., Minute Book, 1897–1913, p. 98, AJA, Cincinnati.

28. Ibid.

29. *Congregation Albert*, p. 22.

30. Charles E. Woodhouse, "History of the Department of Sociology at the University of New Mexico, 1935–1986," pp. 11–12, ms. in possession of its author.

31. See Suzanne Forrest, *The Preservation of the Village* (Albuquerque, 1989), pp. 153–55.

32. Ibid. p. 154.

33. Roy Lujan, "Dennis Chavez and the Roosevelt Era, 1933–1945," Ph.D. diss., University of New Mexico, 1987, pp. 233–36.

34. *Congregation Albert*, pp. 33–34. The *Albuquerque Journal*, April 12, 1938, p. 5, noted that he failed to receive the required two-thirds vote needed for re-election.

35. Congregation Albert, Minute Book, pp. 86, 93, AJA, Cincinati.

36. Ibid., p. 16.

37. Ibid., p. 128.

38. *Congregation Albert*, pp. 31–32.

39. *In Dedication to Congregation B'nai Israel* (December, 1971), p. 31; interview with Jack Meyer, Albuquerque, May 26, 1988.

40. *Albuquerque Journal*, September 21, 1919, p. 8.

41. *In Dedication to B'nai Israel*, p. 31. The date 1915 comes from information provided by Rabbi Solomon E. Starrels of Congregation Albert. See "Religious Directory for New Mexico, 1940," Albuquerque, 1940, p. 119.

42. Interview with Jack Meyer, Albuquerque.

43. *Albuquerque Journal*, January 15, 1941, p. 8; interview with Jack Meyer.

44. *In Dedication to B'nai Israel*, p. 31.

45. *In Dedication to Fifty Years of B'nai Israel Sisterhood*, February 11, 1984.

46. Interview with Jack Meyer.

47. *Albuquerque Journal*, September 11, 1923, p. 3.

48. *Congregation Albert*, p. 31.

49. Interview with Jack Meyer.

50. *Congregation Albert*, p. 20.

51. Receipt in possession of Milton Taichert, Las Vegas, New Mexico.

52. *Albuquerque Journal*, August 5, 1915, p. 8.

53. Ibid., April 3, 1917, p. 8.

54. Melvin I. Urofsky, *American Zionism From Herzl to the Holocaust* (New York, 1975), pp. 31, 85, 89; Jacob Agus, "Current Movements in the Religious Life of American Jewry," *The Jewish People: Past and Present*, v.4 (New York, 1955), pp. 106, 119, 131; Philip Friedman, "Political and Social Movements and Organizations," *The Jewish People: Past and Present*, v.4, pp. 154–55.

55. *Albuquerque Journal*, March 15, 1920, p. 3.

56. Ibid.

57. Ibid., May 11, 1920, p. 3.

58. *Albuquerque Herald*, January 14, 1923, p. 2; Philip Friedman, *The Jewish People: Past and Present*, v.4, p. 147.

59. *Albuquerque Herald*, ibid.

60. See the cited histories of Twitchell, Reeve, Coan, and such volumes as *Representative New Mexicans*, C. S. Peterson, comp. (Denver, 1912), and Ellis A. Davis, ed., *The Historical Encyclopedia of New Mexico* (Albuquerque, 1945) for their flavor.

61. William C. Ilfeld Collection, personal correspondence, October 16, 1919, New Mexico State Records Center and Archives, Santa Fe.

62. *Albuquerque Morning Journal*, May 26, 1921, p. 2.

63. Beatrice Ilfeld Meyer, *Don Luis Ilfeld* (Albuquerque, 1973), p. 15.

64. "Wanderings," tape, courtesy of Jeffrey Brown, History Department, New Mexico State University, April 4, 1988.

65. Perrigo, *Gateway to Glorieta*, p. 37.

66. Ibid., pp. 39, 42.

67. Ibid., pp. 62–63.

68. Based on manuscript census counts for 1900 and 1910.

69. *New Mexico Business Directory, 1911–1912* (Denver, 1911), pp. 441–54; *New Mexico Business Directory, 1921* (Denver, 1921), pp. 306–13.

70. *AJYB*, 1900–1901, v.2, p. 324; *AJYB*, 1907–8, v.9, p. 258; *AJYB*, 1919–20, v.21, p. 431.

71. Linfield, *The Jews*, 1927, p. 100.

72. A. Shinedling, "Las Vegas, New Mexico." p. 29, Histories, AJA, Cincinnati; see also Victoria Rogen, "Jews on the Western Frontier Essay Wins Coveted Scholarship," *Las Vegas Daily Optic*, May 27, 1980, p. 3.

73. See Marta Weigle and Kyle Fiore, *Santa Fe and Taos: The Writer's Era 1916–1941* (Santa Fe, 1982), pp. 5–7.

74. See McKenney's *Business Directory*, 1882–83, p. 339; "Reminiscences of an Old Timer," *El Palacio* 38, no.1–2 (January 2–9, 1935): 12.

75. Carruth, *Business Directory of New Mexico and Arizona*, 1897, p. 149.

76. Reprinted in *El Palacio* 18, no.10–11 (June 1, 1925): 223–29, from "Out West," May 1904.

77. *El Palacio* 5, no.1 (July 1, 1918): 7–8; 7, no.2 (July 31, 1919): 24–26.

78. Davis, ed., *Historical Encyclopedia of New Mexico*, v. 2, p. 1950.

79. Bart Ripp, *Albuquerque Tribune*, November 23, 1987, p. B-1.

80. *The Jewish Encyclopedia* (New York, 1901–6), v.9, cols. 242–43.

81. *AJYB*, 1928–29, v.30, p. 108.

82. Ibid., 1940–41, v.42, p. 253.

83. "The White House, et al., 1912–1939," Institutional History, Special Collections, Zimmerman Library, University of New Mexico.

84. Interview with Walter Kahn, Santa Fe, August 7, 1987.

85. Linfield, *Jews in the United States*, p. 100; *AJYB*, 1940–41, v.42, p. 253.

86. Ibid.; Ibid.

87. Don McAlavy and Harold Kilmer, *High Plains History of East-Central New Mexico* (Clovis, N.M., 1980), pp. 82, 117; Henrietta Wertheim Goldenberg, Autobiographies, AJA, Cincinnati; Twitchell, *New Mexican History*, v.3, pp. 490–91.

88. Twitchell, ibid.; Henrietta W. Goldenberg, ibid.

89. "Memories of Emma Vorenberg Wertheim (Mrs. Joseph)," pp. 5–18, Biographies file, AJA, Cincinnati.

90. Southeastern New Mexico Historical Society, *Eddy County New Mexico to 1981* (Lubbock, Texas, 1982), pp. 251, 329, 424.

91. See "The Weiller Family of Carlsbad, New Mexico: Memoirs of Mrs. Mary E. (Marcel) Weiller of Carlsbad, New Mexico," pp. 1–4, AJA, Cincinnati.

92. Sigurd Johansen, *Rural Organization in a Spanish-American Culture Area* (Albuquerque, 1948), p. 28.

93. Ibid., p. 32.

94. *Las Cruces Bulletin*, July 8, 1971, p. 4.

95. Richard J. Lease, "Eugene J. Stern: Merchant, Farmer and Philanthropist of Las Cruces, New Mexico," *Western States Jewish Historical Quarterly* 9, no.2 (January 1977): 162–63.

96. "Wanderings," tape, Jeffrey Brown, New Mexico State University, April 6, 1988.

97. *Las Cruces Bulletin*, July 8, 1971, p. 1.

98. Lease, "Eugene J. Stern," p. 165.

99. See Irving Telling, "New Mexican Frontiers: A Social History of the Gallup Area 1881–1901," Ph.D. diss., Harvard University, 1952, p.1.

100. Ibid., pp. 3, 51; Gustav Kahn, "Memoirs of Gustav Kahn and the Kahn Family," pp. 74–75, Santa Fe, N.M., 1964, Biographies file, AJA, Cincinnati.

101. Gustav Kahn, ibid., p. 77.

102. Telling, "Gallup," pp. 418, 424.

103. "Sam Danoff—Southwestern Fiddler on the Roof," *Gallup Independent*, August 9, 1972, p. 6B.

104. Hyman O. Danoff, "Indian Traders of the Southwest: The Danoffs of New Mexico," *Western States Jewish Historical Quarterly* 12, no.1 (October 1979): 291–93.

105. Ibid., pp. 297, 300.

106. Gustav Kahn, "Memoirs of Gustav Kahn," pp. 91–92.

107. "Reminiscences of Gus Kahn," p. 3, Sam Moreel, of Gallup, N.M., Biographies, AJA, Cincinnati.

108. "Reminiscences of Walter S. Kahn," ibid., p. 2.

109. "Reminiscences of Gus Kahn," ibid., pp. 7–8.

110. Haldeen Brady, *Pancho Villa at Columbus: The Raid of 1916 Restudied* (El Paso, 1965), pp. 10, 17. This account relates that Villa was seeking a third brother, Sam, who had angered him by selling unsatisfactory commodities. However, Arthur Ravel denied any business dealings with Villa. See letter, *El Paso Jewish Historical Review* 1, no. 2 (Spring 1983): 203–4.

111. Ibid., p. 36; Abraham I. Shinedling, "Letter to the Archives re Louis and Arthur Ravel," October 19, 1964, AJA, Cincinnati.

112. Frank D. Reeve, *History of New Mexico* (New York, 1961), v. 3, p. 282.

113. *Albuquerque Herald*, January 14, 1923, p. 2.

114. *Albuquerque Journal*, April 25, 1934, p. 2; February 27, 1939, p. 3.

115. *Albuquerque Tribune*, December 2, 1938, p. 17.

116. *Albuquerque Tribune*, December 7, 1938, p. 1.

117. *Albuquerque Tribune*, December 7, 1938, p. 10.

118. David M. Chalmers, *Hooded Americanism: The History of the Ku Klux Klan* (Chicago, 1968), pp. 2–3.

119. Ibid., p. 224.

120. Captain Jason W. James, *Memories and Viewpoints* (Roswell, 1928), pp. 152–55.

121. Ibid., p. 135

122. Austin, "Social Survey of Taos County, New Mexico," pp. 10–11, microfilm, Special Collections, Zimmerman Library, University of New Mexico. This item is reproduced by permission of Huntington Library, San Marino, California. AU543.

123. "Alexander Gusdorf," pp. 1–3, Biographies, AJA, Cincinnati.

124. Forrest, *Preservation*, pp. 79–80.

125. Ibid., p. 82.

126. Ibid., pp. 86–87.

127. Ibid., p. 85

128. Ibid., p. 86.

129. George Curry, *George Curry, 1861–1947: An Autobiography*, H. B. Hening, ed. (Albuquerque, 1958), pp. 201–3.

130. Ibid., p. 248.

131. Clarence S. Adams, *Little Town West of the Pecos* (Roswell, 1983), pp. 142–43.

132. Westphall, *Catron*, p. 307.

133. George W. Smith, "New Mexico's Wartime Food Problems, 1917–1918: II (concluded), *NMHR* 19, no.1 (January 1944): 25.

134. Ibid., p. 49.

135. Alice C. Henderson, "New Mexico in the Great War" (continued), *NMHR* 1, no.3 (July 1926): 231–32.

136. See *Who's Who in American Jewry,* 1928[?], v.2 (New York, 1928), 2nd ed., pp. 634–35.

137. Eunice Kalloch and Ruth K. Hall, *The First Ladies of New Mexico* (Santa Fe, 1982), p. 71.

138. P. A. F. W. [Paul A. F. Walter], "Arthur Seligman" *NMHR* 8, no.4 (October 1933): 313.

139. Ibid., p. 316.

140. Rabbi David D. Shor, who served Temple Albert in the post–World War II period, considered Seligman an Episcopalian. See Rabbi Abraham Shinedling, "Jews in the New Mexico Historical Review," mss coll. 128, p. 176, AJA, Cincinnati. Rabbi Shinedling of Albuquerque, who cited Rabbi Shor's view, mused that Christians tend to regard "a *former* Jew, one who has renounced Judaism, *as still being Jewish. This is an error.*" Ibid. However, it should also be noted that Seligman's biography was included in *Who's Who in American Jewry, 1928.*

141. This information came from various New Mexico Blue Books.

142. *Albuquerque Journal,* December 2, 1929, p. 8.

143. Davis, *Historical Encyclopedia of New Mexico,* v. 1, p. 267; v. 2, p. 1031.

144. *Who's Who in American Jewry, 1928,* 2nd ed., v. 2, p. 84.

145. Gustav Kahn, "Memoirs of Gustav Kahn of Santa Fe, New Mexico," pp. 96–97, Biographies file, AJA, Cincinnati; *The New Mexico Blue Book or State Official Register, 1921,* Santa Fe, p. 52.

146. Twitchell, *New Mexican History,* v.3, pp. 490–91; *New Mexico Blue Book, 1921.*

147. Twitchell, ibid., v. 4, pp. 542–43.

148. Reeve, *History of New Mexico*, v. 3, pp. 51–52.

149. Coan, *History of New Mexico*, v. 2, pp. 129–31.

150. US Census Office, *Abstract of the Twelfth Census, 1900* (Washington, 1902), p. 361.

151. Jim F. Heath, "AT&SF," p. 154.

152. Bureau of the Census, *Sixteenth Census of the United States: 1940, Population*, v. 2 (Washington, 1943), pp. 955, 989.

153. Jacob Lestschinsky, "Economic and Social Development of American Jewry," *The Jewish People: Past and Present*, v.4, p. 90.

154. Ibid., p. 82.

155. Ibid., p. 91.

156. Glazer, "Social Characteristics," pp. 14–24; see also Calvin Goldscheider, *Jewish Continuity and Change* (Bloomington, 1986), p. 108.

157. Compiled from Bradstreet's *Commercial Reports* for 1897 and 1925.

158. Hudspeth's, *Albuquerque City Directory 1926* (El Paso).

159. Hudspeth's, *Albuquerque City Directory 1935* (El Paso).

160. Hudspeth's, *Albuquerque City Directory 1940* (El Paso).

161. These data are compiled from Albuquerque city directories for 1926, 1935, 1940.

CHAPTER 6

1. Gerald D. Nash, *The American West in the Twentieth Century* (Englewood Cliffs, N.J., 1973), p. 195.

2. Simmons, *Albuquerque*, p. 366.

3. Ibid., pp. 366–68.

4. Jake W. Spidle, Jr., *The Lovelace Medical Center: Pioneer in American Health Care* (Albuquerque, 1987), p. 50.

5. Ralph L. Edgel, "Manufacturing in New Mexico," *New Mexico Business* 5, no.12 (December 1952): 13–14.

6. R.L.E. and V.T.X., "Employment and Income," *New Mexico Business* 13, no.2: Sec.2 (February 1960): 8.

7. Abraham I. Shinedling, *History of the Los Alamos Jewish Center, Los Alamos, New Mexico (1944 to 1957)* (Albuquerque, 1958), p. 1.

8. Phyllis K. Fisher, *Los Alamos Experience* (Japan Publications, 1985), p. 50. The author recalled celebrating Christmas in 1945 because at Los Alamos "there was no Jewish alternative . . . no evidence

of Jewish worship, and no organized way to join together to celebrate Jewish holidays." For her, the Jewish community came alive in 1946 when Passover was celebrated, pp. 166, 197. However, "The Bulletin," a mimeographed wartime post publication, includes notice of Hebrew Sabbath services in the November 10, 1944 issue. Reprinted in *Los Alamos: The First Forty Years*, Fern Lyon and Jacob Evans, eds. (Los Alamos, N.M., 1984), p. 28.

9. Shinedling, *Los Alamos*, p. 2.

10. Ibid., p. 11; Karen Hack, "The Formation of a Jewish Community in Los Alamos," pp. 10–11, 1991. Unpublished paper.

11. Ibid., p. 25.

12. Rabbi Leonard Helman, "From The Rabbi's Study," *New Mexico Jewish Community Link* 2, no. 6 (June 1982): 5.

13. *AJYB*, 1982, v. 82, pp. 167–68.

14. The data for this table are derived from the following: 1937, *AJYB*, 1944–1945, v.46, p. 495; 1955, *AJYB*, 1956, v.57, p. 124; 1961, *AJYB*, 1961, v.62, p. 62; 1970, *AJYB*, 1970, v.71, p. 345; 1980, *AJYB*, 1982, v.82, pp. 167–68.

15. *AJYB*, 1982, v.82, p. 173.

16. The table rests on tabulations compiled by the author from the forms returned by 498 households involving 1,338 persons, a nonrandom population involving about 20 percent of the total Jewish population of Albuquerque, 1981 JCCA Census, JCCA, Albuquerque. A recent doctoral dissertation, using a random sample of 277 respondents found fairly similar trends in the progression of educational level. See Brigitte K. Goldstein, "Jewish Identification Among the Jews of Albuquerque, New Mexico: The Maintenance of Jewishness and Judaism in the Integrated Residential Setting of a Sunbelt City." Ph.D. diss. University of New Mexico, 1988, p. 161.

17. Nash, *American West*, p. 219.

18. I used congregational membership lists and Albuquerque business directories for the dates noted. In column three, it was necessary to use the business directory for 1981, B'nai Israel membership list for 1981, and the membership list of Temple Albert for 1984. A Jewish Welfare Fund Survey in 1966 found 39.3 percent professional, 24.5 percent merchant, 32.4 percent nonprofessional of 631 persons employed. *Jewish Welfare Fund News and Views* 5, no.6 (October 1966). The major difference between this author's findings and the JWF survey lies in the professional category. Differences of definition could easily

account for differing results. In any case, the rise of professionals as a major group to the displacement of merchants remains clear.

19. Goldstein, "Jewish Identification," pp. 162–63.

20. I have rounded off the figures and ignored the small numbers who attended only elementary and technical schools. That accounts for totals of less than 100 percent, 1981 JCCA Census.

21. Ibid.

22. Ibid.

23. William Graebner, A History of Retirement (New Haven, 1980), p. 215.

24. Jewish Welfare Fund News and Views 5, no.6 (October 1966). The extension of total numbers in the survey is mine, based on two adults per family.

25. Goldstein, "Jewish Identification," p. 160.

26. Shannon Eubanks, "Rio Rancho: Past and Present," New Mexico Business Journal 11, no.7 (July 1987): 89.

27. Interview with Elizabeth Fingard and Beatrice Roth, April 1989.

28. Scrap Book, Rio Rancho Jewish Center; interview with Elizabeth Fingard and Beatrice Roth.

29. Albuquerque Jewish Welfare Fund News 1, no.1 (September 1962).

30. Ibid.

31. The Main Event: The Albuquerque Jewish Community Past, Present, and Future, JCCA files, Albuquerque, [1982].

32. Board Minutes, AJWF, August 24, 1967. See also "Chronology of Major Action," p. 14, AJWF files, Albuquerque.

33. Goldstein, "Jewish Identification," pp. 172–73.

34. Ibid., p. 172.

35. The 1981 JCCA Census, with a relatively small number of examples, shows an 8 percent intermarriage rate in a nonrandom sample. Of twenty-five families of intermarriage with children, nine noted non-Jewish children, six among the eleven reporting Jewish males and three among the fourteen reporting Jewish women. Many of the children, however, appear to be the offspring of earlier marriages. Compiled from the 1981 JCCA Census. See also Goldstein, ibid., pp. 176–77.

36. Ibid., p. 168.

37. Ibid., p. 167.

38. Ibid., p. 168.

39. Ibid.

40. Ibid.

41. Mr. Richard Kaufmann of Albuquerque provided identification of many of these names.

42. Goldstein, "Jewish Identification," p. 168.

43. Ibid., p. 169.

44. Goldstein, "Jewish Identification," p. 194.

45. The author belonged to the Yiddish Club at that time.

46. The author has a playbill in his possession from such a performance.

47. *New Mexico Jewish Community Link* 5, no.6 (June 1976): 1.

48. See *New Mexico Jewish Community Link* 10, no.4 (April 1981): 4.

49. S. P. Goldberg, "Jewish Communal Services: Programs and Finances," *AJYB*, 1971, v. 72, p. 179.

50. Certificate of Incorporation of Albuquerque Jewish Welfare Fund, February 27, 1948, copy, JCCA files, Albuquerque.

51. Goldberg, "Jewish Communal Services," *AJYB*, 1971, v.72, p. 181.

52. Ibid. See "United Jewish Appeal," *Encyclopedia Judaica*, (Jerusalem, 1971) v.15, cols. 1540–41.

53. The figures are from the files of the JCCA Allocation Reports, JCCA files, Albuquerque.

54. *The Main Event*, JCCA files, Albuquerque, [1982].

55. Board Minutes, AJWF, letter from President Lewis R. Sutin to Welfare Fund Contributors, February 21, 1953, JCCA files, Albuquerque.

56. Board Minutes, AJWF, September 28, 1967, JCCA files, Albuquerque.

57. Regular Campaign 1973, Emergency Campaign, JCCA files, Albuquerque.

58. Board Minutes, AJWF, September 26, 1963, JCCA files, Albuquerque.

59. See "U.S. Senate," folder, JCCA files, Albuquerque.

60. Board Minutes, AJWF, July 27, 1967, JCCA files, Albuquerque.

61. Board Minutes, AJWF, Secretary's Report, 1968, JCCA files, Albuquerque.

62. Board Minutes, AJWF, remarks at Annual Meeting, December 3, 1967, JCCA files, Albuquerque.

63. Cathy Robbins, "Albuquerque Jews Losing Invisibility," *Albuquerque Journal*, September 16, 1980, Magazine p. 9.

64. Ibid.

65. *Congregation Albert*, pp. 48–49.

66. Ibid., pp. 49–50.

67. "Sunday Morning Breakfast at Temple Albert," *Century* 3, no. 4 (November 17, 1982): 5.

68. *Congregation Albert*, p. 48.

69. A *Time for Dedication: Temple Albert*, September 8–9, 1984, p. 46.

70. Ibid.

71. Interview with Rabbi John Feldman, Albuquerque, 1989.

72. Board Minutes, JCCA, February 24, 1972, March 23, 1972, April 27, 1972, JCCA files, Albuquerque.

73. *In Dedication to Congregation B'nai Israel*, pp. 33–35.

74. A *Time for Dedication: Temple Albert*, September 8–9, 1984, p. 56.

75. Ibid., p. 32.

76. Ibid., p. 34.

77. Ibid., p. 52.

78. Interview with Rabbi Isaac Celnik, Temple B'nai Israel, May 1988.

79. Ibid.

80. *New Mexico Jewish Community Link* 3, no. 2 (October 1973).

81. *Albuquerque Journal*, June 7, 1983, Magazine p. 5.

82. Ibid.

83. Paula Steinbach, letter from Saul Rosenthal to Paula Steinbach, February 4, 1983, "'Swastika' File," January-June 1983, Rio Grande Historical Collections, New Mexico State University Library, Las Cruces.

84. *Albuquerque Journal*, June 7, 1983, Magazine p. 7.

85. Steinbach, letter from Saul Rosenthal, February 4, 1983, "'Swastika' file," January-June 1983, Rio Grande Historical Collections, New Mexico State University Library, Las Cruces.

86. Ibid. The "Swastika" file contains clippings of the events described.

87. Board Minutes, AJWF, September 26, 1963, JCCA files, Albuquerque. A telephone conversation with Michael Sutin in March 1989 revealed that the materials noted had been deposited with the Denver office of the ADL.

88. The Rio Rancho Jewish Center Scrap Book contains a photograph of its defaced sign, October 4, 1979; Rabbi Isaac Celnik, "Antisemitism in Albuquerque," *New Mexico Jewish Community Link* 11, no. 9 (October 1982): 5.

89. Nancie L. Gonzalez, *The Spanish-Americans of New Mexico* (Albuquerque, 1969), pp. 93–96.

90. Frances L. Swadesh, "The Alianza Movement of New Mexico: The Interplay of Social Change and Public Commentary," *Minorities and Politics*, Henry J. Tobias and Charles E. Woodhouse, eds. (Albuquerque, 1969), pp. 68–70.

91. Ibid., pp. 79–80.

92. *Albuquerque Journal*, September 11, 1967, p. A-2.

93. *Albuquerque Journal*, October 1, 1967, p. F-11. A somewhat fuller quote appears in Richard Gardner, *Grito: Reies Tijerina and the New Mexico Land Grant War of 1967* (Indianapolis, 1970), p. 210.

94. Ibid.

95. *Albuquerque Journal*, October 2, 1967, p. A-10.

96. Interview with Rabbi Isaac Celnik, May 8, 1989.

97. *Albuquerque Journal*, May 15, 1968, p. E-1.

98. *Albuquerque Journal*, May 16, 1968, p. A-2.

99. Telephone conversation with Rabbi David Shor, May 1989, Albuquerque.

100. Ex-governor David Cargo offered this view in a talk at the University of New Mexico on April 22, 1989. Indeed, Cargo noted that he himself was identified as a Jew by Tijerina because he knew a little Yiddish. Cargo is a Catholic. Tijerina has hinted at Jewishness in his own background to a number of persons.

101. David S. Nidel, "Modern Descendants of Conversos in New Mexico—500 Years of Faith," p. 59, December 29, 1980, ms. in possession of its author, Albuquerque.

102. Ibid., pp. 58, 87.

103. Blake, "Secret Signs of Judaism," p. 18.

104. Nidel, "Modern Descendants—500 Years," pp. 59, 62, 87–88.

105. *AJYB*, 1940–41, v.42, p. 253.

106. "Wanderings," tape, New Mexico State University, Las Cruces, April 6, 1988.

107. Richard J. Lease, "Eugene J. Stern: Merchant, Farmer and Philanthropist of Las Cruces, New Mexico," *Western States Jewish Historical Quarterly* 9, no.2 (January 1977): 165.

108. *AJYB*, 1961, v. 62, p. 59.

109. Mr. and Mrs. Leland Trafton, untitled historical summary ms., Freudenthal P. Papers, Box 12, Folder 3, Rio Grande Historical Collections, New Mexico State University Library, Las Cruces. Authors identified by L. E. Freudenthal, January 29, 1965.

110. Lease, "Eugene J. Stern," p. 165.

111. "Wanderings," tape, NMSU, April 6, 1988. A note by Rabbi Abraham Shinedling of Albuquerque places the arrival of the first rabbi at an earlier date, about 1960. "The Founding of the Temple in Las Cruces, New Mexico, Mr. and Mrs. Leland Trafton," Roll 9, *Jewish families and congregations in New Mexico and southern Colorado*, AJA, Cincinnati.

112. Gustav Kahn, "Memoirs," p. 78, Biographies file, AJA, Cincinnati.

113. Ibid., p. 80.

114. "Membership List, October 1981," Temple Beth Shalom Archive, Santa Fe.

115. *AJYB*, 1940–41, v. 42, p. 253; *AJYB*, 1961, v. 62, p. 59; *AJYB*, 1973, v. 74, p. 312; *AJYB*, 1982, v. 82, p. 173.

116. Gustav Kahn, "Memoirs," p. 89.

117. Compiled from Hudspeth's *Santa Fe (Santa Fe County, N.M.) City Directory, 1953*, El Paso.

118. Compiled from Hudspeth's *Santa Fe (Santa Fe County, N.M.) City Directory, 1964*, Dallas.

119. Letter from Robert Burman to Rabbi Malcolm H. Stern, October 23, 1973, Temple Beth Shalom Archive, Santa Fe.

120. Minutes, Temple Board Meeting, October 19, 1975, Temple Beth Shalom Archive, Santa Fe.

121. Minutes, Temple Board Meeting, March 13, 1978, Temple Beth Shalom Archive, Santa Fe.

122. "Membership List, October 1981," Temple Beth Shalom Archive, Santa Fe; Polk's *Santa Fe City (Santa Fe County, N. M.) Direc-*

tory, 1981, Dallas; Polk's *Santa Fe City (Santa Fe County, N. M.) Directory, 1983,* Dallas.

123. *AJYB,* 1940–41, v. 42, p. 253.

124. "Membership List, 1981," in possession of Mr. Seymour A. Beckerman, Roswell.

125. [Judith Feldman], "The Jewish Community in Roswell: A Brief History," pp. 2–3, in possession of Mr. Seymour A. Beckerman, Roswell.

126. Shinkle, *Fifty Years of Roswell History, 1867–1917,* p. 166.

127. "The Jewish Community in Roswell," p. 4.

128. David D. Shor Collection, Miscellaneous files, AJA, Cincinati.

Bibliography

OFFICIAL DOCUMENTS

Annual Report of the Board of Indian Commissioners to the President of the United States, 1873. Washington, 1874.

Annual Report of the Commissioner of Indian Affairs to the Secretary of the Interior for the Year 1876. Washington, 1876.

Appendix to the Congressional Globe for the First Session, Thirty-Second Congress, John C. Rives. New Series, v. 25. Washington, 1852.

Bureau of Indian Affairs, "Letters and Documents Relating to the Bibo and Spiegelberg Families," Record Group 75. Microfilm. Washington, 1954.

Department of the Interior, Census Office. *Compendium of the Tenth Census* (June 1, 1880), Part I, rev. ed. Washington, 1885.

National Archives. *Interior Department Territorial Papers, New Mexico, 1851–1914*. Microfilm. Washington, 1962.

National Archives. *Records of the Comptroller of the Currency, Record Group 101*. "Selected Documents Relating to the Second National Bank of New Mexico, Charter No. 2024." Microfilm. Washington, 1961.

National Archives. *State Department Territorial Papers, 1851–1874*. Microfilm. Washington, 1954.

National Archives. *Population Schedules of the Eighth Census of the United States, 1860: New Mexico*. Microfilm. Washington, 1967.

National Archives. *Population Schedules of the Ninth Census of the United States, 1870: New Mexico*. Microfilm. Washington, 1965.

National Archives. *Population Schedules of the Seventh Census of the United States, 1850: New Mexico*. Microfilm. Washington, 1963.

National Archives. *Population Schedules of the Tenth Census of the Unites States, 1880: New Mexico.* Microfilm. Washington, n. d.

National Archives. *Twelfth Census of Population, 1900: New Mexico.* Microfilm. Washington, [197-?].

N. M. State Records Center. *Territorial Archives of New Mexico, 1850–1911.* Microfilm. Santa Fe, 1971.

Office of Indian Affairs. *The Official Correspondence of James S. Calhoun,* edited by Annie H. Abel. Washington, 1915.

Secretary of the Interior. *Population of the United States in 1860; The Eighth Census.* Washington, 1864.

The Seventh Census of the United States: 1850. Washington, 1853.

62d Congress. 2d session. *Occupation of Mexican Territory,* Doc. No. 896. Washington, 1912.

U.S. Bureau of the Census. *Fourteenth Census of the United States Taken in the Year 1920. Population,* v. 1. Washington, 1921.

U.S. Bureau of the Census. *Sixteenth Census of the United States, 1940. Population: Mother Tongue.* Washington, 1943.

U.S. Bureau of the Census. *Sixteenth Census of the United States, 1940. Population* v. 2. Washington, 1943.

U.S. Bureau of the Census. *Thirteenth Census, 1910: New Mexico.* Microfilm. Washington, [1982?].

U.S. Bureau of the Census. *Twelfth Census of the United States Taken in the Year 1900. Population,* v. 1. Washington, 1901.

U.S. Bureau of the Census. *Twelfth Census of Population 1900: New Mexico.* Microfilm. Washington, 1970.

U.S. Census Office. *Abstract of the Twelfth Census of the United States, 1900,* Washington, 1902.

U.S. Congress. Senate. Reports of the Immigration Commission, *Emigration Conditions in Europe* v. 12. 61st Congress, 3rd session. Senate Document 748. Washington, 1911.

U.S. Congress. Senate. Reports of the Immigration Commission. *Statistical Review of Immigration,* v. 20. 61st Congress. 3rd session. Senate Document 756. Washington, 1911.

ARCHIVAL MATERIALS

Amberg and Elsberg. "Bill on Confederacy," New Mexico State Records Center and Archives, Santa Fe.

American Jewish Archives, Mr. and Mrs. Leland Trafton, "The Founding of the Temple in Las Cruces, N. M.," Jewish families and congregations in New Mexico and southern Colorado, roll 9, p. 4. [Filmed between 1982 and 1986], AJA, Cincinnati.

Manuel Alvarez Papers. New Mexico State Records Center and Archives, Santa Fe.

Bernalillo County District Court Records. Civil Case #350. New Mexico State Records Center and Archives, Santa Fe.

Bibo Family. "Interview with Mr. Leroy Bibo and Mrs. Max Weiss, children of Solomon Bibo." February 21, 1969. Charter Oak, California. Box no. 2802. American Jewish Archives, Cincinnati.

B'nai B'rith Cemetery Association. Lodge no. 336. Albuquerque, New Mexico. "Minute Book and Cemetery Books, 1892–1917." Box 681. American Jewish Archives, Cincinnati.

B'nai B'rith Lodge no. 336, Albuquerque, New Mexico. "Minutes, 1883–1898." Box no. x-81, American Jewish Archives, Cincinnati.

B'nai B'rith Lodge no. 336, Albuquerque, New Mexico. "Registration Book of Membership, 1883–1936." Box no. 2311. American Jewish Archives, Cincinnati.

Carrasco-Sanchez Family, American Jewish Archives, Cincinnati.

Catron, Thomas B. "Letter Books." Special Collections, Zimmerman Library, University of New Mexico.

Congregation Albert. Albuquerque, New Mexico. "Minute Book, 1897–1913." American Jewish Archives, Cincinnati.

Congregation Montefiore. Las Vegas. Miscellaneous Records, 1880–1964. American Jewish Archives, Cincinnati.

Dun, R. G., and Co. "Western Territories," 3 vols. Baker Library, Graduate School of Business Administration, Harvard University.

Economic Records. Unidentified Business Ledger, 1848–49. New Mexico State Records Center and Archives, Santa Fe.

Executive Record Book no. 1. New Mexico State Records Center and Archives, Santa Fe.

First National Bank Records. Santa Fe, New Mexico. "Letter Books." Archive no. 177. Special Collections, Zimmerman Library, University of New Mexico.

Freudenthal Family Papers. "Family Correspondence." Rio Grande Historical Collections, New Mexico State University Library, Las Cruces.

Fur Traders—Extranjeros. History File no. 9, New Mexico State Records Center and Archives, Santa Fe.

Hebrew Ladies Benevolent Society. "Minutes," January 1904–February 2, 1920. Las Vegas, New Mexico. In possession of Milton Taichert, Las Vegas, New Mexico.

Henderson, Jr., Rev. Clifton H. and Jean Woodburn Henderson, comps. "Directory and Maps of the Masonic Cemetery, 1876–1979." [Silver City, New Mexico?], n. d.

William C. Ilfeld Collection. "Personal Correspondence, February 25, 1867—December 24, 1921." New Mexico State Records Center and Archives, Santa Fe.

"Jewish Circumcision Record" (1867–1905, Denver). DeGolyer Library and Fikes Hall of Special Collections, Southern Methodist University.

Jewish Community Council of Albuquerque. "Albuquerque Jewish Welfare Fund, Inc., Minutes, 1948–1980." Albuquerque.

Jewish Community Council of Albuquerque. "Jewish Community Council of Albuquerque Survey, August 1981." Albuquerque.

Jewish Community Council of Albuquerque. "Regular Campaign 1973, Emergency Campaign." Albuquerque.

Kingsbury, John M. "Correspondence, 1858–1860. Letters to James J. Webb." DeGolyer Library and Fikes Hall of Special Collections, Southern Methodist University.

"Membership Lists, 1918–19, 1920–21," Diamond Anniversary. Box no. 1. Temple Albert Archives, Albuquerque.

New Mexico Supreme Court Records, 1872, no. 7. New Mexico State Records Center and Archives, Santa Fe.

William J. Parish, "Papers, 1700–1964." Archive no. 276. Special Collections, Zimmerman Library, University of New Mexico.

Rio Rancho Jewish Center, Scrapbook. Rio Rancho, New Mexico.

Emanuel Rosenwald Collection no. 220. Special Collections, Zimmerman Library, University of New Mexico.

Rosenwald Family. "Materials Depicting the History of the Rosenwald Family," May 12, 1910. Miscellaneous. American Jewish Archives, Cincinnati.

San Miguel District Court Records. Criminal Folder nos. 231a, 333, 434. New Mexico State Records Center and Archives, Santa Fe.

Schuyler, Ted. Letter to Henry J. Tobias, December 20, 1983.

Shinedling, Abraham I., "References to and texts on New Mexico Jews in the Volumes of the *New Mexico Historical Review* 1, no. 1 (1926) to 36, no. 2 (April 1961)." May 1961. Mss coll. no. 128 20/6. American Jewish Archives, Cincinnati.

Shinedling, Abraham I. (with Milton Taichert). "The Las Vegas, New Mexico (the Montefiore Congregation) and the Jewish Community of Las Vegas, New Mexico." Histories. American Jewish Archives, Cincinnati.

David D. Shor Collection. Miscellaneous file. American Jewish Archives, Cincinnati.

Silver City Public Library. "David Abraham," "I. N. Cohen," "Max Schutz." Biographical folders. Silver City, New Mexico.

Spiegelberg Bros. "Bad Accounts," 1881. Jewish Merchants. New Mexico State Records Center and Archives, Sante Fe.

Flora Spiegelberg Collection no. 18. Special Collections, Zimmerman Library, University of New Mexico

"'Swastika' File." January-June 1983. Rio Grande Historical Collections, New Mexico State University, Las Cruces.

Temple Albert Archives. "Membership List, July 1, 1919," Box no 1. Diamond Anniversary. Albuquerque.

Temple Beth Shalom. "Temple Board Minutes." Temple Beth Shalom Archive, Santa Fe.

Temple Beth Shalom. "Membership List, October 1981." Temple Beth Shalom Archive, Santa Fe.

Territory of New Mexico vs. James H. Carelton. New Mexico State Records Center and Archives, Santa Fe.

Trafton, Leland, Mr. and Mrs. "The Founding of the Temple in Las Cruces, New Mexico," 1965. Freudenthal P. Papers, Box 12, Folder 3. Rio Grande Historical Collections, New Mexico State University Library, Las Cruces.

"The White House, et al., 1912–1939." Institutional History. Special Collections, Zimmerman Library, University of New Mexico.

PUBLISHED SOURCE MATERIALS

Bieber, Ralph P. "The Papers of James J. Webb, Santa Fe Merchant, 1844–1861." *Washington University Studies* 11 (1923–24).

Bloom, Lansing B., ed. "Historical Society Minutes, 1859–1863." *New Mexico Historical Review* 18, no. 3 (July 1943): 247–311.

Bradstreet, J. M., and Son. *Bradstreet's Commercial Reports* 30 (January 6, 1872); 116 (January 1897), New York.

Bradstreet's Book of Commercial Ratings 229 (April 1925), New York.

Carruth, J. A. *Business Directory of Arizona and New Mexico for 1897.* Las Vegas, N.M., 1897.

Dun, R. G., and Co. *The Mercantile Agency Reference Book* 67 (January 1885), New York.

Hudspeth. *Albuquerque City Directory*, 1926, 1935, 1940. El Paso, Texas.

Hudspeth. *Santa Fe (Santa Fe County, N.M.) City Directory, 1953.* El Paso, Texas, 1953.

Hudspeth. *Santa Fe (Santa Fe County, N.M.) City Directory, 1964.* Dallas, 1965.

McKenney. *Business Directory of the Principal Towns of Central and Southern California, Arizona, New Mexico, Southern Colorado, and Kansas.* Oakland and San Francisco, 1882–83.

The New Mexico Blue Book or State Official Register, 1921. Santa Fe, New Mexico.

New Mexico Business Directory including El Paso, Texas, 1903–4. Denver, 1903.

New Mexico Business Directory including El Paso, Texas, with Denver and Foreign Classifications, 1911–1912. Denver, 1911.

New Mexico State Business Directory including El Paso, Texas with Los Angeles and Foreign Classifications, Denver, 1921.

Polk. *Santa Fe (Santa Fe County, N.M.) City Directory, 1981.* Dallas.

Polk. *Santa Fe (Santa Fe County, N.M.) Directory, 1983.* Dallas.

Roberts, C. O'Conor. *Albuquerque City Directory and Business Guide for 1896.* Albuquerque, 1896.

Theisen, Lee Scott, ed. "Frank Warner Angel's Notes on New Mexican Territory, 1878." *Arizona and the West* 18, no. 4 (Winter 1976): 333–70.

INTERVIEWS

Rabbi Isaac Celnik, Albuquerque, 1989.

Rabbi John Feldman, Albuquerque, 1989.

Elizabeth Fingard and Beatrice Roth, Rio Rancho, 1989.

Walter Kahn, Santa Fe, 1987.

Jack Meyer, Albuquerque, 1987.

Louis M. Prager, Roswell, 1986.

Milton Taichert, Las Vegas, 1986.

UNPUBLISHED MEMOIRS

Floersheim, Carl. "Biography of Solomon Floersheim." 1959. Biographies file, American Jewish Archives, Cincinnati.

Goldenberg, Henrietta Wertheim. "Autobiography." October 30, 1958. Biographies file, American Jewish Archives, Cincinnati.

Kahn, Gustav. "Memoirs of Gustav Kahn and the Kahn Family." Santa Fe, New Mexico, 1964. Biographies file, American Jewish Archives, Cincinnati.

Kahn, Walter, and Gus Kahn. "Reminiscences of Sam Moreel, of Gallup, New Mexico." November 1963. Biographies file, American Jewish Archives, Cincinnati.

Minces, Elizabeth Nordhaus. "The Family: Early Days in New Mexico." Albuquerque, August 1980. In possession of John Feldman, Albuquerque.

Prager, Louis M. "My Memories of Roswell, 1903–1978." Tape. Chaves County Historical Museum, Roswell, N.M.

"Wanderings." Two tapes. April 6, 1988. Courtesy of Dr. Jeffrey Brown, New Mexico State University, Las Cruces.

Weiller, Mrs. Mary E. (Marcel). "The Weiller Family of Carlsbad, New Mexico: Memoirs of Mrs. Mary E. (Marcel) Weiller of Carlsbad, New Mexico." Biographies file, American Jewish Archives, Cincinnati.

Weimer, C. D. "Alexander Gusdorf." Taos, N.M., 1956. Biographies file. American Jewish Archives, Cincinnati.

Wertheim, Emma Vorenberg (Mrs. Joseph). "Memoirs, covering the period 1861–1965." Carlsbad, N.M., 1965. Biographies file, American Jewish Archives, Cincinnati.

PUBLISHED MEMOIRS

Bell, William A. *New Tracks in North America*. New York, 1870.

Bloom, L. B. "Bourke on the Southwest, VII." *New Mexico Historical Review* 10, no. 1 (January 1935): 271–322.

Curry, George. *George Curry, 1861–1947: An Autobiography*, edited by H. B. Hening. Albuquerque, 1958.

Danoff, Hyman O. "Indian Traders of the Southwest: The Danoffs of

New Mexico." *Western States Jewish Historical Quarterly* 12, no. 1 (October 1979): 291–303.

Fierman, Floyd S. "Nathan Bibo's Reminiscences of Early New Mexico." *El Palacio* 68, no.4 (Winter 1961): 231–57.

———. "Nathan Bibo's Reminiscences of Early New Mexico," *El Palacio* 69, no.1 (Spring 1962): 40–59.

Fisher, Phyllis K. *Los Alamos Experience*. New York, 1985.

Huning, Franz. *Trader on the Santa Fe Trail: Memoirs of Franz Huning*. Albuquerque, 1973.

James, Captain Jason W. *Memories and Viewpoints*. Roswell, 1928.

Lesinsky, Henry. *Letters Written by Henry Lesinsky to His Son*. New York, 1924.

McKay, R. H. *Little Pills: An Army Story*. Pittsburg, Kan., 1918.

Meline, James F. *Two Thousand Miles on Horseback, Santa Fe and Back*. Albuquerque, 1966.

Meyer, Beatrice I. *Don Luis Ilfeld*. Albuquerque, 1973.

Peyton, John Rowzee. *A Virginian in New Mexico, 1773*. Santa Fe, 1967.

"Roswell was 'Pearl of the Pecos'—1880." *Old Timers' Review* 4, no. 1 (Autumn 1982): 7.

"Reminiscences of an Old Timer." *El Palacio* 38, nos. 1–2 (January 2–9, 1935): 12.

Shinkle, James D. *Reminiscences of Roswell Pioneers*. Roswell, N. M., 1966.

Spiegelberg, Flora. "Tribute to Archbishop Lamy of New Mexico." *El Palacio* 36, nos. 3–4 (January 17–24, 1934): 22–25. (Reprinted from *The Jewish Chronicle*.)

Segale, Sister Blandina. *At the End of the Santa Fe Trail*. Columbus, Ohio, 1932.

Thompson, Waddy. *Recollections of Mexico*. New York, 1846.

Webb, James J. *Adventures in the Santa Fe Trade 1844–1847*. Ralph B. Bieber, ed. Glendale, Calif., 1931.

Whitlock, V. H. (Ol' Waddy). *Cowboy Life on the Llano Estacado*. Norman, Oklahoma, 1970.

Wise, Isaac M. *Reminiscences*, trans. and edited by David Philipson. 2nd edition. New York, 1945.

Wislizenus, A. *Memoir of a Tour to Northern Mexico*. Washington, 1848.

ENCYCLOPEDIAS, COLLECTED WORKS, ANNUALS

American Jewish Year Book, 1899–1982. Philadelphia, New York.

Encyclopedia Judaica, 16 vols. Jerusalem and New York, 1972.

Davis, Arthur Ellis, ed. *Historical Encyclopedia of New Mexico*, 2 vols. Albuquerque, 1945.

New Mexico Historical Records Survey. "Religious Directory for New Mexico, 1940." Albuquerque, N.M., 1940.

The Jewish Encyclopedia, 12 vols. New York, 1901–06.

Peterson, C. S. *Representative New Mexicans*. Denver, 1912.

Southeastern New Mexico Historical Society, Carlsbad, N.M. *Eddy County, New Mexico to 1981*. Lubbock, Texas, 1982.

Speer, William S., ed. *The Encyclopedia of the New West*. Marshall, Texas, 1881.

Who's Who in American Jewry, 1928. 2 vols. 2nd edition. New York, 1928.

COMMEMORATIVE PUBLICATIONS

Centennial Celebration, Santa Fe, New Mexico, July 4, 1876. Santa Fe, N.M., 1876.

In Dedication to Congregation B'nai Israel, December 1971. Albuquerque.

In Dedication to Fifty Years of B'nai Israel Sisterhood, February 11, 1984. Albuquerque.

A Time for Dedication, Temple Albert September 8 and 9, 1984.

SECONDARY WORKS

Adams, Clarence S. *Little Town West of the Pecos—1909*. Roswell, N.M., 1983.

Agus, Jacob. "Current Movements in the Religious Life of American Jewry." *The Jewish People: Past and Present*, v. 4, pp. 97–141. New York, 1955.

Anderson, George B. *History of New Mexico: Its Resources and People*. 2 vols. Los Angeles, 1907.

Atherton, Lewis E. *The Frontier Merchant in Mid-America*. Columbia, Missouri, 1971.

Bancroft, Hubert, H. *History of Arizona and New Mexico. The Works of Hubert H. Bancroft*, v. 17. San Francisco, 1889.

Bannon, John Francis, ed. *Bolton and the Spanish Borderlands.* Norman, Okla., 1964.

Braddy, Haldeen. *Pancho Villa at Columbus: The Raid of 1916 Restudied.* El Paso, 1965.

Callon, Milton W., "Chanukah Comes to Las Vegas." *Denver Westerners Monthly Roundup* 26, no. 9–10 (September–October 1970): 285–305.

Chalmers, David M. *Hooded Americanism: The History of the Ku Klux Klan.* Chicago, 1968.

Chávez, Fray Angélico. *My Penitente Land: Reflections on Spanish New Mexico.* Albuquerque, 1966.

———. "New Names in New Mexico." *El Palacio* 64, no. 9–10 (September–October 1957): 291–318.

———. "New Names in New Mexico" (concluded). *El Palacio* 64, no. 11–12 (November–December 1957): 367–80.

———. *Origins of New Mexico Families.* Santa Fe, 1954.

Coan, Charles F. *A History of New Mexico,* 3 vols. Chicago, 1925.

Cohen, Martin A. "Introduction," *The Jewish Experience in Latin America,* 2 vols. New York, 1971.

———. "Some Misconceptions About the Crypto-Jews in Colonial Mexico." *American Jewish Historical Quarterly* 61, no. 4 (June 1972): 277–93.

Colton, Ray C. *The Civil War in the Western Territories: Arizona, Colorado, New Mexico, and Utah.* Norman, Oklahoma, 1959.

Dike, Sheldon H. "The Territorial Post Offices of New Mexico." *New Mexico Historical Review* 34, no. 1 (January 1959): n.p.

———. "The Territorial Post Offices of New Mexico," continued. *New Mexico Historical Review* 34, no. 3 (July 1959): n.p.

R. L. E. and V. T. X. "Employment and Income." *New Mexico Business* 13, no. 2, sec. 2 (February 1960): 5–10.

Edgel, Ralph L. "Manufacturing in New Mexico." *New Mexico Business* 5, no. 12 (December 1952): 3–14.

Eubanks, Shannon. "Rio Rancho: Past and Present." *New Mexico Business Journal* 11, no. 7 (July 1987): 89–93.

Fierman, Floyd S. "The Frontier Career of Charles Clever." *El Palacio* 85, no. 4 (Winter 1979–80): 2–6, 34–35.

———. *Guts and Ruts: The Jewish Pioneer on the Trail in the American Southwest.* New York, 1985.

———. *The Impact of the Frontier on a Jewish Family: The Bibos.* El Paso, 1961.

———. "Jewish Pioneering in the Southwest: A Record of the Freudenthal—Lesinsky—Solomon Families." *Arizona and the West* 2, no. 1 (Spring 1960): 54–72.

———. "*Merchant-Bankers of Early Santa Fe, 1844–1893.*" *Southwestern Studies* 1 (El Paso, 1964).

———. "The Staabs of Santa Fe: Pioneer Merchants in New Mexico Territory." *Rio Grande History* 13 (New Mexico State University, 1983): 2–23.

———. "The Triangle and the Tetragrammaton: A Note on the Cathedral at Santa Fe." *New Mexico Historical Review* 37, no. 4 (October 1962): 309–21.

Forrest, Suzanne. *The Preservation of the Village: New Mexico's Hispanics and the New Deal.* Albuquerque, 1989.

Frazer, Robert W. *Forts of the West.* Norman, Oklahoma, 1965.

———. "Purveyors of Flour to the Army: Department of New Mexico, 1849–1861." *New Mexico Historical Review* 47, no. 3 (July 1972): 213–38.

Freudenthal, Louis E., comp. *A Century of Freemasonry at Las Cruces, 1867–1967.* N. p., 1967.

Friedman, Philip. "Political and Social Movements and Organizations." *The Jewish People: Past and Present*, v. 4, pp. 142–86. New York, 1955.

"Martin Gardesky." *New Mexico Historical Review* 16, no. 1 (January 1941): 119–20.

Gardner, Richard. *Grito: Reies Tijerina and the New Mexico Land Grant War of 1967.* Indianapolis, 1970.

Gerber, David. "Ethnics, Enterprise, and Middle Class Formation: Using the Dun and Bradstreet Collection for Research in Ethnic History." *The Immigration History Newsletter* 12, no. 1 (May 1980): 1–7.

Glanz, Rudolf. "The Immigration of German Jews Up to 1880." *YIVO Annual of Jewish Social Science* 2–3 (1947–48): 81–99.

———. "Notes on Early Jewish Peddling in America." *Jewish Social Studies* 7, no. 2 (April 1945): 119–36.

Glazer, Nathan. "Social Characteristics of American Jews, 1654–1954." *American Jewish Year Book* 56 (1955): 3–41.

Goldberg, S. P. "Jewish Communal Services: Programs and Finances." *American Jewish Year Book* 72 (1971): 179–229.

Goldscheider, Calvin. *Jewish Continuity and Change: Emerging Patterns in America*. Bloomington, Ind., 1986.

Goldstein, Fanny. "Sixty Years Ago on the Santa Fe Trail." *The Jewish Advocate* (November 22, 1935).

Gonzalez, Nancie L. *The Spanish-Americans of New Mexico: Heritage of Pride*, revised and enlarged edition. Albuquerque, 1969.

Graebner, William. *A History of Retirement: The Meaning and Function of an American Institution, 1885–1978*. New Haven, 1980.

Greenleaf, Richard E. "The Inquisition in Eighteenth-Century New Mexico" *New Mexico Historical Review* 60, no. 1 (January 1985): 29–60.

———. *The Mexican Inquisition of the Sixteenth Century*. Albuquerque, 1969.

Greer, Richard R. "Origins of the Foreign-Born Population of New Mexico During the Territorial Period." *New Mexico Historical Review* 17, no. 4 (October 1942): 281–87.

Hall, Martin H. *Sibley's New Mexican Campaign*. Austin, Texas, 1960.

Hammond, George P. "Don Juan de Oñate and the Founding of New Mexico." *New Mexico Historical Review* 1, no. 1 (January 1926): 42–77.

Hansen, Marcus L. *The Atlantic Migration, 1607–1860*. Cambridge, Mass., 1941.

Hauben, Paul J. *The Spanish Inquisition*. New York, 1969.

Helman, Rabbi Leonard. "From the Rabbi's Study." *New Mexico Jewish Community Link* 2, no. 6 (June 1982): 5.

Henderson, Alice Corbin. "New Mexico in the Great War, (continued): The Women's Part." *New Mexico Historical Review* 1, no. 3 (July 1926): 231–45.

Hirshler, Eric E., ed. *Jews from Germany in the United States*. New York, 1955.

Hodge, F. W. "A Virginian in New Mexico in 1773–74." *New Mexico Historical Review* 4, no. 3 (July 1929): 239–73.

Hordes, Stanley M. "The Inquisition as Economic and Political Agent: The Campaign of the Mexican Holy Office Against the Crypto-Jews in the Mid-Seventeenth Century." *The Americas* 39, no. 1 (July 1982): 23–38.

Horgan, Paul. *The Centuries of Santa Fe.* New York, 1956.

———. *Lamy of Santa Fe: His Life and Times.* New York, 1975.

Horn, Calvin. *New Mexico's Troubled Years: The Story of the Early Territorial Governors.* Albuquerque, 1963.

Hornbein, Marjorie. "Dr. John Elsner, A Colorado Pioneer." *Western States Jewish Historical Quarterly* 13, no. 4 (July 1981): 291–302.

"Jewish Community-Survey Report." *Jewish Welfare Fund News* 5, no. 6 (October 1966).

Jocknick, Sidney. *Early Days on the Western Slope of Colorado and Campfire Chats with Otto Mears, the Pathfinder, from 1870 to 1883, Inclusive.* Denver, 1913.

Johansen, Sigurd. *Rural Social Organization in a Spanish-American Culture Area.* Albuquerque, 1948.

Jones, Oakah L., Jr. *Los Paisanos: Spanish Settlers on the Northern Frontier of New Spain.* Norman, Oklahoma, 1979.

Kalloch, Eunice, and Ruth K. Hall. *The First Ladies of New Mexico.* Santa Fe, 1982.

Karp, Abraham J. "What's American About American Jewish History: The Religious Scene." *American Jewish Historical Quarterly* 52, no. 4 (June 1963): 283–94.

Keleher, William A. *The Fabulous Frontier.* Santa Fe, 1945. (New introduction, 1982.)

Kohler, Max J. "Some Jewish Factors in the Settlement of the West." *Publications of the American Jewish Historical Society* 16 (1907): 23–32.

Kraines, Oscar "Louis Sulzbacher, Justice of the Supreme Court of Puerto Rico, 1900–1904." *Jewish Social Studies* 13, no. 2 (April 1951): 127–32.

Lamar, Howard R. *The Far Southwest 1846–1912: A Territorial History.* New York, 1970.

———. "Political Patterns in New Mexico and Utah Territories 1850–1900." *Utah Historical Quarterly* 28, no. 4 (October 1960): 363–87.

Lamb, Blaine P. "Fifty-Four Years on the Southwest Frontier: Nathan Benjamin Appel in New Mexico, Arizona, and Southern California." *Western States Jewish History* 16, no. 2 (January 1984): 125–33.

Lang, Herbert H. "The New Mexico Bureau of Immigration, 1880–

1912." *New Mexico Historical Review* 51, no. 3 (July 1976): 193–214.

Langston, LaMoine "Red." *A History of Masonry in New Mexico (1877–1977)*. Roswell, N.M., n.d.

Larson, Robert W. *New Mexico Populism: A Study of Radical Protest in a Western Territory*. Boulder, Colorado, 1974.

Latimer, Roman L. "Spiegelberg Brothers: Bankers and Merchants to New Mexico Territory." *Numismatic Scrapbook Magazine* 38, whole no. 432 (February 1972): 118–44.

Lavender, David. *The Big Divide*. New York, 1948.

Lawson, Michael L. "Flora Langermann Spiegelberg: Grand Lady of Santa Fe." *Western States Jewish Historical Quarterly* 8, no. 4 (July 1976): 291–308.

Lease, Richard J. "Eugene J. Stern: Merchant, Farmer, and Philanthropist of Las Cruces, New Mexico." *Western States Jewish Historical Quarterly* 9, no. 2 (January 1977): 161–66.

Lestschinsky, Jacob. "Economic and Social Development of American Jewry." *The Jewish People: Past and Present*, v. 4, pp. 56–96. New York, 1955.

Levinson, Robert E. "American Jews in the West." *The Western Historical Quarterly* 5, no. 3 (July 1974): 285–94.

Liebman, Seymour B. *The Jews in New Spain: Faith, Flame and the Inquisition*. Coral Gables, Florida, 1970.

Linfield, Harry S. *The Jews in the United States, 1927: A Study of Their Number and Distribution*. New York, 1929.

———. *Statistics of Jews and Jewish Organizations: Historical Review of Ten Censuses, 1850–1937*. New York, 1939.

Lyon, Fern, and Jacob Evans, eds. *Los Alamos: The First Forty Years*. Los Alamos, N.M., 1984.

Martinez, Demetria. "Hispanic Priest Finds Jewish Roots." *Albuquerque Journal*, Section C, July 27, 1986, pp. 1, 3.

McAlavy, Don, and Harold Kilmer. *High Plains History of East Central New Mexico*. Clovis, N.M., 1980.

McCall, Samuel W. *For the Honor of the Nation*. New York, 1939.

McDermott, John Francis. "The Remarkable Life and Adventures of John Eugene Leitensdorfer." *Bulletin of the Missouri Historical Society* 15, no. 2 (January 1959): 105–17.

McNitt, Frank. *The Indian Traders*. Norman, 1962.

Meketa, Jacqueline Dorgan. *Louis Felsenthal: Citizen-Soldier of Territorial New Mexico.* Albuquerque, 1982.

Miller, Darlis A. *The California Column in New Mexico.* Albuquerque, 1982.

Moore, Deborah Dash. *B'nai B'rith and the Challenge of Ethnic Leadership.* Albany, 1981.

Moorhead, Max L. *New Mexico's Royal Road: Trade and Travel on the Chihuahua Trail.* Norman, Oklahoma, 1958.

Nash, Gerald D. *The American West in the Twentieth Century: A Short History of an Urban Oasis.* Englewood Cliffs, N.J., 1973.

Newman, Simeon H., III. "The Santa Fe Ring: A Letter to the *New York Sun.*" *Arizona and the West* 12, no. 3 (Autumn 1970): 269–88.

Nidel, David S. "Modern Descendants of Conversos in New Mexico." *Western States Jewish History* 16, no. 3 (April 1984): 249–62.

Noggle, Burl. "Anglo Observers of the Southwest Borderlands, 1875–1890: The Rise of a Concept." *Arizona and the West* 1, no. 2 (Summer 1959): 105–31.

Parish, William J. *The Charles Ilfeld Company: The Rise and Decline of Mercantile Capitalism in New Mexico.* Cambridge, Mass., 1961.

———. "The German Jew and the Commercial Revolution in Territorial New Mexico 1850–1900." *New Mexico Historical Review* 35, no. 1 (January 1960): 1–29.

———. "The German Jew and the Commercial Revolution in Territorial New Mexico 1850–1900" (concluded). *New Mexico Historical Review* 35, no. 2 (April 1960): 129–50.

Perrigo, Lynn. *Gateway to Glorieta: A History of Las Vegas, New Mexico.* Boulder, 1982.

Rabinowitz, Howard N. "Albuquerque: City at a Crossroads." *Sunbelt Cities: Politics and Growth Since World War II*, edited by Richard M. Bernard and Bradley R. Rice. Austin, Texas, 1983.

Reeve, Frank D. *History of New Mexico*, 3 vols. New York, 1961.

Ripp, Bart. "Jewels from the Desert." *Albuquerque Tribune*, Section B, November 23, 1987, pp. 1, 8.

Robbins, Cathy. "Albuquerque Jews Losing Invisibility." *Albuquerque Journal Magazine*, September 16, 1980, p. 9

Rogen, Victoria. "Jews on the Western Frontier Essay Wins Coveted Scholarship." *Las Vegas Daily Optic*, May 27, 1980, p. 3.

Rollins, Sandra Lea. "Jewish Indian Chief." *Western States Jewish Historical Quarterly* 1, no. 4 (July 1969): 151–63.

Rosenbaum, Robert J. *Mexicano Resistance in the Southwest*. Austin, Texas, 1981.

Rothenberg, Gunther, author; Israel C. Carmel, research. *Congregation Albert, 1897–1972*. Albuquerque, 1972.

Salomon, H. P. "The Jews in New Spain" review essay. *American Jewish Historical Quarterly* 62, no. 2 (December 1972): 190–201.

Santos, Richard G. "Chicanos of Jewish Descent in Texas." *Western States Jewish Historical Quarterly* 15, no. 4 (July 1983): 327–33.

Scholes, France V. "Church and State in New Mexico, 1610–1650." *New Mexico Historical Review* 12, no. 1 (January 1937): 78–106.

———. "Troublous Times in New Mexico, 1659–1670." *New Mexico Historical Review* 12, no. 4 (October 1937): 380–452.

———. "Troublous Times in New Mexico, 1659–1670." *New Mexico Historical Review* 15, no. 4 (October 1940): 369–417.

——— "Troublous Times in New Mexico, 1659–1670." *New Mexico Historical Review* 16, no. 3 (July 1941): 313–27.

Schroeder, Adolf E. "The Survival of German Traditions in Missouri." *The German Contribution to the Building of the Americas*, edited by Gerhard K. Friesen and Walter Schatzberg. Hanover, N.H., 1977.

Sharfman, Harold I. *Jews on the Frontier*. Chicago, 1977.

Shinedling, Abraham I. *History of the Los Alamos Jewish Center (1944 to 1957)*. Albuquerque, 1958.

Shinkle, James D. *Fifty Years of Roswell History—1867–1917*. Roswell, N.M., 1964.

Simmons, Marc. *Albuquerque*. Albuquerque, 1982.

———. *New Mexico: A History*. New York, 1977.

Smith, George W. "New Mexico's Wartime Food Problems, 1917–1918: II (concluded)." *New Mexico Historical Review* 19, no. 1 (January 1944): 1–54.

Spicer, Edward H. *A Short History of the Indians of the United States*. New York, 1969.

Spidle, Jake W., Jr. *The Lovelace Medical Center: Pioneers in American Health Care*. Albuquerque, 1987.

Stanley, F., pseud. (Crocciola, Stanley Francis Louis). *Fort Union (New Mexico)*. N. p., 1953.

———. *Ciudad Santa Fe, Territorial Days 1846–1912*. Pampa, Texas, 1965.

Stern-Taeubler, Selma. "The Motivation of the German-Jewish Emigration to America in the Post-Mendelssohnian Era." *Essays in American Jewish History*. Cincinnati, 1958.

"Sunday Morning Breakfast at Temple Albert." *Century* 3, no. 4 (November 17, 1982): 5.

Swadesh, Frances L.. "The Alianza Movement of New Mexico: The Interplay of Social Change and Public Commentary." *Minorities and Politics*, edited by Henry J. Tobias and Charles E. Woodhouse. Albuquerque, 1969.

Thomas, David Yancey. *A History of Military Government in Newly Acquired Territory of the United States*. New York, 1904.

Thompson, Mrs. Harry, et al. *Clayton, the Friendly Town in Union County, New Mexico*. Denver, Colorado, 1962.

Tobias, Henry J. *The Jews in Oklahoma*. Norman, 1980.

Tobias, Henry J., and Charles E. Woodhouse. "New York Investment Bankers and New Mexico Merchants: Group Formation and Elite Status Among German-Jewish Businessmen." *New Mexico Historical Review* 65, no. 1 (January 1990): 21–47.

Twitchell, Ralph E. *The Leading Facts of New Mexican History*, 5 vols. Albuquerque, 1917.

———. *Old Santa Fe: The Story of New Mexico's Ancient Capital*. Chicago, 1925.

Urofsky, Melvin I. *American Zionism from Herzl to the Holocaust*. New York, 1975.

Valle, Victor. "The Exodus of New Mexico's 'Hidden Jews.'" *Los Angeles Times*, part VI, July 15, 1988, p. 34.

Van Cleave, Errett. "Credit on the Santa Fe Trail: Business Pioneering in Pueblo Regions." *Credit and Financial Management* 41 (October 1939): 16–17.

P. A. F. W. [Paul A. F. Walter], "Arthur Seligman," *New Mexico Historical Review* 8, no. 4 (October 1933): 306–16.

Weigle, Marta, and Kyle Fiore. *Santa Fe and Taos: The Writer's Era, 1916–1941*. Santa Fe, 1982.

Westphall, Victor. *Thomas Benton Catron and His Era*. Tucson, Arizona, 1973.

UNPUBLISHED SECONDARY WORKS
AND MISCELLANY

Atencio, Tomas, and Stanley M. Hordes. "The Sephardic Legacy in New Mexico: A Prospectus." Southwest Hispanic Research Institute, University of New Mexico, 1987.

Austin, Mary. "Social Survey of Taos County, New Mexico," 1919. Microfilm. Special Collections, Zimmerman Library, University of New Mexico.

Blake, Fay F. "Signs of Secret Judaism in New Mexico," Albuquerque, 1983. Manuscript in possession of its author.

Carmel, Israel C. "Laying of Cornerstone, Congregation Albert Synagogue by the Most Worshipful Grand Lodge Ancient Free Accepted Masons of New Mexico, Albuquerque, New Mexico, September 3, 1899." Temple Albert Archives, Box no. 1 Archives.

[Feldman, Judith]. "The Jewish Community in Roswell: A Brief History." Roswell, n.d. Manuscript in possession of Seymour A. Beckerman, Roswell, N.M.

Goode, Alex D. [Cimonce, pseud.]. "A History of Jewish Economic Life from 1830 to 1860 in the United States," Hebrew Union College, Cincinnati, 1933.

Nidel, David S. "Modern Descendants of Conversos in New Mexico—500 Years of Faith." Manuscript in possession of its author.

Spiegelberg, Lehman. "Commerce of Santa Fe," 1884. American Jewish Archives, Cincinnati.

Tigges, Linda. "Land Use Patterns in Santa Fe, 1885–1886." Manuscript in possession of its author.

Woodhouse, Charles E. "History of the Department of Sociology at the University of New Mexico, 1935–1986." Manuscript in possession of its author.

DISSERTATIONS AND THESES

Bailey, David T. "Stratification and Ethnic Differentiation in Santa Fe, 1860 and 1870." Ph.D. diss., University of Texas at Austin, 1975.

Goldstein, Brigitte K. "Jewish Identification Among the Jews of Albuquerque, New Mexico: The Maintenance of Jewishness and Judaism in the Integrated Setting of a Sunbelt City," Ph.D. diss., University of New Mexico, 1988.

Heath, Jim F. "A Study of the Influence of the Atchison, Topeka, and

Santa Fe Railroad Upon the Economy of New Mexico 1878 to 1900." M. A. thesis, University of New Mexico, 1955.

Hoover, Herbert. "History of the Republican Party in New Mexico, 1867–1952." Ph.D. diss., University of Oklahoma, 1966.

Lamb, Blaine P. "Jewish Pioneers in Arizona, 1850–1920." Ph.D. diss., Arizona State University, 1982.

Larralde, Carlos Montalvo. "Chicano Jews in South Texas." Ph.D. diss., University of California at Los Angeles, 1978.

Lehmann, Terry J. "Santa Fe and Albuquerque 1870–1890: Contrast and Conflict in the Development of Two Southwestern Towns." Ph.D. diss., Indiana University, 1974.

Lujan, Roy "Dennis Chavez and the Roosevelt Era, 1933–1945." Ph.D. diss., University of New Mexico, 1987.

Naegle, Conrad K. "The History of Silver City, New Mexico, 1870–1886." M. A. thesis, University of New Mexico, 1943.

Rebord, Bernice Ann. "A Social History of Albuquerque 1880–1885." M. A. thesis, University of New Mexico, 1947.

Shane, Karen D. "Edmund G. Ross: Governor of New Mexico, 1885–1889." M. A. thesis, University of New Mexico, 1983.

Telling, Irving. "New Mexican Frontiers: A Social History of the Gallup Area 1881–1901." Ph.D. diss., Harvard University, 1952.

Index